COGNITIVE–BEHAVIOURAL INTERVENTIONS WITH PSYCHOTIC DISORDERS

Cognitive–Behavioural Interventions with Psychotic Disorders features new psychological treatments for people experiencing enduring and persistent psychotic symptoms. It has contributions from leading researchers and clinicians in the field who are currently engaged in relevant research and clinical practice. Their approach reflects the growing interest amongst mental health professionals in psychological methods of psychosis management as a complement or as an alternative to traditional psychopharmacological methods. **Gillian Haddock, Peter D. Slade** and an experienced team of contributors describe the latest research in this area and demonstrate, using case examples, how research can be translated into clinical practice. This is a practical and informative book for all professionals who work with people experiencing severe mental health problems as well as for trainers and managers.

Gillian Haddock is Tutor in Clinical Psychology at the University of Manchester and Honorary Consultant Clinical Psychologist for South Manchester University Hospitals NHS Trust. She is currently researching psychological treatments for psychosis.

Peter D. Slade is Head of the Clinical Psychology Department at the University of Liverpool and has been involved for many years in the psychological investigation and treatment of psychotic disorders.

COGNITIVE–BEHAVIOURAL INTERVENTIONS WITH PSYCHOTIC DISORDERS

*Edited by Gillian Haddock
and Peter D. Slade*

London and New York

First published 1996
by Routledge
11 New Fetter Lane, London EC4P 4EE

Simultaneously published in the USA and Canada
by Routledge
29 West 35th Street, New York, NY 10001

Reprinted in 1997

Typeset in Times by
Keystroke, Jacaranda Lodge, Wolverhampton

Printed and bound in Great Britain by
Clays Ltd, St Ives plc

British Library Cataloguing in Publication Data
A catalogue record for this book is available from the British Library

Library of Congress Cataloguing in Publication Data
A catalogue record for this book has been requested
ISBN 0–415–10289–8 (hbk)
ISBN 0–415–10290–1 (pbk)

CONTENTS

Part III: Integrating with other therapeutic strategies

LIST OF FIGURES

LIST OF TABLES

NOTES ON CONTRIBUTORS

Richard P. Bentall is Professor of Clinical Psychology at the Department of Clinical Psychology, University of Liverpool.

Max Birchwood is Professor of Psychology, University of Birmingham and Consultant Clinical Psychologist and Head of Academic Section, Northern Birmingham Mental Health Trust, All Saints Hospital, Birmingham.

Paul Chadwick is Honorary Lecturer in Clinical Psychology at the School of Psychology, University of Birmingham and Clinical Psychologist for Northern Birmingham Mental Health Trust.

Jennifer C. Day is a Research Pharmacist at the School of Nursing, University of Manchester.

Sandra Escher is a journalist at the Social Psychiatry Unit, University of Limburg, Netherlands.

David Fowler is Lecturer in Clinical Psychology, Health Policy and Practice Unit, University of East Anglia, Norwich.

Philippa Garety is Associate and Academic Course Director, Oxford Clinical Psychology Training Course, Warneford Hospital, Oxford.

Gillian Haddock is Tutor in Clinical Psychology, School of Psychiatry and Behavioural Sciences, University of Manchester and Honorary Consultant Clinical Psychologist for South Manchester University Hospitals NHS Trust.

Lorna Hogg is Clinical Psychologist, Littlemoor Hospital, Oxford.

David Kingdon is Consultant Psychiatrist at Bassetlaw Hospital, Nottinghamshire.

Elizabeth Kuipers is Reader in Clinical Psychology at the Institute of Psychiatry, London.

Marius Romme is Professor of Social Psychiatry at the Social Psychiatry Unit, University of Limburg, Netherlands.

Peter D. Slade is Professor of Clinical Psychology and Head of the Department of Clinical Psychology, University of Liverpool.

Nicholas Tarrier is Professor of Clinical Psychology at the Department of Clinical Psychology, School of Psychiatry and Behavioural Sciences, University of Manchester and Director of Psychology Services for South Manchester University Hospitals NHS Trust.

Douglas Turkington is Consultant Psychiatrist at St Nicholas Hospital, Newcastle and the Newcastle Cognitive Therapy Centre.

Lawrence Yusupoff is Clinical Psychology Senior Fellow, Department of Clinical Psychology, School of Psychiatry and Behavioural Sciences, University of Manchester and Honorary Consultant Clinical Psychologist for South Manchester University Hospitals NHS Trust.

PREFACE

The major treatment for psychotic disorders in the UK during the past 40 years has involved the use of psychopharmacological agents. While such drugs have clearly revolutionised the management of patients who suffer with severe mental health problems, such as schizophrenia, they have not proved to be the complete answer. The reasons for this include the failure of many patients to respond fully to neuroleptic medication, the problem of severe side-effects experienced by others and the unwillingness for some patients to accept medication. In addition, the outcome of adopting a primarily psychopharmacological approach to mental health has been that professionals have limited their verbal interactions with patients to establishing their diagnosis and deciding on appropriate medication.

More recently, the *Zeitgeist* has changed, such that, an increasing number of mental health professionals have become interested in talking to their patients, and attempting to understand their symptoms. This led a number of researchers and professionals to organise a one day conference in June 1991 on 'Psychological Approaches to the Management of Psychosis' at the University of Liverpool. We set a maximum attendance figure at 130, but finally accepted 150 and had to turn away a large number of others who wished to attend. It was clear to all the organisers that there were many mental health professionals who wished to explore the possible value of these methods as an adjunct to, or as an alternative to, traditional psychopharmacological approaches in the management of psychosis. All of the speakers who were at the conference agreed to contribute chapters to this book and, in addition, other contributions were commissioned.

The crucial principles which were highlighted during this conference and which are reiterated in this book include the following:

1. The importance of listening and attempting to make sense of the patients' symptoms and problems.
2. The importance of acknowledging the meaning and role of the symptoms in the person's life.
3. The importance of attempting to develop and refine more effective

treatments for those people experiencing persistent and distressing symptoms.
4. The importance of future research in order to demonstrate the useful-ness of these techniques so that they can become incorporated into routine services.

This book attempts to give an overview of the literature on psychological management of psychosis, together with recent innovative research from experienced clinicians and researchers in the field of severe mental health problems. Although there is an emphasis on research, the authors have attempted to demonstrate their approaches in clinical examples making this a useful text for a wide range of mental health professionals.

Gillian Haddock and Peter D. Slade

ACKNOWLEDGEMENTS

The editors would like to acknowledge Mary Gregg, Alison Davies and Jean Haddock for their help in the preparation of this manuscript.

Part I

HISTORICAL BACKGROUND

1

FROM COGNITIVE STUDIES OF PSYCHOSIS TO COGNITIVE–BEHAVIOUR THERAPY FOR PSYCHOTIC SYMPTOMS

Richard P. Bentall

INTRODUCTION

In the past few years a small number of researchers, mainly from Great Britain, have advocated the development of cognitive–behavioural interventions for psychotic patients, either as direct therapies for specific symptoms (e.g. Bentall *et al.*, 1994a; Chadwick and Birchwood, 1994; Chadwick and Lowe, 1990; Fowler and Morley, 1989; Garety *et al.*, 1994; Haddock *et al.*, 1993; see Chapters 3, 4 and 7 of this book); as a way of enhancing patients' coping skills (e.g. Tarrier *et al.*, 1990; Tarrier *et al.*, 1993; see Chapter 5 of this book); or as part of a normalising strategy designed to make patients more accepting of what would otherwise be disturbing experiences (e.g. Kingdon and Turkington, 1991, 1994; see Chapter 6 of this book). These authors have argued for renewed optimism about the prospects for developing individual psychological therapies adequate for the needs of the most seriously disturbed psychiatric patients, and have suggested that research into such therapies should be vigorously pursued as a matter of priority. In this chapter, I will show that this kind of optimism is consistent with recent advances in the understanding of the psychological mechanisms involved in psychotic symptomatology, and I will illustrate these advances by describing some of the investigations which my colleagues and I have carried out at Liverpool University. Before describing these recent advances, however, it will be useful to identify some inaccurate but widely held assumptions about the nature of psychotic disorders which in the past have tended to impede the development of psychological therapies for psychotic patients.

3

RICHARD P. BENTALL

PESSIMISM AND THE BIOLOGICAL *ZEITGEIST*

Paradoxically, recent advances in the cognitive–behavioural treatment of psychotic disorders have occurred following a period in which the scientific *Zeitgeist* has emphasised the importance of biological determinants of psychotic behaviour and de-emphasised the value of psychological theories and interventions. Nancy Andreasen (1984), in a popular account of the biological approach in psychiatry entitled *The Broken Brain*, looks forward to a time when the average psychiatric interview will be fifteen minutes in duration, when the starting point for psychiatric interventions will always be a diagnosis agreed according to operational criteria such as those given in the American Psychiatric Association's Diagnostic and Statistical Manual (APA, 1987), and in which the most frequently used forms of psychiatric treatment will be those which involve adjusting the relative balance of different kinds of neurotransmitters in the brain by means of sophisticated medications. More recently, Samuel Guze has argued that, 'There can be no such thing as a psychiatry which is too biological' (Guze, 1989, p. 315) and has suggested that disciplines such as neurochemistry and molecular genetics, rather than psychology, provide the vital background knowledge necessary for modern psychiatric practice.

Andreasen, Guze and other biological psychiatrists clearly see psychological treatments as having at best a marginal role in the management of severe mental illness. At its most extreme, this attitude has amounted to an almost complete rejection of social and psychotherapeutic methods of treatment (Herbst, 1987). Non-psychiatrists have at times also been sceptical about the value of individual psychological therapies for psychotic patients, although perhaps to a lesser degree. The psychologists Mueser and Berenbaum (1990), for example, in an editorial review published in a major psychiatric journal, concluded that outcome studies employing dynamic psychotherapy with 'schizophrenic' patients had been so disappointing that no further studies could be justified. However, these authors did recognise the value of behavioural and family therapies for ameliorating psychotic symptoms. Similarly, Alan Bellack (1992), a psychologist who has made important contributions to our understanding of the social deficits of 'schizophrenic' patients, recently argued that it is unlikely that cognitive rehabilitation treatments will prove efficacious with psychotic patients because the cognitive deficits underlying schizophrenia are poorly understood and because such therapies have not proved useful for patients suffering from brain damage. On Bellack's view, instead of trying to treat core symptoms and deficits, psychologists should try and develop ways of helping schizophrenic patients cope with the limitations imposed on them by their disease. This point of view is particularly striking as, only six years earlier, Bellack (1986) had written a paper entitled 'Schizophrenia: Behaviour therapy's forgotten child' in which he had chastised clinical

4

psychologists for their failure to take the psychological treatment of psychosis seriously.

It will be useful, in passing, to examine two arguments which have been used to justify pessimism about the value of psychological therapies for psychotic patients. First, as Spring and Ravdin (1992) note, many researchers and clinicians have believed that the relative success of biological therapies means that research into the psychological treatment of psychosis is not warranted. On this view, the proven efficacy of neuroleptic medication indicates that costly and time consuming research into the psychological treatment of psychotic symptoms and behaviours is not necessary. However, this would be to adopt an over-generous view of the successes of biological interventions. While there is no doubt that a proportion of psychotic patients benefit from neuroleptic medications (Marder, 1992), even advocates of the biological approach admit that few patients, if any, can be said to be 'cured' by them (Andreasen, 1984). Moreover, recent research has indicated that a sizeable proportion of psychotic patients do not respond to medication at all (Brown and Herz, 1989), and that some may even do worse as a result of this kind of treatment (Warner, 1985). The efficacy of neuroleptic drugs is further limited by the substantial adverse effects associated with this kind of treatment, which are viewed as a serious impediment to therapy by some authors and a scandalous form of iatrogenesis by others (Breggin, 1993). Interestingly, in one of the few carefully conducted studies of attitudes towards neuroleptic medication, it was found that both patients and practising psychiatrists regarded side-effects as about as distressing to patients as the symptoms the drugs are used to treat (Finn *et al.*, 1990). Indeed, the acknowledged inadequacy of currently available medical treatments for psychosis remains one of the main motivations for research into novel neuroleptics. Pessimism about the value of psychological therapies for psychotic patients cannot therefore be justified on the grounds that biological treatments already 'do the job'.

A second, related argument has been that pessimism is warranted by the past failure of psychological therapies with psychotic patients, for example psychodynamic therapies (Mueser and Berenbaum, 1990). However, this argument cannot be sustained without presuming that the psychological treatment studies published to date exhaust the possible range of psychological interventions which might be carried out with psychotic patients. There is, of course, no reason to believe that the innovative skills of psychological researchers are any more limited than those of biological investigators. Indeed, the argument from past failure, if applied in the wake of the disappointing results of medical interventions already alluded to, would probably halt further research into chemotherapy overnight. History has no message for researchers in either the psychological or the biological domains.

5

What, then, has been the real cause of pessimism about psychological treatments for psychotic disorders? I would like to suggest that two conceptual fallacies have been at the root of this pessimism. These fallacies have been implicit in much of the biological theorising about psychotic behaviour which has been so popular in the recent past. The first is the assumption that psychotic disorders can be divided into a small number of discrete syndromes or symptom clusters. The second is the assumption that psychotic symptoms, because they reflect anatomical and physiological abnormalities in the brain, are not meaningful. I will suggest that neither of these assumptions survives close scrutiny of the relevant evidence. Furthermore, I will show how rejection of these assumptions has important implications for the future development of cognitive–behavioural treatments for psychotic patients.

ASSUMPTIONS ABOUT PSYCHOSIS AND COGNITIVE INTERVENTIONS

Most of the current research into psychopathology takes as its starting point systems of psychiatric classification derived from the work of Kraepelin and others in the latter years of the last century (see Berrios and Hauser, 1988 and Boyle, 1991 for critical historical accounts). Although his methods would be judged unsophisticated by modern standards, Kraepelin was one of the first psychiatric researchers to collect information systematically about both the phenomenology of psychiatric disorders and their outcome as revealed by the careers of the patients whom he followed-up over many years. Kraepelin made the assumption (which was reasonable for the time) that phenomenological course and outcome data would converge to reveal a method of classifying psychiatric disorders which would ultimately lead to aetiological discoveries:

> Judging from our experience in internal medicine it is a fair assumption that similar disease processes will produce identical symptom pictures, identical pathological anatomy and an identical aetiology. If, therefore, we possessed a comprehensive knowledge of any of these three fields – pathological anatomy, symptomatology, or aetiology – we would at once have a uniform and standard classification of mental diseases. A similar comprehensive knowledge of either of the other two fields would give us not just as uniform and standard classifications, but all of these classifications would exactly coincide.
>
> (Kraepelin, 1907; quoted in Reider, 1974, pp. 260–1)

Following this kind of reasoning, Kraepelin, in the edition of his great textbook of psychiatry published in 1896, first collapsed a group of syndromes (previously described at various different times by Morel, Hecker and Kahlbaum) into the one disorder 'dementia praecox', so described because of its apparent early age of onset and chronic, deteriorating course. Contrasted against dementia praecox (renamed 'schizophrenia' by Bleuler in 1911) was the second major group of serious psychiatric disorders, the 'manic depressive psychoses' which, Kraepelin argued, generally began later in life and had a better outcome. This distinction, which has informed most subsequent attempts at psychiatric classification (see Boyle, 1991 for a historical account of developments from Kraepelin's time to the present), has been described as one of the cornerstones of modern psychiatry (Kendell and Gourlay, 1970).

It is hard to overestimate the impact of Kraepelin's system on both biological and psychological research into psychosis. The implication of his method of classification is that patients should be studied according to diagnostic grouping. Although patients diagnosed as schizophrenic according to his system present with diverse symptoms, it is assumed that these symptoms all reflect a common underlying disease process. Hence the most common research paradigm employed in psychological research into psychosis involves comparing a group of patients diagnosed as 'schizophrenic' with a group of individuals diagnosed as 'normal' (and perhaps, in order to control for the non-specific effects of illness, a group of patients diagnosed as suffering from some other kind of psychiatric disorder). Sarbin and Mancuso (1980) surveyed the *Journal of Abnormal Psychology* (formerly the *Journal of Abnormal and Social Psychology*) between the years 1959 and 1978, finding that 374 papers totalling 2,472 pages, or 15.3 per cent of the journal space, used the presence or absence of a diagnosis of schizophrenia as an independent variable in this way. There has been no sign that this trend has decreased in the years since Sarbin and Mancuso's survey. This strategy can only hope to be successful, however, if those diagnosed as 'schizophrenic' have something in common which is absent in the case of the comparison groups.

When choosing dependent variables for research, most psychologists investigating psychotic behaviour have taken their lead from Bleuler (1911/1950), who assumed that schizophrenic symptoms reflect a core disorder of thinking. Investigators have thus tried to identify gross cognitive abnormalities in broadly defined groups of patients, usually without making any reference to the particular symptoms experienced by those patients (Harvey and Neale, 1983). It is important in this context to distinguish between research into cognitive *deficits* and research into cognitive *biases*. Cognitive deficits are typically measured using emotionally neutral tasks and concern what the patient can or cannot do; they are said to be present when there is some gross disorder of mental functioning, for example an inability to attend to relevant information in the presence of distracting information (said to be a common feature of schizophrenia; cf. Neale and Oltmanns, 1980). They are important because they are likely to provide evidence pertaining to the role of neuropsychological impairments in

7

psychiatric disorders. Indeed, it is natural to look for disorders in the biological mechanisms sustaining cognition when content-nonspecific abnormalities in the ability to attend, memorise and reason are observed.

Cognitive biases, on the other hand, are said to be present when the individual shows an abnormal tendency to process some kinds of information as opposed to others (for example, a tendency to notice and recall information which is negatively self-referent), and are typically studied by requiring individuals to remember or think about emotionally significant material. Cognitive biases are important to study because human mental life has the property described by philosophers as 'intentionality'. That is to say, it is a feature of all mental states (thoughts, desires, beliefs and what in ordinary language are known as intentions) that they are always *about* something (Tallis, 1991). This human ability to represent the world internally and to respond to that representation is in turn dependent upon the ability to process information according to its content.

Consistent with the view that psychotic disorders reflect underlying biological dysfunctions, most psychological research into cognitive processes in psychosis has focused on deficits. There is, indeed, good evidence that such deficits can often be found in patients suffering from psychotic disorders (see Frith and Done, 1987; Gray *et al.*, 1991; and Hemsley, 1992, 1993 for recent integrative accounts of these findings). However, this emphasis on deficits has meant that the possible contributory role of cognitive biases in psychosis has been almost entirely neglected by investigators even though such biases have been clearly implicated in the neurotic disorders (Bentall, 1992a). To some extent, this prejudice is consistent with Jaspers' (1963) influential view that psychotic symptoms are 'ununderstandable' and do not reflect patients' personalities and experiences. At the extreme, this prejudice manifests itself in the assertion that psychotic experiences such as delusions are completely meaningless and, 'Empty speech acts, whose informational content refers to neither world or self. They are not the symbolic expression of anything' (Berrios, 1991, p. 12). This kind of model of psychotic behaviour has clear implications for the development of psychotherapeutic strategies for psychotic patients. If psychosis reflects, at the psychological level, a core deficit in information processing then any successful therapeutic strategy will have to rectify this underlying cognitive deficit.

Towards this end, Meichenbaum (1977) and his colleagues developed a technique called 'self-instructional training' (SIT) which, although eventually evaluated across a wide range of clinical conditions, was initially employed with patients diagnosed as suffering from chronic schizophrenia (Meichenbaum and Cameron, 1973). These authors assumed that the attentional deficits presumed to underlie the symptoms of schizophrenia were the product of a failure of verbal self-regulation. In order to overcome this deficit, therefore, patients would have to learn to control their own attentional processes by means of self-directed speech which might be overt (talking to self) or, after sufficient practice, covert (verbal thought). In SIT, the patient is explicitly taught to do this, first by watching the therapist talk to himself while solving a series of intellectual puzzles, second by talking to himself while being prompted by the therapist, and finally by learning to talk to himself silently or covertly. Meichenbaum and Cameron claimed that this procedure resulted in marked improvements in patients' performance on a series of intellectual tasks, and that this improvement generalised so that the patients' speech became significantly less disordered. Unfortunately, a subsequent study by Margolis and Sherberg (1976) failed to replicate this finding. More recently, in a study conducted by myself and others, in which we compared the effects of different kinds of self-instruction strategies, we found that, although improvements in performance on specific intellectual tasks could be achieved in chronically ill patients, these improvements failed to generalise even to quite similar tasks, let alone to clinically interesting measures (Bentall et al., 1987).

In the past few years, the hope of developing cognitive interventions which would address core schizophrenic deficits has been revived by a number of researchers who have attempted to train attentional performance directly, often using computer tasks. Whilst a few promising case studies have been reported (e.g. Adams et al., 1981), the only systematic evaluation of this kind of approach which has so far been carried out has been reported by Hans Brenner and his colleagues in Germany. These investigators have described an Integrated Psychological Therapy consisting of five subprogrammes designed to ameliorate the cognitive and social deficits presumed to be characteristic of schizophrenia. The entire programme takes approximately three months of weekly sessions, and begins with interventions targeted at basic cognitive skills (for example, by training on card sorting tasks and word problems), progresses to interventions in which those skills are applied to social situations (for example, recognition of emotional expressions) and culminates in sessions devoted to interpersonal problem solving. Results from preliminary studies with this treatment programme are consistent with those obtained with SIT: initial rapid gains on the cognitive training tasks do not appear to be followed by general improvements in the social domain (Brenner et al., 1992). Interestingly, there is some evidence that symptomatic improvements are evident only in those patients who show positive changes in self-esteem during therapy (Brenner, 1989).

Given that these kinds of cognitive-behavioural interventions do not appear to result in the resolution of patients' main difficulties, and especially given that improvements in cognitive skills do not seem to result in symptomatic improvement, it is perhaps time to subject the assumptions informing these interventions to careful scrutiny.

RICHARD P. BENTALL

ARE PREVAILING ASSUMPTIONS ABOUT PSYCHOSIS JUSTIFIED?

The question of classification

I have discussed the scientific limitations of the schizophrenia diagnosis at length elsewhere (Bentall *et al.*, 1988; Bentall, 1992b,c; see also the *Journal of Mental Health*, volume 2, number 3, 1993 for a debate about these issues) and the relevant arguments can only be outlined briefly here. It should be recognised that, for any diagnostic classification to be scientifically useful, it has to be both *reliable* and *valid*. Reliability refers to the extent to which different investigators can agree about who merits the diagnosis and who does not. In order to resolve past disagreements about the fundamental features of schizophrenia, a number of investigators have proposed operational criteria for the disorder, perhaps the most widely used of which are those contained in the revised third edition of the *American Psychiatric Association's Diagnostic and Statistical Manual* (DSM-III-R; APA, 1987). Unfortunately, different operational criteria proposed by different investigators tend to diagnose different patients as schizophrenic (Brockington *et al.*, 1978; Farmer *et al.*, 1993; McGuffin *et al.*, 1991) so that disagreements between clinicians about who is schizophrenic have been replaced by 'A babble of precise but differing formulations of the same concept' (Brockington *et al.*, 1978, p. 387).

The validity of a diagnosis refers to the extent to which it can be said to be meaningful, and can be determined only by a series of tests. For example, the diagnosis of schizophrenia should refer to a cluster of symptoms which tend to occur together. Research in which multivariate statistical techniques have been applied to symptom data has generally failed to reveal such a cluster of symptoms (Blashfield, 1984); indeed a number of authors have recently argued that there are two (Crow, 1980) or perhaps even three independent syndromes of positive symptoms (delusions and hallucinations), negative symptoms and cognitive disorganisation (Klimidis *et al.*, 1993; Liddle, 1987; Minas *et al.*, 1992). Similar clusters have been identified in factor-analytic studies of schizotypal traits (assessed using questionnaire measures of mild schizophrenic experiences) in normal subjects (Bentall *et al.*, 1989; Kendler and Hewitt, 1992; Muntaner *et al.*, 1988). This latter finding suggests that, not only do schizophrenic symptoms fail to cluster in the manner predicted by Kraepelin's account, but also that those symptoms lie on continua with normal functioning, with psychotic experiences at the extreme end of those continua.

A different way in which the validity of a diagnostic classification can be assessed is by examining the extent to which it predicts important variables such as outcome and response to treatment. However, the outcome of psychotic disorders appears to be extremely variable and is better predicted by social factors than symptom variables (Ciompi, 1984; Sartorius *et al.*,

1987). Moreover, as I have already indicated, although neuroleptics are usually regarded as the treatment of choice for schizophrenia, many 'schizophrenic' patients do not respond to this kind of treatment. Indeed, in those few trials in which different kinds of medication have been randomly assigned irrespective of diagnosis, a diagnosis-specific pattern of neuroleptic drug response has not been identified (Kendell, 1989).

If schizophrenia is a disorder which has no consistent pattern of symptoms, which has no particular course and which responds to no particular treatment, it is unlikely that one kind of core cognitive deficit can account for its many manifestations (Bentall *et al.*, 1988). Rather different symptoms will reflect different cognitive abnormalities, and cognitive–behavioural treatment programmes will have to take this complication into account.

The question of intentionality

This returns us to the point raised earlier about the kinds of cognitive abnormalities studied by schizophrenia researchers. It will be recalled that most contemporary approaches to psychosis have failed to pay attention to the content of symptoms, and that some authors have even argued that psychotic symptoms are generally meaningless. Interestingly, this was not an assumption made by Kraepelin, who recognised the role of personality and experience in determining the content of psychotic experiences, even when these experiences reflected undoubted cerebral pathology:

> Even where clear-cut external agents are involved (e.g. a head injury or poisoning) . . . there is an interplay of forces at work: the nervous system of the affected individual, the deficits inherited from past generations and his own personal history . . . these preconditions are especially important when considering forms of the illness which do not arise from external injury, but from circumstances of the individual concerned . . . it seems absurd to propose that syphilis causes patients to believe that they are the proud possessors of cars . . . rather the general desires of such people are reflected in their delusions . . . if these observations approximate the truth we will have to look for the key to the understanding of the clinical picture primarily in characteristics of the individual patient . . . his expectations play a decisive role.
> (Kraepelin, 1920; quoted in Berrios and Hauser, 1988, p. 814)

In the case of positive psychotic symptoms, at least, their meaningfulness should be evident on even a cursory examination. For example, delusions tend to concern certain themes, most often of persecution or grandiosity, which invariably reflect the patient's concern about his or her position in the social universe (Sims, 1988). Similarly, hallucinations are usually constrained by content, so that patients' voices make particular kinds of remarks, often negatively self-referent accusations or instigations (Bentall, 1990a). With regard to the speech disorders associated with psychosis, these become most obvious when patients 'intermingle' emotionally salient themes from their past into their conversations (Harrow and Prosen, 1978). The implication of these observations is that researchers, in addition to expecting a different pattern of cognitive abnormalities corresponding to each type of symptom, will also have to expect that some of the most important abnormalities will take the form of cognitive biases rather than deficits.

This is an appropriate point at which to introduce some of my own research into delusions and hallucinations which has explicitly focused on the role of content-specific information processing in the abnormal experiences of psychotic patients. When discussing this research I will try to indicate briefly the relevance of these findings for the design of effective cognitive–behavioural interventions.

COGNITIVE PROCESSES AND PERSECUTORY DELUSIONS

Our research into psychotic beliefs has focused on persecutory delusions and has been informed by the hypothesis that such beliefs are a function of the same kinds of variables which affect normal beliefs and attitudes. A crude, heuristic model showing how some of these variables are inter-related is shown in Figure 1.1. In this model (which is admittedly a simplification), belief-relevant information in the world is perceived by the individual, who then makes certain inferences about that data and arrives at a belief. A truly rational individual would then seek further evidence to either refute or support the belief, but research indicates that normal subjects are generally very bad at this (Gilhooly, 1983).

It is possible that the abnormal beliefs observed in psychiatric patients

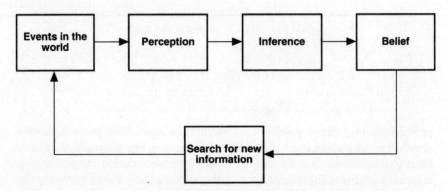

Figure 1.1 A simple model of belief acquisition indicating possible loci of causal variables influencing the formation and maintenance of delusional beliefs (reproduced with permission from Bentall, 1990b)

reflect abnormalities at any of these stages. With regard to environmental information which may provide the context for delusion formation, some authors have argued that deluded patients come from families (Heilbrun and Norbert, 1972; Kaffman, 1983) or social circumstances (Mirowsky and Ross, 1983) characterised by aversive control, inflexible rules, powerlessness and the threat of victimisation. Perceptual processes have also been implicated in the genesis of some kinds of delusions, since misperceived stimuli may sometimes provide fuel for irrational beliefs. Maher (Maher, 1974; Maher and Ross, 1984), for example, has argued that all delusional systems reflect rational attempts to explain anomalous experiences such as hallucinations or abnormal bodily sensations. Although this idea cannot be accepted uncritically because of the dissociations observed between abnormal beliefs and abnormal perceptions (Chapman and Chapman, 1988) it does seem likely that perceptual deficits are implicated in some delusions. For example, Ellis and Young (1990) have argued that the Capgras delusion (the belief that a loved one has been replaced by a robot or imposter) is partially the consequence of a disorder of the neuropsychological processes sustaining facial recognition, so that the patient fails to experience a feeling of familiarity when greeting someone who should be very familiar.

One way in which core cognitive processes can influence the availability of belief-relevant information to the individual is through mechanisms of attention. Ullman and Krasner (1969) argued long ago that persecutory delusions might be maintained by selective attention to threatening events. Consistent with this, we have found that deluded patients show abnormal attention to threat-related words on an emotional Stroop task (Bentall and Kaney, 1989). On this kind of task, a variant of a procedure first described by Stroop (1935), subjects are shown words printed in different colours and are asked to ignore the meaning and just name the colours. In practice, it is very difficult not to pay attention to the meaning of the words, and this slows down naming of the colours. In our study, we found that deluded patients were particularly slow when naming threat-related but not control words. In subsequent studies we have been able to show that deluded subjects have an abnormal tendency (compared to normal and depressed controls) to remember threat-related propositions during a story recall task (Kaney et al., 1992) and to remember both threat-related and depression-related words during a free recall task (Bentall et al., in press).

Most of our research on delusions has, however, focused on reasoning processes using the framework of attribution theory (Hewstone, 1989), which provides models of how people make inferences about the causes of events affecting themselves and other people. Attributional accounts have already been offered for those types of depression marked by low self-esteem. In particular, Abramson et al. (1978) have argued that depressed people make relatively internal, stable and global attributions for negative events. That is to say, if something unpleasant happens the depressed person

13

is likely to explain the event in terms of a cause internal to him or herself, which is unlikely to change and which will affect all areas of life (for example, explaining exam failure in terms of lack of intelligence). While the evidence that this cognitive style is causal in depression is at best equivocal, there is modest evidence that depression characterised by low self-esteem is indeed associated with this style of reasoning (Brewin, 1988).

In our first study of attributional processes in patients suffering from persecutory delusions (Kaney and Bentall, 1989), we gave Peterson *et al.*'s (1982) Attributional Style Questionnaire (ASQ) to deluded patients, psychiatric controls and normal subjects. This questionnaire requires subjects to think of possible causes for hypothetical positive and negative events (e.g. 'You go on a date and it turns out badly'; 'You win a prize'). Subjects then self-rate the causes they have generated on bipolar scales of internality (the extent to which the cause is due to themselves rather than other people or circumstances), stability (the extent to which the cause is likely to be present in the future) and globalness (the extent to which the cause will affect other areas of the respondent's life). Because the persecuted patients in our study all showed substantial depressive symptomatology, we matched them with psychiatric controls on the basis of scores on the Beck Depression Inventory. As we had anticipated, the deluded patients made excessively external, stable and global attributions for negative events. They were also observed to make excessively internal, global and stable attributions for positive events. In other words, if something went wrong they tended to blame this on other people or circumstances, whereas if something went right they showed an equally systematic tendency to credit themselves (see Figure 1.2). Subsequent analyses indicated that it was specifically the self-ratings of the deluded subjects which were abnormal, rather than the causes they generated (Kinderman *et al.*, 1992); these subjects often generated causes for negative events which were rated by independent judges as internal (e.g. failing to get a job because 'I can't get it together') but self-rated these attributions as external (due to other people or circumstances).

This finding was substantially replicated by Candido and Romney (1990), who studied non-depressed paranoids, depressed paranoids and depressed controls. In this study depressed paranoids were found not to differ from non-depressed paranoids on attributions for negative events, but were less inclined to make extreme internal attributions for positive events. These observations can be accounted for by assuming that deluded patients have an exaggerated 'self-serving bias' (Bentall, 1994; Bentall *et al.*, 1994b). The 'self-serving bias' is the tendency to attribute positive outcomes to self and negative outcomes to external causes, which has been demonstrated in a much lesser form in normal subjects in many experiments (Taylor, 1988). It is reasonable to assume that this bias is a mechanism for maintaining self-esteem.

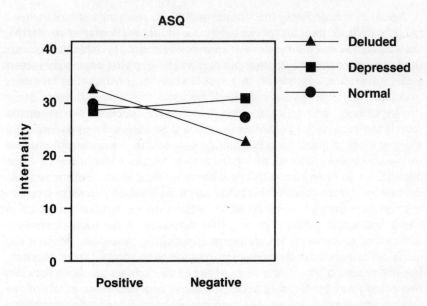

Figure 1.2 Deluded, depressed and normal subjects' attributions of causality (ratings of internality versus externality) for hypothetical positive and negative events on Peterson *et al.*'s Attributional Style Questionnaire. High scores indicate that subjects attribute blame for events to self, low scores indicate that they attribute blame to other people or circumstances. (Data from Kaney and Bentall, 1988; reproduced with permission from Bentall, 1994)

In a demonstration that the self-serving bias is relatively absent in depressives, Alloy and Abramson (1979) used a contingency judgement task. We therefore tried a version of their experimental procedure with patients suffering from persecutory delusions (Kaney and Bentall, 1992). Subjects were asked to play two computer games in which they had to make choices between stimuli presented on a screen. Starting with twenty points, incorrect choices led to the loss of one point and correct choices led to a gain of one point. Unknown to the subjects, the games were preprogrammed so that the outcome was predetermined, with one game (the 'lose game') leading to a net loss of points and the other game (the 'win game') leading to a gain of points. After each game the subjects were asked to estimate their degree of control over outcomes. Consistent with the hypothesis that persecutory delusions are the product of an abnormal self-serving bias, the deluded patients, in comparison with the normals, exhibited a strong tendency to claim more control in the win as opposed to the lose condition. The normal control subjects also showed this bias but to a significantly lesser degree. The depressed group, on the other hand, like those in Alloy and Abramson's study, were sadder but wiser and claimed very little control over the outcome of either game.

We have extended our attributional analysis by studying the explanations made by deluded patients for the behaviour of others (Bentall *et al.*, 1991b), showing that deluded subjects have an abnormal tendency to blame the actor (and not circumstances or other people) when observing negatively valued social interactions. However, in a recent study of attributional processes in deluded patients (Lyon *et al.*, 1994) we have investigated in more detail the hypothesis that delusions have a defensive function. We predicted that, if attributions for negative events could be elicited from patients in a manner which avoided them becoming aware that they were being required to allocate blame, patients with persecutory delusions would respond like depressives. In order to test this prediction, we used an attribution measure devised by Winters and Neale (1985) which is disguised as a story comprehension task. Subjects were asked to listen to stories involving themselves which had either positive or negative outcomes. After each story, they were asked to answer a few simple multiple choice questions. Most of the questions required simple factual information to be recalled from the story, but one question after each story required the subject to chose between two equally valid inferences about the cause (internal or external) of the outcome portrayed. As we had anticipated, both deluded and depressed subjects blamed themselves more for negative than for positive outcomes on this test. However, when given a more conventional attributional style measure the deluded subjects, as in previous experiments, attributed positive outcomes to self and negative outcomes to others.

Taken together, these findings provide strong support for the view that there is a motivational component to delusional beliefs. Specifically, it seems that deluded subjects construct their persecutory hypotheses in order to avoid awareness of discrepancies between how they perceive themselves to be and how they would like to be (Bentall *et al.*, 1994). In our most recent investigations we have therefore begun to search for methods of probing the self-concept of deluded patients. One such technique which we have employed (Bentall and Kaney, submitted) makes use of the phenomenon of 'self-referent encoding', the tendency to remember specifically information which relates to ourselves. Depressed deluded subjects, non-depressed deluded subjects, depressed and normal controls were required to complete a questionnaire in which they were asked to endorse as 'true' or 'not true' of themselves positive and negative trait words. Both groups of deluded subjects, like the normal controls, endorsed as true of themselves far more positive than negative trait words, whereas the depressed subjects endorsed an approximately equal number of negative and positive words. Immediately afterwards, the subjects were asked to remember as many of the trait words as possible. Consistent with their pattern of responses on the questionnaire, the normal subjects recalled more of the positive words which they had endorsed as true of themselves than the negative words which they had endorsed. However, when their recall of endorsed words was examined, both groups of deluded subjects, like the depressives, recalled an approximately equal number of negative and positive words. Thus, whether or not they were depressed, the deluded subjects' endorsement scores were similar to those of the normal subjects, and seemed to indicate a relatively positive view of the self. The same subjects' recall scores, however, were similar to those of the depressed subjects and seemed to indicate a negative view of the self.

In this study, subjects also completed the Dysfunctional Attitude Scale (Dobson and Shaw, 1986) which measures beliefs or attitudes which delineate excessively rigid and perfectionistic criteria for evaluating personal performance and self-worth (e.g. 'I should be able to please everybody'; 'I cannot be happy unless most people I know admire me'). High scores on this scale usually indicate a high degree of discrepancy between perceptions of the self and the ideal self, and are therefore associated with a negative view of the self. As expected, and consistent with the recall data, both the depressed deluded subjects and the non-depressed deluded subjects, like the depressed patients, scored abnormally high on this questionnaire.

Given that the beliefs of deluded patients seem to have the function of preventing negatively self-referent thoughts from entering consciousness, it is not surprising that they are reluctant to give the beliefs up in the face of counter-arguments or contradicting evidence. It therefore follows that therapeutic interventions which avoid direct challenges to patients' delusional systems should be more effective than therapeutic strategies which involve confronting patients with the apparent irrationality of their beliefs. Consistent with this analysis, a number of authors have reported cognitive–behavioural interventions which seem to achieve some degree of belief modification in deluded patients, either because they involve the therapist challenging at first only beliefs which are peripheral to the main delusional system (Watts et al., 1973; Hartman and Cashman, 1983) or because they require the patient to devise tests of his or her beliefs and to collaborate with the therapist in observing the outcomes of those tests (Chadwick and Lowe, 1990; Garety et al., 1994; see also Chapters 4 and 7 of the present volume).

COGNITIVE PROCESSES AND AUDITORY HALLUCINATIONS

Any understanding of the psychological processes responsible for hallucinatory experiences must be informed by a number of key observations. First, although hallucinations are usually attributed to schizophrenia (Sartorius et al., 1974), they are sometimes reported by people who are otherwise normal and who do not regard themselves as psychiatrically ill (Romme and Escher, 1989 and see Chapter 8). Second, considerable cultural differences exist in the experience of hallucinations, both in the extent to which they are reported by people who regard themselves as normal (Bourguignon, 1970), and in the modality of hallucinations reported to clinicians by patients in different parts of the world (Al-Issa, 1978). Third, clinical studies indicate that hallucinations are most likely to occur during periods of stress (Slade, 1973). Consistent with this observation, psychophysical studies indicate that the onset of hallucinations is associated with changes in psychophysical arousal (Cooklin *et al.*, 1983). Fourth, research also indicates that patients are more likely to report hallucinations when deprived of sensations or when exposed to unpatterned stimulation such as white noise (Margo *et al.*, 1981). Fifth, some studies have indicated that auditory hallucinations tend to be associated with subvocalisation or micromovements of the speech muscles (e.g. Inouye and Shimizu, 1970; Green and Preston, 1981). Finally, there is also evidence that auditory hallucinations tend to be blocked by concurrent verbal tasks such as reading or speaking aloud (e.g. Margo *et al.*, 1981; James, 1983).

A number of authors have suggested that these kinds of findings can be accommodated by supposing that hallucinatory experiences occur when private or mental events are misattributed to an external or alien source. This kind of model explains the apparent association between auditory hallucinations and subvocalisation, which accompanies normal thinking (McGuigan, 1978). It also explains why verbal tasks, which block the stream of ongoing subvocal activity, tend to inhibit hallucinatory experiences. However, the exact mechanisms responsible for this kind of misattribution remain a topic of some debate. Hoffman (1986) has argued that hallucinating patients suffer from a discourse planning disorder so that they experience their subvocalisations as unintended; against this no consistent relationship has been observed between hallucinations and speech disorders (Slade and Bentall, 1988). Frith and Done (1987), on the other hand, have argued that all positive symptoms reflect a deficit in an internal neuropsychological monitoring mechanism responsible for identifying the source of perceived events. Following a detailed review of the available psychological literature on hallucinations, I similarly proposed that it is the hallucinator's decision about the source of events which is abnormal but, instead of attributing this kind of error to a defect in a hypothetical neuropsychological mechanism, argued that it might reflect both top-down processes (patients' beliefs and expectations about what kinds of events are likely to occur) together with specific (perhaps neuropsychological) deficits in the ability to discriminate between internal events and external events (Bentall, 1990a). Consistent with existing evidence on hallucinations, this account carries the implication that distinguishing between internally generated and externally generated auditory sensations should be most difficult under conditions of stress and unpatterned stimulation (see Figure 1.3). This account also explains the observed cultural differences in the experience of hallucinations if it is

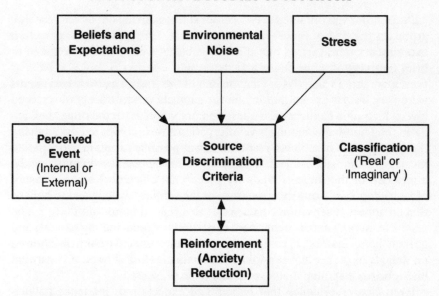

Figure 1.3 A model of auditory hallucinations showing the influence of different
variables on an individual's classification of perceived events as 'real' or
'imaginary' (from Slade and Bentall, 1988)

assumed that an individual's classification of an event as 'real' or 'imaginary'
will be influenced by culturally encoded beliefs about what kinds of events
are likely to occur in the real world.

In an experiment designed to access deficits in the ability to discriminate
between internally generated and externally generated events, Bentall *et al.*
(1991a) reported a study of hallucinating patients, deluded and normal
controls using a 'reality monitoring' paradigm. Adapting a method from the
work of Johnson and Raye (1981), subjects were required to generate
answers to simple clues (e.g. 'Think of a vehicle beginning with C') and listen
to a list of similar paired associates (e.g. 'Country–Norway'). One week later,
the subjects were asked to identify the source of items from a list containing
the answers they had given to clues, the associates they had heard and new
foils. Both hallucinating patients and deluded controls were less accurate
than the normal controls and there was no difference between the two
psychotic groups on the total number of errors made. However, when the
type of errors made were studied, the hallucinators, in comparison with
the deluded subjects, were found to be more likely to misclassify their
own answers to clues as words they had heard. Although this finding is
consistent with the view that hallucinators have some difficulty in identifying
their own thoughts as self-generated, the group differences were relatively
small and were probably not sufficient to account for the hallucinator's
tendency to hear voices.

Evidence that patients' beliefs and expectations are implicated in hallucinations was obtained in two earlier studies carried out by our research group. In the first of these (Bentall and Slade, 1985), two signal detection experiments were carried out in which subjects were required to listen to brief episodes of white noise and determine whether or not a voice was present; in fact a voice was present on half of the trials. The two experiments were very similar except that in one the subjects were students who scored low or high on a hallucination questionnaire whereas, in the other, hallucinating and non-hallucinating psychotic patients were compared. By studying the exact pattern of subjects' responses it was possible to obtain two separate measures from each subject: a measure of *perceptual sensitivity* (roughly, a measure of the subjects' auditory perceptual efficiency) and a measure of *perceptual bias* (roughly, a measure of the subjects' willingness to believe that an apparent sensation corresponds to a real stimulus 'out there'). The results from both experiments were very similar. Hallucinating patients and normal 'hallucinators', in comparison with their respective controls, showed no deficits in perceptual sensitivity, but hallucinators showed a consistent bias towards assuming that a voice had been presented.

Even clearer evidence that beliefs and expectations influence hallucinations was obtained in a subsequent study (Young *et al.*, 1987). In this study hallucinating and non-hallucinating psychotic patients were again compared, as were students who scored high or low on a hallucination questionnaire. Replicating an earlier study by Mintz and Alpert (1972), we were able to show that the psychiatric and normal hallucinators, in comparison with their respective controls, were much more likely to be influenced by suggestions to hallucinate (for example the suggestion, 'Close your eyes and listen to the recording "Jingle Bells"' when no such recording was played).

One implication of these findings is that patients might be taught to reattribute their voices to themselves. If it is the case that patients' misattribution of their thoughts to an external source at least in part reflects their beliefs and expectations, then focusing on those beliefs and expectations may be of particular therapeutic value. In Liverpool, we have begun to develop a therapeutic programme which specifically draws patients' attention to the content of their voices and the beliefs they have about the voices' origins (Haddock *et al.*, 1993; Bentall *et al.*, 1994a; see Chapter 3). A somewhat similar approach has been developed by Chadwick and Birchwood (1994; see also Chapter 4) who have focused on patients' beliefs about the omnipotence of their voices. Although these kinds of therapeutic strategies are at a relatively early stage of development they seem to hold out considerable promise for the future treatment of hallucinating patients.

CONCLUSIONS

In this chapter I have argued that progress towards adequate psychological treatments for psychotic patients has been impeded by some of the assumptions commonly held about psychosis. In particular, it is often assumed that psychotic disorders fall into a few discrete categories, and that the symptoms experienced by psychotic patients have no meaning. Phenomenological and experimental research supports neither of these assumptions. Future psychological research into psychosis should therefore focus on particular manifestations of psychopathology, i.e. the symptoms, and measure content-specific information processing biases as well as gross cognitive deficits. There is nothing particularly antibiological about this approach; after all, it is difficult to see how biological abnormalities cause psychotic experiences without an adequate understanding of the psychological functions implemented by the relevant biological systems. Psychological research of the kind I have outlined should, therefore, lead to models of psychopathology which integrate biological and psychological findings (Bentall, 1991).

The main advantage of such developments for patients would be the design of cognitive–behavioural interventions that accurately target those cognitive abnormalities which underlie particular symptoms. Cognitive–behavioural interventions for psychosis remain in their infancy (Slade, 1990) but, as I outlined at the outset, there are good grounds for optimism about future developments. Further refinements of existing approaches, the development of innovative strategies, carefully conducted single case studies and controlled trials are required to identify precisely which therapeutic methods are most efficacious in which circumstances, and which patients are most likely to benefit. The following chapters attempt to address some of these issues.

ACKNOWLEDGEMENT

An earlier version of this chapter was published under the title 'Des études cognitives sur la psychose à la thérapie cognitivo-comportementale des symptômes psychotiques: à la recherche d'interventions psychologiques à l'ère de la psychiatrie biologique' in *Psychothérapie Cognitive Des Psychoses Chroniques*, edited by O. Chambion and M. Marie-Cardine, Masson: Paris, 1993. Much of the research described in this chapter was supported by research grants to the author from the UK Medical Research Council (for studies of the psychological treatment of hallucinations, with P.D. Slade) and the Wellcome Trust (for studies of cognitive processes in psychotic symptomatology).

REFERENCES

Abramson, L. Y., Seligman, M. E. P. and Teasdale, J. D. (1978) 'Learned helplessness in humans: Critique and reformulation', *Journal of Abnormal Psychology* 78: 40–74.

Adams, H. E. and Suther, P. (eds) (1984) *Comprehensive Handbook of Psychopathology*, New York: Plenum.

Adams, H. E., Malatesta, V., Brantley, P. J. and Turkat, I. D. (1981) 'Modification of cognitive processes: a case study of schizophrenia', *Journal of Consulting and Clinical Psychology* 49: 460–4.

Al-Issa, I. (1978) 'Social and cultural aspects of hallucinations', *Psychological Bulletin* 84: 570–87.

Alloy, L. B. and Abramson, L. Y. (1979) 'Judgement of contingency in depressed and non-depressed students: Sadder but wiser?', *Journal of Experimental Psychology: General* 108: 441–85.

American Psychiatric Association (1987) *Diagnostic and Statistical Manual of Mental Disorders*, 3rd edition, revised, Washington: APA.

Andreasen, N. C. (1984) *The Broken Brain: The Biological Revolution in Psychiatry*, New York: Harper and Row.

Bellack, A. S. (1986) 'Schizophrenia: Behavior therapy's forgotten child', *Behavior Therapy* 17: 199–214.

Bellack, A. S. (1992) 'Cognitive rehabilitation for schizophrenia: Is it possible? Is it necessary?', *Schizophrenia Bulletin* 18: 43–50.

Bentall, R. P. (1990a) 'The illusion of reality: A review and integration of psychological research on hallucinations', *Psychological Bulletin* 107: 82–95.

—— (1990b) 'The syndromes and symptoms of psychosis: Or why you can't play twenty questions with the concept of schizophrenia and hope to win', in R. P. Bentall (ed.) *Reconstructing Schizophrenia*, London: Routledge.

—— (ed.) (1990c) *Reconstructing Schizophrenia*, London: Routledge.

—— (1991) 'Explaining and explaining away insanity', in R. Tallis and H. Robinson (eds) *Pursuit of Mind*, London: Carcanet.

—— (1992a) 'Psychological deficits and biases in psychiatric disorders', *Current Opinion in Psychiatry* 5: 825–30.

—— (1992b) 'The classification of schizophrenia', in D. J. Kavanagh (ed.) *Schizophrenia: An Overview and Practical Handbook*, London: Chapman and Hall.

—— (1992c) 'Reconstructing psychopathology', *The Psychologist* 5: 61–5.

—— (1994) 'Cognitive biases and abnormal beliefs: Towards a model of persecutory delusions', in A. S. David and J. Cutting (eds) *The Neuropsychology of Schizophrenia*, London: Lawrence Erlbaum Associates.

Bentall, R. P. and Kaney, S. (1989) 'Content specific processing and persecutory delusions: An investigation using the emotional Stroop test', *British Journal of Medical Psychology* 62: 355–64.

Bentall, R. P. and Kaney, S. (submitted) 'The defensive function of persecutory delusions: Dysfunctional attitudes and self-referent encoding'.

Bentall, R. P. and Slade, P. D. (1985) 'Reality testing and auditory hallucinations: A signal-detection analysis', *British Journal of Clinical Psychology* 24: 159–69.

Bentall, R. P., Higson, P. J. and Lowe, C. F. (1987) 'Teaching self-instructions to chronic schizophrenic patients: Efficacy and generalization', *Behavioural Psychotherapy* 15: 58–76.

Bentall, R. P., Jackson, H. F. and Pilgrim, D. (1988) 'Abandoning the concept of "schizophrenia": Some implications of validity arguments for psychological research into psychotic phenomena', *British Journal of Clinical Psychology* 27: 156–69.

Bentall, R. P., Claridge, G. S. and Slade, P. D. (1989) 'The multidimensional nature of schizotypal traits: A factor-analytic study with normal subjects', *British Journal of Clinical Psychology* 28: 363–75.

Bentall, R. P., Baker, G. and Havers, S. (1991a) 'Reality monitoring and psychotic hallucinations', *British Journal of Clinical Psychology* 30: 213–22.

22

Bentall, R. P., Kaney, S. and Dewey, M. E. (1991b) 'Paranoia and social reasoning: An attribution theory analysis', *British Journal of Clinical Psychology* 30: 13–23.

Bentall, R. P., Haddock, G. and Slade, P. D. (1994a) 'Cognitive–behaviour therapy for persistent auditory hallucinations: From theory to therapy', *Behavior Therapy* 25: 51–66.

Bentall, R. P., Kinderman, P. and Kaney, S. (1994b) 'Self, attributional processes and abnormal beliefs: Towards a model of persecutory delusions', *Behaviour Research and Therapy* 32: 331–41.

Bentall, R. P., Kaney, S. and Bowen-Jones, K. (forthcoming) 'Persecutory delusions and recall of threat-related, depression-related and neutral words', *Cognitive Therapy and Research*.

Berrios, G. (1991) 'Delusions as "wrong beliefs": A conceptual history', *British Journal of Psychiatry* 159, Suppl. 14: 6–13.

Berrios, G. and Hauser, R. (1988) 'The early development of Kraepelin's ideas on classification: A conceptual history', *Psychological Medicine* 18, 813–21.

Blashfield, K. (1984) *The Classification of Psychopathology: NeoKraepelinian and Quantitative Approaches*, New York: Plenum.

Bleuler, E. (1950) *Dementia Praecox or the Group of Schizophrenias* (originally published 1911, English translation; E. Zinkin), New York: International Universities Press.

Bourguignon, E. (1970) 'Hallucinations and trance: An anthropologist's perspective', in W. Keup (ed.) *Origins and Mechanisms of Hallucinations*, New York: Plenum.

Boyle, M. (1991) *Schizophrenia: A Scientific Delusion*, London: Routledge.

Breggin, P. (1993) *Toxic Psychiatry*, London: Fontana.

Brenner, H. D. (1989) 'The treatment of basic psychological dysfunctions from a systematic point of view', *British Journal of Psychiatry* 155 (suppl. 5): 24–83.

Brenner, H. D., Hodel, B., Volker, R. and Corrigan, P. (1992) 'Treatment of cognitive dysfunctions and behavioral deficits in schizophrenia', *Schizophrenia Bulletin* 18: 21–6.

Brewin, C. (1988) *Cognitive Foundations of Clinical Psychology*, Hove: Lawrence Erlbaum Associates.

Brockington, I. F., Kendell, R. E. and Leff, J. P. (1978) 'Definitions of schizophrenia: Concordance and prediction of outcome', *Psychological Medicine* 8: 387–98.

Brown, W. A. and Herz, L. R. (1989) 'Response to neuroleptic drugs as a device for classifying schizophrenia', *Schizophrenia Bulletin* 15: 123–9.

Candido, C. and Romney, D. M. (1990) 'Attributional style in paranoid vs depressed patients', *British Journal of Medical Psychology* 63: 355–63.

Chadwick, P. and Birchwood, M. (1994) 'Challenging the omnipotence of voices', *British Journal of Psychiatry* 164: 190–201.

Chadwick, P. and Lowe, C. F. (1990) 'The measurement and modification of delusional beliefs', *Journal of Consulting and Clinical Psychology* 58: 225–32.

Chapman, L. J. and Chapman, J. P. (1988) 'The genesis of delusions', in T. F. Oltmans and B. A. Maher (eds) *Delusional Beliefs*, New York: Wiley.

Ciompi, L. (1984) 'Is there really a schizophrenia?: The long term course of psychotic phenomena', *British Journal of Psychiatry* 145: 636–40.

Cooklin, R., Sturgeon, D. and Leff, J. P. (1983) 'The relationship between auditory hallucinations and spontaneous fluctuation of skin conductance in schizophrenia', *British Journal of Psychiatry* 142: 47–52.

Crow, T. J. (1980) 'The molecular pathology of schizophrenia: More than one disease process?', *British Medical Journal* 280: 66–8.

David, A. S. and Cutting, J. (eds) (1994) *The Neuropsychology of Schizophrenia*, London: Lawrence Erlbaum Associates.

23

Dobson, K. S. and Shaw, B. F. (1986) 'Cognitive assessment with major depressive disorders', *Cognitive Therapy and Research* 10: 13–30.
Ellis, H. D. and Young, A. W. (1990) 'Accounting for delusional misidentifications', *British Journal of Psychiatry* 157: 239–48.
Farmer, A., Jones, I., Williams, J. and McGuffin, P. (1993) 'Defining schizophrenia: Operational criteria', *Journal of Mental Health* 2: 209–22.
Finn, S. E., Bailey, J. M., Schultz, R. T. and Faber, R. (1990) 'Subjective utility ratings of neuroleptics in treating schizophrenia', *Psychological Medicine* 35: 843–8.
Fowler, D. and Morley, S. (1989) 'The cognitive–behavioural treatment of hallucinations and delusions: A preliminary study', *Behavioural Psychotherapy* 17: 267–82.
Frith, C. D. and Done, D. J. (1987) 'Towards a neuropsychology of schizophrenia', *British Journal of Psychiatry* 153: 437–43.
Garety, P. A., Kuipers, L., Fowler, D., Chamberlain, F. and Dunn, G. (1994) 'Cognitive–behavioural therapy for drug-resistant psychosis', *British Journal of Medical Psychology* 67: 259–71.
Gilhooly, K. (1983) *Thinking*, London: Academic Press.
Gray, J. A., Feldon, J., Rawlins, J. N. P., Hemsley, D. R. and Smith, A. D. (1991) 'The neuropsychology of schizophrenia', *Behavioural and Brain Sciences* 14: 1–84.
Green, P. and Preston, M. (1981) 'Reinforcement of vocal correlates of auditory hallucinations by auditory feedback: A case study', *British Journal of Psychiatry* 139: 204–8.
Guze, S. (1989) 'Biological psychiatry: Is there any other kind?', *Psychological Medicine* 19: 315–23.
Haddock, G., Bentall, R. P. and Slade, P. D. (1993) 'Psychological treatment of chronic auditory hallucinations: Two case studies', *Behavioural and Cognitive Psychotherapy* 21: 335–46.
Hafner, H., Gattaz, W. G. and Janzarik, W. (eds) (1987) *Search for the Causes of Schizophrenia*, Berlin: Springer.
Harrow, M. and Prosen, M. (1978) 'Intermingling and disordered logic as influences on schizophrenic thought', *Archives of General Psychiatry* 35: 1213–18.
Hartman, L. M. and Cashman, F. E. (1983) 'Cognitive–behavioural and psychopharmacological treatment of delusional symptoms: A preliminary report', *Behavioural Psychotherapy* 11: 50–61.
Harvey, P. D. and Neale, J. M. (1983) 'The specificity of thought disorder to schizophrenia: Research methods in their historical perspective', in B. Maher (ed.) *Progress in Experimental Personality Research*, volume 12, New York: Academic Press.
Heilbrun, A. B. and Norbert, N. (1972) 'Style of adaption to aversive maternal control and paranoid behaviour', *Journal of Genetic Psychology* 121: 145–53.
Hemsley, D. R. (1992) 'Disorders of perception and cognition in schizophrenia', *Revue Européenne de Psychologie Appliquée* 42: 104–14.
—— (1993) 'A simple (or simplistic?) cognitive model for schizophrenia', *Behaviour, Research and Therapy* 7: 633–45.
Herbst, K. G. (ed.) (1987) *Schizophrenia*, London: Mental Health Foundation.
Hewstone, M. (1989) *Causal Attribution: From Cognitive Processes to Collective Beliefs*, Oxford: Blackwell.
Hoffman, R. E. (1986) 'Verbal hallucinations and language production processes in schizophrenia', *Brain and Behavioural Sciences* 9: 503–48.
Inouye, T. and Shimizu, A. (1970) 'The electromyographic study of verbal hallucination', *Journal of Nervous and Mental Disease* 151: 415–22.

James, D. A. E. (1983) 'The experimental treatment of two cases of auditory hallucinations', *British Journal of Psychiatry* 143: 515–16.

Jaspers, K. (1963) *General Psychopathology* (translated by J. Hoenig and M. W. Hamilton), Manchester: Manchester University Press.

Johnson, M. K. and Raye, C. L. (1981) 'Reality monitoring', *Psychological Review* 88: 67–85.

Kaffman (1983) 'Paranoid disorders: Family sources of the delusional system', *Journal of Family Therapy* 5: 107–16.

Kaney, S. and Bentall, R. P. (1989) 'Persecutory delusions and attributional style', *British Journal of Medical Psychology* 62: 191–8.

—— (1992) 'Persecutory delusions and the self-serving bias: Evidence from a contingency judgement task', *Journal of Nervous and Mental Disease* 180: 773–80.

Kaney, S., Wolfenden, M., Dewey, M. E. and Bentall, R. P. (1992) 'Persecutory delusions and the recall of threatening and non-threatening propositions', *British Journal of Clinical Psychology* 31, 85–7.

Kavanagh, D. J. (ed.) (1992) *Schizophrenia: An Overview and Practical Handbook*, London: Chapman and Hall.

Kendell, R. E. (1989) 'Clinical validity', in L. N. Robins and J. E. Barrett (eds) *The Validity of Psychiatric Diagnosis*, New York: Raven Press.

Kendell, R. E. and Gourlay, J. A. (1970) 'The clinical distinction between the affective psychoses and schizophrenia', *British Journal of Psychiatry* 117: 261–6.

Kendler, K. S. and Hewitt, J. (1992) 'The structure of self-report schizotypy in twins', *Journal of Personality Disorders* 6: 1–17.

Kinderman, P., Kaney, S., Morley, S. and Bentall, R. P. (1992) 'Paranoia and the defensive attributional style: Deluded and depressed patients' attributions about their own attributions', *British Journal of Medical Psychology* 65: 371–83.

Kingdon, D. G. and Turkington, D. (1991) 'The use of cognitive–behaviour therapy with a normalising rationale in schizophrenia', *Journal of Nervous and Mental Disease* 179: 207–11.

—— (1994) *Cognitive–behavioural Therapy of Schizophrenia*, Hove: Lawrence Erlbaum Associates.

Klimidis, S., Stuart, G. W., Minas, I. H., Copolov, D. L. and Singh, B. S. (1993) 'Positive and negative symptoms in psychoses: Re-analysis of published SAPS and SANS global ratings', *Schizophrenia Research* 9: 11–18.

Liddle, P. F. (1987) 'The symptoms of chronic schizophrenia: a re-examination of the positive–negative dichotomy', *British Journal of Psychiatry* 151: 145–51.

Lyon, H. M., Kaney, S. and Bentall, R. P. (1994) 'The defensive function of persecutory delusions: Evidence from attribution tasks', *British Journal of Psychiatry* 164: 637–46.

McGuffin, P., Farmer, A. and Harvey, I. (1991) 'A polydiagnostic application of operational criteria in studies of psychotic illness', *Archives of General Psychiatry* 48: 764–70.

McGuigan, F. J. (1978) *Cognitive Psychophysiology: Principles of Covert Behaviour*, Englewood Cliffs, New Jersey: Prentice-Hall.

Maher, B. A. (1974) 'Delusional thinking and perceptual disorder', *Journal of Individual Psychology* 30: 98–113.

—— (ed.) (1983) *Progress in Experimental Personality Research*, volume 12, New York: Academic Press.

Maher, B. A. and Ross, J. S. (1984) 'Delusions', in H. E. Adams and P. Suther (eds) *Comprehensive Handbook of Psychopathology*, New York: Plenum.

Marder, S. R. (1992) 'Pharmacological treatment of schizophrenia', in D. J. Kavanagh (ed.) *Schizophrenia: An Overview and Practical Handbook*, London: Chapman and Hall.

Margo, A., Hemsley, D. R. and Slade, P. D. (1981) 'The effects of varying auditory input on schizophrenic hallucinations', *British Journal of Psychiatry* 139: 122–7.

Meichenbaum, D. M. (1977) *Cognitive–behaviour Modification*, New York: Plenum.

Meichenbaum, D. M. and Cameron, R. (1973) 'Training schizophrenics to talk to themselves: A means of developing attentional controls', *Behavior Therapy* 4: 515–34.

Minas, I. H., Stuart, G. W., Klimidis, S., Jackson, H. J., Singh, B. S. and Copolov, D. L. (1992) 'Positive and negative symptoms in the psychoses: Multidimensional scaling of SAPS and SANS items', *Schizophrenia Research* 8: 143–56.

Mintz, S. and Alpert, M. (1972) 'Imagery vividness, reality testing and schizophrenic hallucinations', *Journal of Abnormal Psychology* 19: 310–16.

Mirowsky, J. and Ross, C. E. (1983) 'Paranoia and the structure of powerlessness', *American Sociological Review* 48: 228–39.

Mueser, K. T. and Berenbaum, H. (1990) 'Psychodynamic treatment of schizophrenia: Is there a future?', *Psychological Medicine* 20: 253–62.

Muntaner, C., Garcia-Sevilla, L. and Fernandez, A. (1988) 'Personality dimensions, schizotypal and borderline personality traits and psychosis proneness', *Personality and Individual Differences* 9: 257–68.

Neale, J. and Oltmans, T. F. (1980) *Schizophrenia*, New York: Wiley.

Oltmans, T. F. and Maher, B. A. (eds) *Delusional Beliefs*, New York: Wiley.

Peterson, C., Semmel, A., Von Baeyer, C., Abramson, L. Y., Metlasky, G. I. and Seligman, M. P. E. (1982) 'The Attributional Style Questionnaire', *Cognitive Therapy and Research* 6: 287–300.

Reider, O. (1974) 'The origin of our confusion about schizophrenia', *Psychiatry* 37: 197–208.

Robins, L. N. and Barrett, J. E. (eds) (1989) *The Validity of Psychiatric Diagnosis*, New York: Raven Press.

Romme, M. and Escher, A. (1989) 'Hearing voices', *Schizophrenia Bulletin* 15: 209–16.

Sarbin, T. R. and Mancuso, J. C. (1980) *Schizophrenia: Diagnosis or Moral Verdict?*, Oxford: Pergamon.

Sartorius, N., Shapiro, R. and Jablensky, A. (1974) 'The international pilot study of schizophrenia', *Schizophrenia Bulletin* 1: 21–5.

Sartorius, N., Jablensky, A., Ernberg, G., Leff, J., Korten, A. and Gulibant, W. (1987) 'Course of schizophrenia in different countries: Some results of a WHO comparative 5 year follow-up study', in H. Hafner *et al.* (eds) *Search for the Causes of Schizophrenia*, Berlin: Springer.

Sims, A. (1988) *Symptoms in the Mind*, London: Ballière Tindall.

Slade, P. D. (1973) 'The psychological investigation and treatment of auditory hallucinations: a second case report', *British Journal of Medical Psychology* 46: 293–6.

Slade, P. D. (1990) 'The behavioural and cognitive treatment of psychotic symptoms', in R. P. Bentall (ed.) *Reconstructing Schizophrenia*, London: Routledge.

Slade, P. D. and Bentall, R. P. (1988) *Sensory Deception: A Scientific Analysis of Hallucination*, London and Sydney: Croom Helm.

Spring, B. J. and Ravdin, L. (1992) 'Cognitive remediation in schizophrenia: Should we attempt it?', *Schizophrenia Bulletin* 18: 15–26.

Stroop, J. R. (1935) 'Studies of interference in serial verbal reactions', *Journal of Experimental Psychology* 18: 643–62.

Tallis, R. (1991) 'A critique of neuromythology', in R. Tallis and H. Robinson (eds) *Pursuit of Mind*, London: Carcanet.

Tallis, R. and Robinson, H. (eds) (1991) *Pursuit of Mind*, London: Carcanet.

Tarrier, N., Harwood, S., Yusopoff, L., Beckett, R. and Baker, A. (1990) 'Coping strategy enhancement (CSE): A method of treating residual schizophrenic symptoms', *Behavioural Psychotherapy* 18: 283–93.

Tarrier, N., Beckett, R., Harwood, S., Baker, A., Yusopoff, L. and Ugarteburu, I. (1993) 'A trial of two cognitive–behavioural methods of treating drug-resistant residual psychotic symptoms in schizophrenia: I Outcome', *British Journal of Psychiatry* 162: 524–32.

Taylor, S. E. (1988) *Positive Illusions*, New York: Basic Books.

Ullmann, L. P. and Krasner, L. (1969) *A Psychological Approach to Abnormal Behaviour*, Englewood Cliffs, New Jersey: Prentice-Hall.

Warner, R. (1985) *Recovery from Schizophrenia: Psychiatry and Political Economy*, London: Routledge and Kegan Paul.

Watts, F. N., Powell, E. G. and Austin, S. V. (1973) 'The modification of abnormal beliefs', *British Journal of Medical Psychology* 46: 356–63.

Winters, K. C. and Neale. J. M. (1985) 'Mania and low self-esteem', *Journal of Abnormal Psychology* 94: 282–90.

Young, H. F., Bentall, R. P., Slade, P. D. and Dewey, M. E. (1987) 'The role of brief instructions and suggestibility in the elicitation of hallucinations in normal and psychiatric subjects', *Journal of Nervous and Mental Disease* 175: 41–8.

2

A HISTORICAL OVERVIEW OF PSYCHOLOGICAL TREATMENTS FOR PSYCHOTIC SYMPTOMS

Peter D. Slade and Gillian Haddock

INTRODUCTION

Psychological treatments for psychotic symptoms have been available for more than thirty years, without becoming well recognised or accepted into general treatment settings. During this period, psychotic disorders have been viewed as primarily biologically determined and therefore only amenable to biological treatments such as neuroleptic medication. During the early 1990s, the value of psychological treatments has become increasingly recognised as a viable treatment for a wide range of disorders, even where these have clear biological underpinnings. It is not surprising, therefore, that psychological treatments have become a focus of interest in the field of psychotic disorders.

The following historical overview traces the development of behavioural and cognitive–behavioural treatments for psychotic patients over the last few decades. The review will focus mainly on positive psychotic symptoms (that is, hallucinations and delusions). The most recent developments are described in the subsequent chapters of this book. It should be noted, however, that no attempt is made in this chapter to cover more general psychotherapeutic and psychodynamic approaches to psychosis.

The historical analysis is interesting in that it reflects changing attitudes and approaches to severe mental health problems, and behaviour in general, over the past thirty years. Thus, the first behavioural approaches used in the treatment of psychosis in the 1960s and early 1970s were firmly based on conditioning principles, both operant and classical, and were generally viewed as methods of behavioural modification or behavioural engineering. The former operant approaches were inspired by the laboratory studies of B. F. Skinner (1953) and his basic thesis that all behaviour is determined and controlled by the environment. Behaviour of all kinds, including that of psychotic patients, could therefore only be changed by therapists intervening actively and directly. The behavioural 'engineering' analogy was strongly held at the time, both because of the impact of Skinner's ideas, and as a result of the high profile accorded to Science and Technology in the 1960s. The latter was given its own Government Ministry, for the first time in the United Kingdom, by the Labour Government of that era.

In the 1970s and early 1980s an intermediate position held sway, whereby the main psychological treatments explored (i.e. social skills training, life skills training and family management) were focused on a mixture of behaviour modification principles and empowering principles. That is, they were approaches which both attempted to change the behaviour of patients and their relatives, while at the same time providing them with the tools to help themselves (i.e. empowering approaches).

Finally, in the latter part of the 1980s and beyond, we saw the emphasis placed firmly on the value of empowerment approaches. That is, the task of the therapist was no longer to 'change the behaviour of the patient', but rather to 'help the client to change their own behaviour, if they wished to do so'. Subsequent chapters will describe the current methods which are being used to achieve this latter objective. We shall now go back in history to trace in more detail the changes which have occurred in our thinking and practice over the past thirty years.

OPERANT METHODS

Treatment programmes derived from operant conditioning principles have been applied to both positive schizophrenic symptoms (hallucinations and delusions) and to schizophrenic pathology more generally (see reviews by Slade, 1990 and Slade and Bentall, 1988, 1989). Each of these applications will now be briefly described.

Hallucinations

Lindsley (1959; 1963) reported one of the first attempts to bring hallucinations under operant control. He investigated the behaviour of 80 psychotic patients using a six-foot square laboratory containing a chair and a small plunger and delivery tray. Following on from his direct observations of hallucinating patients, he defined a hallucination as 'a high frequency of vocalisation by a patient alone in a room'. He then tried to modify the latter vocalisations by reinforcing either (a) plunger pulling for sweets – a distracting procedure, or (b) vocalisation rate. He failed to secure the differential effect he sought and therefore concluded that verbal psychotic symptoms were under some form of internal control which resisted positive reinforcement. In contrast with Lindsley's conclusions, a number of clinicians have reported positive therapeutic gains using operant methods with hallucinating patients (Nydegger, 1972; Haynes and Geddy, 1973; Anderson and Alpert, 1974; Davis et al., 1976; Heron and DeArmond, 1978).

A good example of the clinical application of operant methodology to hallucinations is provided in the Nydegger (1972) study. This involved a 20-year-old man with a diagnosis of schizophrenia whose symptoms included auditory and visual hallucinations, social withdrawal and delusions. Following a careful examination of these symptoms it was concluded that the auditory hallucinations occurred when the patient was in a conflict situation requiring a difficult decision on his part. The conflict was usually resolved by his voices telling him what to do. Nydegger instructed the patient not to refer to his voices but to call them his thoughts, thereby accepting responsibility for them. The therapist and nursing staff then gave social approval for any speech involving personal responsibility such as talk about decisions and thoughts. Within two months no more hallucinations or behaviours associated with them were reported. Although there are a number of studies which have shown that reductions in psychotic symptoms can occur as a result of similar approaches, it is difficult to assess whether the symptoms really reduce in severity or whether the patient learns not to discuss them with the relevant staff. For a fuller review of operant approaches to hallucinations the reader is referred to Slade and Bentall, 1988.

Delusions

Operant methods have been used in the treatment of delusions by a number of researchers (e.g. Richard et al. 1960; Ayllon and Haughton, 1964; Liberman et al., 1973; Wincze et al., 1972). For example, Liberman et al. (1973) described a study in which four chronic paranoid patients were given daily therapy sessions. The main reinforcer was 'an evening chat' where patients could choose to talk to a therapist they liked, could talk about anything, and the session was held in a comfortable and private place where coffee, fruit, doughnuts, etc. were served. The length of this chat was dependent on the amount of rational speech the patients had shown in the daily sessions. Within 15 days the patients were showing between 200–600 per cent increases in rational talk during interviews, and this improvement generalised well to the evening chat. Unfortunately, there was no obvious generalisation of this improvement to the ward situation. A study by Wincze et al. (1972) compared the effectiveness of providing social reinforcement or token reinforcement (discussed below) as a reinforcer when psychotic patients exhibited non-delusional talk. They found that both were effective at reducing the occurrence of delusional talk.

Token economy

Token economy regimes represent a form of behavioural engineering which was, in theory, applicable to all types of psychotic symptoms (Kazdin,

1982). In practice, however, they were particularly suited to the reversal of negative symptoms (such as social withdrawal; see Chapter 9).

Token economy regimes were introduced into large psychiatric hospitals in the 1960s in the USA with dramatic results. In the early 1970s they were imported into the UK and produced good, but less dramatic, results. These regimes typically involved selecting a group of suitable psychotic patients within an institution, transferring them to a selected ward, and selecting and training a set of nursing staff in the application of the token economy approach. The latter involves the identification of desirable behaviours (e.g. self-care skills, laying tables, cleaning, bed making, and social interaction) and the rewarding of these immediately with tokens, which could later be exchanged for more substantial rewards such as cigarettes, television viewing, magazines, drinks or weekend leave.

The principle on which token economy regimes were based was operant conditioning, in which the immediate rewarding of desirable behaviour was considered to be the essential ingredient. However, a seminal study by Baker *et al.* (1977) demonstrated that contingent reinforcement (which is considered to be the essential feature of operant conditioning) was not responsible for the observed changes. By contrast, it was concluded that the positive therapeutic effects were due to the better organisation of the ward and the increased staff–patient interactions fostered by the token economy regime.

OTHER BEHAVIOURAL ENGINEERING METHODS

Systematic desensitisation

This technique has been used in a number of reported single-case studies of psychotic patients, focusing particularly on patients with hallucinations and delusions (see review by Slade and Bentall, 1988). One example is the single-case study reported by the first author (Slade, 1972), who used imaginal systematic desensitisation with an 18-year-old paranoid man who had a diagnosis of schizophrenia. The man's voices were triggered by the presence of, or thoughts about, his father. Fourteen outpatient sessions led to a reduction of reported voices from 16 to 6 per cent, which further reduced to 2 per cent during a five week follow-up period. However, this was accompanied by the development of depressive symptoms, an outcome which merits further study.

Aversion therapy

The use of electrical aversion therapy has been reported by a number of writers (Bucher and Fabricatore, 1970; Weingaertner, 1971; Alford and Turner, 1976; Turner *et al.*, 1977). For example, Bucher and Fabricatore

31

(1970) treated a 47-year-old man who had experienced auditory hallucinations for five years using this method. They gave the patient a shock box and instructed him to self-administer an electric shock every time he heard his voices. Within ten days the patient reported that he was free of voices, and although he subsequently developed 'background' voices, he said (perhaps not surprisingly) that he did not want any further treatment!

Weingaertner (1971) carried out one of the few controlled studies in this field, but found that electrical aversion therapy was no more successful than a placebo or a waiting-list control group, while Alford and Turner (1976) and Turner et al. (1977) found positive, but limited, results for this method. Again, it is possible that patients learn not to report their symptoms to staff when subjected to this aversive form of treatment rather than the symptoms actually disappearing.

The other form of aversion therapy treatment which has been used with this client group involves the use of white noise as the aversive stimulus. The method was pioneered by Watts and Clements (1971) with a man who had a diagnosis of schizophrenia. It involved administering a blast of white noise whenever the person reported hearing his voices. The method was used subsequently by the first author and his colleagues with four patients with considerable success (Fonagy and Slade, 1982; Slade et al., 1986). Two out of the four patients lost their voices completely, while the other two were greatly improved. Indeed, one of the latter patients asked to stop the treatment as he found it very effective and did not know whether he wanted to lose his voices completely; while the other patient stopped reporting her 'good voices', because she apparently did not want to lose them. The clear message from these observations is that, for some patients, psychotic symptoms are an important part of their lives, indicating that therapists should be cautious in attempting treatments which aim to remove the occurrence of symptoms without first assessing the potential consequences of this on the individual. This principle fits well with the themes expounded in later chapters of this book.

Belief modification

Although later becoming famous for his work in depression, Beck (1952) was one of the first people to publish a case study which reported his attempts to modify a patient's delusional beliefs. This approach was further developed by the belief modification procedure of Watts et al. (1973). Using the principle of 'psychological reactance' outlined by Brehm (1966), it was argued by Watts et al. that direct rejection of a patient's delusional beliefs would only result in a strengthening of the belief. This observation was later confirmed by Milton et al. (1978) who compared confrontation of delusional beliefs with a belief modification procedure with two small groups of patients. The authors found that for both groups, conviction in the beliefs decreased initially, but when the groups were followed up after six weeks, they found that the conviction in the beliefs of the confrontation group had increased to above pre-treatment levels, whereas the conviction of the belief modification group remained at post-treatment levels. The belief modification procedure, they concluded, aims to modify beliefs by minimising the 'psychological reactance' which could result in a strengthening of the belief. Four basic principles underpin the approach, namely:

1. Less psychological reactance will be triggered when discussing weakly held beliefs. The therapist should therefore start with weakly held beliefs and then work up through those that are held increasingly more strongly (cf., the principle of systematic desensitisation).
2. In order to avoid direct confrontation, the therapist should not explicitly require the patient to abandon his or her own beliefs and accept those of the therapist. It is therefore made clear to the patient that the therapist simply wishes to discuss the beliefs and alternative possibilities.
3. In order to facilitate this indirect approach, only the evidence on which a belief is based is discussed and not the reality of the belief itself.
4. The therapist encourages the subject to voice their own arguments against their beliefs, rather than those of the therapist.

Watts *et al.* (1973) presented two single case studies in which this procedure was compared with a baseline control, relaxation and desensitisation. Only the belief modification procedure produced a significant reduction in the reported strength of delusional beliefs in both cases. Hartman and Cashman (1983) have also described a form of cognitive–behavioural treatment which included a belief modification procedure. Two out of three patients experiencing delusions were treated and showed some benefits from this approach.

More recently, Chadwick and Lowe (1990; 1994) have reported successful interventions with patients experiencing delusions using a form of verbal questioning, belief modification and experimental reality testing. They have treated twelve patients who had been experiencing delusions for at least two years. The intervention consisted of identifying the nature of the delusions, sensitively helping the individual to question the evidence underlying the belief and developing behavioural experiments designed to test out the reality of this evidence. For example, a patient who believed strongly that he could predict the next item during television presentations was helped to design an experiment to test this out. A news programme was video-taped and the individual watched the tape, stopped it at various points and then attempted to predict the next item. The evidence from this experiment was used to help the individual modify his belief. Chadwick and Lowe (1994) report that, following treatment, of the twelve patients seen, five had rejected their beliefs completely and a further five reported a reduction in the conviction with which they held their belief. For those patients whose conviction in their belief decreased, there was an accompanying decrease in depression following treatment. For other clinical applications of this general approach the reader is referred to the chapters in Part II of this volume.

SOCIAL SKILLS AND LIFE SKILLS TRAINING APPROACHES

Social skills training (SST)

Social anxiety and deficits in social functioning are generally viewed as core problems for individuals with psychotic disorders. It is not surprising therefore that attempts to modify the social functioning of psychotic patients have received much attention. The main focus of this approach has been the application of social skills training (SST) to such patients (Hersen and Bellack, 1976; Liberman *et al.*, 1989; Wallace *et al.*, 1985; Halford and Hayes, 1991). The general model underpinning this approach was developed by Argyle and Kendon (1967) and views social functioning as a set of skills which have to be learned and practised. SST therefore attempts to identify social skill deficits in patients and to teach or train those skills. Although it is not possible to review all of the studies relating to SST in this chapter, a number of authors have reported positive results of SST during the training period. Unfortunately, as yet, less promising results have been found with regard to generalisation of skills to the naturalistic setting (Halford and Hayes, 1991).

Life skills training

Life skills training is a broader concept than SST and involves training patients in the basic skills required to live as independently as possible. A specific example of this approach was described by Brown (1982). Brown outlined a day-patient programme, which took place over seven weeks each week-day. The seven training modules were:

1. interpersonal skills training
2/3. nutrition and meal planning (two modules)
4. health and hygiene
5. managing money
6. pre-vocational issues, and
7. the use of community resources and social networks.

The important feature of this programme was the emphasis on training as opposed to treatment. Thus, instead of simply advising patients to take their medicine, psychiatrists gave lectures and seminars to patients about the value and possible side-effects of medication. Although the initial effects of life skills training programmes seem favourable, the longer-term effects are unknown.

EMPOWERING APPROACHES

Counter-stimulation/distraction

One of the early approaches to empowering patients to control their own symptoms is that of counter-stimulation or distraction. Erickson and Gustafson (1968), based on the idea that auditory hallucinations stem from patient's misinterpreting their own inner speech, taught two hallucinating patients to use their vocal chords for other purposes in order to establish control over their auditory hallucinations. The approaches included humming and gargling. Both patients reported that this was useful as an immediate method of control but that their voices did not disappear for good.

This early report was followed by a number of laboratory studies in the 1970s and early 1980s (Slade, 1974; Alford and Turner, 1976; Turner *et al.*, 1977; Margo *et al.*, 1981) in which the effects of different forms of external input on auditory hallucinations were investigated. These studies demonstrated an inhibitory effect of various types of distracting task, particularly those which required an overt response on the part of the patient (e.g. speech) or were attention-grabbing (e.g. an interesting talk). For example, Margo *et al.* (1981) examined the effects of nine different types of distraction material on the frequency, clarity and loudness of seven patients' auditory hallucinations. The types of distraction material used included: listening to white noise, listening to pop music, reading out loud, listening to an interesting or boring story, listening to irregular and regular electronic blips and listening to a passage in Afrikaans (which none of the patients understood). They also used a sensory deprivation condition which involved wearing headphones and eye-shields and, finally, a control condition. The authors found that all conditions, except white noise and sensory deprivation, were effective in reducing the severity of patients' hallucinations. Reading out loud was the most effective strategy and the approaches which were least effective included those which the authors considered to be least meaningful (e.g. listening to a boring story was less effective than listening to an interesting story, listening to irregular electronic blips was less effective than the boring story). These findings have recently been replicated by Gallagher *et al.* (1994).

A number of authors have further investigated the use of distracting material as a treatment for hallucinations. Feder (1982) reported a case of a patient with a three year history of intermittent auditory hallucinations. The patient was advised to use stereo headphones in conjunction with a radio when hearing voices. The patient reported a complete cessation of his voices while he wore the headphones but no change during the times he did not wear them.

35

Hustig *et al.* (1990) conducted a larger study on the effect of headphone music on persistent auditory hallucinations in ten patients with a diagnosis of schizophrenia. They allowed subjects to choose two tapes, one which they viewed to be relaxing, the other which they viewed to be stimulating. They hypothesised that the relaxing music would be more effective at reducing the frequency of hallucinations than the stimulating music. Of the ten subjects, one dropped out of the study because she found the effects of the stimulating tape unpleasant. Of the remaining nine subjects, neither the relaxing nor the arousing tape had a superior influence on the frequency of hallucinations for the group overall. Three subjects reported a reduction in frequency of their hallucinations regardless of the type of music. Although analysis of group data did not show differences between the effects of the relaxing and arousing tape, the authors argued that inspection of individual data revealed a trend towards the relaxing tape being superior. A notable feature of this experiment was that the five subjects who reported a general improvement while listening to tapes experienced pleasant or innocuous hallucinations whereas the subject who dropped out of the study and the remaining subjects experienced unpleasant and/or hostile voices. The authors concluded that the approach could be useful for people who have only innocuous voices, rather than negative ones. This may be true but it is also the case that people who have innocuous voices are less likely to request help than those who have negative ones. The value of listening to tapes as a therapeutic tool must therefore be investigated further. Morley (1987), in a similar study investigating the effect of music through headphones on auditory hallucinations, obtained only temporary reductions in the severity of hallucinations. Nelson *et al.* (1991) encouraged twenty patients to use three types of distraction approaches at different times. The approaches included using a personal stereo, using earplugs (discussed below) and sub-vocal counting. Of the twenty patients, a number found that the approaches were helpful, particularly the personal stereo, although only seven patients continued to use the approach in the long term.

The general conclusion from these reports is that counter-stimulation or distraction techniques usually enable patients to obtain immediate relief from their voices but that the benefit disappears with the termination of the distracting stimulus. A controlled clinical trial comparing distraction therapy (which uses all of the techniques described above) with an alternative type of focusing therapy, will be described by Haddock, Bentall and Slade in Chapter 3.

Earplug therapy

The use of earplugs to control auditory hallucinations was first suggested by Paul Green (1978). The suggestion stemmed from Green's theory that hallucinations resulted from defective interhemispheric transfer. That is, he suggested that input to the non-dominant hemisphere might be interfering with that to the dominant hemisphere. He therefore suggested that wearing an earplug in the left ear could reduce this interference and thereby reduce the experience of auditory hallucination. A number of clinical researchers have reported on attempts to use this simple procedure, most reports being positive (James, 1983; Birchwood, 1986; Done *et al.*, 1986; Morley, 1987). One thing that has been clearly established in these studies is that the effective ear is not always the left ear, so that the theory underpinning the procedure remains in doubt (Morley, 1987). However, from a clinical standpoint, it is clear that earplug therapy is simple, inexpensive and has no known medical or psychological complications. It therefore may be worth trying with medication-resistant patients.

Self-instructional training (SIT)

SIT is a form of psychological treatment in which patients are taught to 'talk to themselves' in order to help them organise, regulate and control their own behaviour. This procedure was first used by Meichenbaum and Cameron (1973) to improve the performance of schizophrenic patients on a variety of cognitive tasks and to reduce psychotic speech. Subsequent research has, however, questioned the extent to which the improvements generalise spontaneously to other tasks or types of behaviour (Bentall *et al.*, 1987). This is, of course, a general problem running through many of the approaches discussed above.

Focusing and self-monitoring approaches

In contrast to the approaches described above, which have attempted to direct attention away from the experience, some authors have encouraged patients to focus on, or monitor the occurrence of, their symptoms. For example, Rutner and Bugle (1969) encouraged a woman to record her experience of auditory hallucinations. This resulted in a reduction in the frequency of her voices and was followed-up by the recording chart being displayed publicly, allowing staff to positively reinforce her improvement. A total elimination of voices was observed using this combination of focusing and reinforcement.

Self-monitoring was also emphasised as a focusing approach in a later study. Reybee and Kinch (1973), who called their approach 'focusing', treated two patients diagnosed as suffering from chronic schizophrenia who were experiencing auditory hallucinations. Initially, the patients were required to monitor their voices retrospectively at several intervals during the day. No change in hallucination occurrence was noted using this procedure. It was only when the patients were asked to monitor their

37

voices concurrently during laboratory sessions that reductions in hallucination frequency were seen. A further focusing approach was described by
Greene (1978). He suggested that the experience of auditory hallucinations
involved the least personal responsibility on the part of the sufferer and
the most responsibility on external control. He described this as a form
of avoidance and emphasised that focusing on the voices was the only
way to overcome hallucinatory experiences. He proposed that patients be
educated about the nature of their experiences (i.e. informed that they
are internally generated and represent 'talking to oneself'). Patients in
Greene's study were encouraged to refer to their voices in the first person
singular (i.e. that the voices were their own thoughts). Greene (1978)
reported successfully using this technique with two female patients, both
of whom reported that their voices had disappeared once they had fully
accepted and implemented the first person singular approach. An approach
which shows some similarities to the work of Greene has been described
by Fowler and Morley (1989), who reported a study with five individuals
who were hearing voices. Their subjects were encouraged to bring on and
then dismiss their hallucinations in order to facilitate reattribution of the
voices from external to internal sources (i.e. to demonstrate that the voices
were under their own control rather than that of an external source). They
also utilised some distraction techniques concurrently. Only one patient
showed a reduction in the frequency of their voices, but four out of the five
patients reported that the control they perceived they had over their voices
had increased.

Problem solving training

In order to help empower patients to help themselves, a problem solving
approach was advocated in the 1980s and implemented with schizophrenic
patients (Wallace and Boon, 1983; Hansen et al., 1985). The essence of the
approach is to use scenarios which patients have particular difficulty with,
for example chatting up a member of the opposite sex, help them analyse
the situation and then achieve a feasible solution.

Hansen et al. (1985) exemplified this approach in their study with seven
patients who had a diagnosis of schizophrenia. The procedure involved five
stages, which were the following: problem identification; goal definition;
solution generation; evaluation of alternatives; and selection of the best
solution. Hansen et al. found that this was a viable approach and produced
positive results which appeared to transfer to non-training problems.
The benefits of training also appeared to be maintained at one and four
month follow-up. This approach has recently also been used by Tarrier and
colleagues in their treatment for positive psychotic symptoms (Tarrier et
al., 1993; see Chapter 11).

SUMMARY AND CONCLUSIONS

The history of applying behavioural and cognitive–behavioural treatments to psychotic disorders has been beset by a number of problems. First has been the reluctance of clinicians to consider such treatments suitable and therefore to attempt to apply them to patients. Second, it has to be said that some of the early approaches were crude, both theoretically and in their clinical application. Third has been the problem that most psychological treatments have been tried only with chronic psychotic patients. The major exception is the recent study of Drury (1994) which demonstrated a marked reduction in hospital stay in those psychotic patients treated with energetic cognitive–behavioural therapy, as compared to routine treatment and a control treatment.

The following chapters outline and describe various cognitive–behavioural approaches which have been developed from the earlier techniques described above and which are now being implemented more generally.

REFERENCES

Alford, G. S. and Turner, S. M. (1976) 'Stimulus interference and conditioned inhibition of auditory hallucinations', *Journal of Behaviour Therapy and Experimental Psychiatry* 7: 155–60.

Anderson, L. T. and Alpert, M. (1974) 'Operant analysis of hallucination frequency in a hospitalised schizophrenic', *Journal of Behaviour Therapy and Experimental Psychiatry* 5: 13–18.

Argyle, M. and Kendon, A. (1967) 'The experimental analysis of social behaviour', in L. Berkowitz (ed.) *Advances in Experimental Social Psychology*, volume 3, New York: Academic Press.

Ayllon, T. and Haughton, E. (1964) 'Modification of symptomatic behaviour of mental patients', *Behaviour Research and Therapy* 2: 87–9.

Baker, R., Hall, J. N., Hutchinson, K. and Bridge, G. (1977) 'Symptom changes in chronic schizophrenic patients on a token economy: a controlled experiment', *British Journal of Psychiatry* 131: 381–93.

Barlow, D. (ed.) (1985) *Clinical Handbook of Psychological Disorders*, New York: Guildford Press.

Beck, A. T. (1952) 'Successful out-patient psychotherapy of a chronic schizophrenic with a delusion based on borrowed guilt', *Psychiatry* 15: 305–12.

Bentall, R. P. (ed.) (1990) *Reconstructing Schizophrenia*, London and New York: Routledge.

Bentall, R. P., Higson, P. J. and Lowe, C. F. (1987) 'Teaching self-instructions to chronic schizophrenics: efficacy and generalisation', *Behavioural Psychotherapy* 15: 58–76.

Berkowitz, L. (ed.) (1967) *Advances in Experimental Social Psychology*, volume 3, New York: Academic Press.

Birchwood, M. (1986) 'Control of auditory hallucinations through occlusion of monaural auditory input', *British Journal of Psychiatry* 149: 104–7.

Birchwood, M. and Tarrier, N. (eds) (1994) *Psychological Management of Schizophrenia*, Chichester: Wiley.

Brehm, J. W. (1966) *A Theory of Psychological Reactance*, New York: Academic Press.

Brown, M. (1982) 'Maintenance and generalisation of issues in skills training with chronic schizophrenics', in J. P. Curran and P. M. Monti (eds) *Social Skills Training: A Practical Handbook for Assessment and Treatment*, London: Guildford Press.

Bucher, B. and Fabricatore, J. (1970) 'Use of patient-administered shock to suppress hallucinations', *Behaviour Therapy* 1: 382–5.

Chadwick, P. D. J. and Lowe, C. F. (1990) 'The measurement and modification of delusional beliefs', *Journal of Consulting and Clinical Psychology* 58: 225–32.

—— (1994) 'A cognitive approach to measuring and modifying delusions', *Behaviour, Research and Therapy* 32: 355–67.

Curan, J. P. and Monti, P. M. (eds) (1982) *Social Skills Training: A Practial Handbook for Assessment and Treatment*, London: Guildford Press.

Davis, J. R., Wallace, C. J., Liberman, R. P. and Finch, B. E. (1976) 'The use of a brief isolation to suppress delusional and hallucinatory speech', *Journal of Behaviour Therapy and Experimental Psychiatry* 7: 269–75.

Done, D. J., Frith, C. D. and Owens, D. C. (1986) 'Reducing persistent auditory hallucinations by wearing an earplug', *British Journal of Clinical Psychology* 25: 151–2.

Drury, V. (1994) 'Recovery from acute psychosis', in M. Birchwood and N. Tarrier (eds) *Psychological Management of Schizophrenia*, Chichester: Wiley.

Erickson, G. D. and Gustafson, G. J. (1968) 'Controlling auditory hallucinations', *Hospital and Community Psychiatry* 19: 327–9.

Feder, R. (1982) 'Auditory hallucinations treated by radio headphones', *American Journal of Psychiatry* 139: 1188–90.

Fonagy, P. and Slade, P. D. (1982) 'Punishment versus negative reinforcement in the aversive conditioning of auditory hallucinations', *Behaviour Research and Therapy* 20: 483–92.

Fowler, D. and Morley, S. (1989) 'The cognitive–behavioural treatment of hallucinations and delusions: A preliminary study', *Behavioural Psychotherapy* 17: 267–82.

Gallagher, A. G., Dinan, T. G. and Baker, L. J. V. (1994) 'The effects of varying auditory input on schizophrenic hallucinations: a replication', *British Journal of Medical Psychology* 67: 67–76.

Green, P. (1978) 'Defective interhemispheric transfer in schizophrenia', *Journal of Abnormal Psychology* 87: 472–80.

Greene, R. J. (1978) 'Auditory hallucination reduction: First person singular', *Journal of Contemporary Psychology* 9: 167–70.

Halford, W. K. and Hayes, R. L. (1991) 'Psychological rehabilitation of schizophrenia: Recent findings on social skills training and family psychoeducation', *Clinical Psychology Review* 11: 23–44.

Hansen, D. J., Lawrence, J. S. and Cristoff, K. A. (1985) 'Effects of interpersonal problem-solving training with chronic aftercare patients on problem-solving component skills and effectiveness of solutions', *Journal of Consulting and Clinical Psychology* 53: 167–74.

Hartman, L.M. and Cashman, F.E. (1983) 'Cognitive–behavioural and psychopharmacological treatment of delusional symptoms: a preliminary report', *Behavioural Psychotherapy* 11: 50–61.

Haynes, S. N. and Geddy, P. (1973) 'Suppression of psychotic hallucinations through time-out', *Behavior Therapy* 4: 123–7.

Heron, D. P. and DeArmond, D. (1978) 'The use of time-out in controlling hallucinatory behaviour in a mentally retarded adult', *Bulletin of the Psychonomic Society* 11: 115–16.

Hersen, M. and Bellack, A. S. (1976) 'Social skills training for chronic psychiatric patients: Rationale, research findings and future directions', *Comprehensive Psychiatry* 17: 559–80.

Hustig, H. H., Tran, D. B., Hafner, R. J. and Miller, R. J. (1990) 'The effect of headphone music on persistent auditory hallucinations', *Behavioural Psychotherapy* 18: 273–81.

James, D. A. E. (1983) 'The experimental treatment of two cases of auditory hallucinations', *British Journal of Psychiatry* 143: 515–16.

Kazdin, A. E. (1982) 'The token economy: A decade later,' *Journal of Applied Behaviour Analysis* 15: 431–55.

Liberman, R. P., De Risi, W. J. and Mueser, K. T. (1989) *Social Skills Training With Psychiatric Patients*, New York: Pergamon Press.

Liberman, R. P., Teigen, J., Patterson, R. and Baker, V. (1973) 'Reducing delusional speech in chronic paranoid schizophrenics', *Journal of Applied Behaviour Analysis* 6: 57–64.

Lindsley, O.R. (1959) 'Reduction in rate of vocal psychotic symptoms by differential positive reinforcement', *Journal of the Experimental Analysis of Behaviour* 2: 269.

—— (1963) 'Direct measurement and functional definition of vocal hallucinatory symptoms', *Journal of Nervous and Mental Disease* 136: 293–7.

Mallya, A. R. and Shen, W. W. (1983) 'Radio in the treatment of auditory hallucinations', *American Journal of Psychiatry* 140: 1264–5.

Margo, A., Hemsley, D. R. and Slade, P. D. (1981) 'The effects of varying auditory input on schizophrenic hallucinations', *British Journal of Psychiatry* 139: 122–7.

Meichenbaum, D. M and Cameron, R. (1973) 'Training schizophrenics to talk to themselves: a means of developing attentional control', *Behavior Therapy* 4: 515–34.

Milton, F., Patwa, V.K. and Hafner, R.J. (1978) 'Confrontation versus belief modification in persistently deluded patients', *British Journal of Medical Psychology* 51: 127–30.

Morley, S. (1987) 'Modification of auditory hallucinations: experimental studies of headphones and ear-plugs', *Behavioural Psychotherapy* 15: 252–71.

Nelson, H. E.,Thrasher, S. and Barnes, T. R. E. (1991) 'Practical ways of alleviating auditory hallucinations', *British Medical Journal* 302: 327.

Nydegger, R. V. (1972) 'The elimination of hallucinatory and delusional behaviour by verbal conditioning and assertive training: a case study', *Journal of Behaviour Therapy and Experimental Psychiatry* 3: 225–7.

Reybee, J. and Kinch, B. (1973) 'Treatment of auditory hallucinations using focusing', Unpublished study.

Richard, H. C., Dignam, P. J. and Horner, R. F. (1960) 'Verbal manipulations in a psychotherapeutic relationship', in L. P. Ullman and L. Krasner (eds) *Case Studies in Behaviour Modification*, New York: Reinhart and Winston.

Rutner, I. T. and Bugle, C. (1969) 'An experimental procedure for the modification of psychotic behaviour', *Journal of Consulting and Clinical Psychology* 33: 651–3.

Skinner, B. F. (1953) *Science and Human Behaviour*, New York: Macmillan.

Slade, P. D. (1972) 'The effects of systematic desensitisation on auditory hallucinations', *Behaviour, Research and Therapy* 10: 85–91.

—— (1974) 'The external control of auditory hallucinations: an information theory analysis', *British Journal of Social and Clinical Psychology* 13: 73–9.

—— (1990) 'The behavioural and cognitive treatment of psychotic symptoms', in

R. P. Bentall (ed.) *Reconstructing Schizophrenia*, London and New York: Routledge.

Slade, P. D. and Bentall, R. P. (1988) *Sensory Deception: A Scientific Analysis of Hallucination*, London: Croom Helm.

—— (1989) 'Psychological Treatments for Negative Symptoms', *British Journal of Psychiatry* 155 (supplement 7): 133–5.

Slade, P. D., Judkins, M., Clark, P. and Fonagy, P. (1986) unpublished study.

Tarrier, N., Beckett, R., Harwood, S., Baker, A., Yusupoff, L. and Ugarteburu, I. (1993) 'A trial of two cognitive–behavioural methods of treating drug-resistant residual positive symptoms in schizophrenic patients: 1. Outcome', *British Journal of Psychiatry* 162: 524–32.

Turner, S. M., Hersen, M. and Bellack, A. S. (1977) 'Effects of social disruption, stimulus interference and aversive conditioning on auditory hallucinations', *Behaviour Modification* 1: 249–58.

Ullman, L. P. and Krasner, L. (eds) (1960) *Case Studies in Behaviour Modification*, New York: Reinhart and Winston.

Wallace, C. J. and Boon, S. E. (1983) 'Cognitive factors in the social skills of schizophrenic patients: implications for treatment', Nebraska symposium on motivation: Theories of schizophrenia and psychoses.

Wallace, C. J., Boon, S. E., Donohue, C. P. and Foy, D. W. (1985) 'The chronically mentally disabled: independent living skills training', in D. Barlow (ed.), *Clinical Handbook of Psychological Disorders*, New York: Guildford Press.

Watts, F. and Clements, J. (1971) 'The modification of schizophrenic hallucinations and associated delusions: a case report', unpublished paper.

Watts, F. N., Powell, G. E. and Austin, S. V. (1973) 'The modification of abnormal beliefs', *British Journal of Medical Psychology* 46: 359–63.

Weingaertner, A. H. (1971) 'Self-administered aversive stimulation with hallucinating hospitalised schizophrenics', *Journal of Consulting and Clinical Psychology* 36: 422–9.

Wincze, J. P., Leitenberg, H. and Agras, W. S. (1972) 'The effects of token reinforcement on the delusional verbal behaviour of chronic paranoid schizophrenics', *Journal of Applied Behaviour Analysis* 5: 247–62.

Part II

COGNITIVE–BEHAVIOURAL INTERVENTIONS FOR PSYCHOTIC DISORDERS

Part II

COGNITIVE-BEHAVIORAL
INTERVENTIONS
FOR PSYCHOTIC
DISORDERS

3

PSYCHOLOGICAL TREATMENT OF AUDITORY HALLUCINATIONS: FOCUSING OR DISTRACTION?

Gillian Haddock, Richard P. Bentall
and Peter D. Slade

As reviewed in the previous chapter, many different psychological approaches have been employed in the treatment of auditory hallucinations. Despite the diversity in the techniques used and their differing theoretical under-pinnings, it is clear that the approaches share some common themes. In an earlier review of the literature, Slade and Bentall (1988) argued that many of the psychological approaches used in the treatment of hallucinations tended to fit into three main categories: those which involved distraction from the hallucinations, those which involved focusing on the hallucinations and those for which anxiety reduction was the target for intervention. Although this continues to be the case for many researchers, more recently, many have seen the need to use a combination of these approaches to produce comprehensive treatment strategies which address the multiple needs of people with enduring psychotic symptoms (Tarrier *et al.*, 1993; Fowler, 1992; Kingdon and Turkington, 1991; 1994; also see Chapters 5, 6 and 7 of this book). As a result of this, it is still unclear which elements of the therapeutic process are producing the most benefit and whether par-ticular types of approaches suit particular types of symptoms or individuals. For example, it is possible that purely employing a distraction- or focusing-based treatment may not be sufficient to bring about long-lasting changes to a patient's experience of auditory hallucinations. Indeed, as pointed out in the previous chapter, in some studies which have employed self-directed distraction techniques, the beneficial effects appear to be restricted to the time when the individual is engaged in the technique and do not appear to generalise outside this. Conversely, focusing approaches which aim to encourage the individual to pay more attention to their experience may be distressing for some individuals, especially when the content of the

45

hallucinations is unpleasant. As a result of the above observations, in this chapter we describe a study, as yet only partially completed, in which we have attempted to compare the relative merits of focusing and distraction approaches in the management of auditory hallucinations.

Evidence from previous studies indicates that both approaches would be effective in reducing the severity of persistent auditory hallucinations, although in this study we hypothesised that focusing would have additional benefits as compared to distraction. For example, it has been hypothesised that hallucinations arise because of a faulty monitoring process which results in internally generated verbal material being attributed to an alien source (Bentall, 1990; Frith, 1992, see Chapter 1). As a consequence, it may be hypothesised that focusing on the experience would reduce the likelihood that such a misattribution will occur. In addition, if patients' reality monitoring skills can be improved through focusing, by helping them to recognise that their hallucinations arise from an internal source, then this approach should be more likely to produce continued or long-term benefits than distraction therapy. Finally, given that beliefs and expectations about the origin and content of verbal stimuli are important factors which determine whether a perceived event is attributed to an external source (Young *et al.*, 1987; Chadwick and Birchwood, 1994), this provides further support for the notion that focusing, which allows the exploration and modification of these beliefs, should be a more effective treatment than distraction. Taken together, these three arguments suggest that, although both distraction and focusing may have short-term positive effects on hallucinations, lasting therapeutic benefits are more likely to be achieved by focusing.

INTERVENTION STUDY

Patients recruited for this study were suffering from auditory hallucinations which had been persistent for six months or more, were experienced as unpleasant, had not responded significantly to neuroleptic medication and were experienced at least two to three times per week. It was also requested from referrers that potential patients had a diagnosis of schizophrenia and that, in the event that a patient was accepted for treatment, medication would be kept stable for the period of treatment and for a follow-up period of six months.

Following referral, patients were assessed using the following battery of tests:

1. The Present State Examination, ninth edition (Wing *et al.*, 1974).
2. A cognitive–behavioural assessment of hallucinations (the Hallucination Interview Schedule) which assessed the frequency and duration of voices, their content, coping strategies, physical characteristics and

origin of voices, as well as the person's beliefs and attributions regarding their voices.
3. Patients were also asked to complete the Rosenberg Self-esteem Scale (Rosenberg, 1965).

Following assessment, which took between one and three sessions, patients who met the inclusion criteria were informed that they would receive between eighteen and twenty weeks of therapy with a clinical psychologist who was attempting to develop new ways of helping people who experienced voices which did not involve medication. Patients were then randomly assigned to either a distraction treatment group or a focusing treatment group. Twenty-six people were eventually assigned to either the focusing or the distraction group. The following eight referrals to the study were then assigned to a waiting list control group.

The two treatment groups had the following in common. Each approach consisted of eighteen to twenty weekly sessions which lasted approximately one hour. At the beginning of each session, patients were requested to complete a Hospital Anxiety and Depression scale (HAD; Zigmond and Snaith, 1983) and complete the Personal Questionnaire Rapid Scaling technique (PQRST; Mulhall, 1978) which was used to elicit patients' ratings of their hallucinations. The PQRST symptom statements were chosen by the authors to provide an assessment of the following areas: frequency of voices over the past week, the distress caused by the voices, the disruption to life caused by the voices and the amount to which the patients believed the voices to be their own thoughts. In addition, patients in both groups were asked to complete a daily hallucination diary before going to bed each night. They were asked to rate frequency, loudness, distressfulness and hostility of the voices on a scale from one to nine, as well as to write a brief account of their daily activities.

Session one, for both treatment groups, involved thoroughly introducing the patients to the assessment measures and allowing them sufficient time to become familiar with them. This session also served to provide a thorough rationale and description of the approach being used and was a useful session for deepening of rapport and for addressing any questions which the patient had. Following session one, the treatment sessions were quite different. An outline of the different procedures is given below.

Distraction approach

The assumption behind this approach was that the more the patients could distract themselves from their voices the better, it being hypothesised that this should allow the voices to extinguish. The treatment consisted of a combination of a number of distraction or counter-stimulation techniques (many of which were outlined in Chapter 2) plus others which were especially designed for the study. Patients were asked to use each technique for one week and review progress in the following session. Techniques were presented during treatment in the following order.

Personal stereo therapy
(see, e.g. Feder, 1982; Morley, 1987; Nelson *et al.*, 1991).

This part of the treatment involved patients being provided with a personal stereo on which they could listen to the radio or play a cassette. They were asked to listen to music through headphones each time they heard their voices or, if their voices were continuous, to use the stereo at particular times during the day or night. Patients were asked to record after each use how effective the stereo had been at distracting them from their voices on a scale from zero to ten, where a score of ten indicated that the voices had been blocked out completely and a score of zero indicated that the voices had not been blocked out at all.

Following a period of listening to music through headphones, patients were asked to spend the following week listening to different material. This was usually talking programmes on Radio 4, based on the rationale that these would be more meaningful and hence would be more effective at distracting the patient from their voices (Margo *et al.*, 1981; Gallagher *et al.*, 1994). Patients were asked to rate out of ten how effective the talking programmes were at distracting them from their voices each time they used the technique. At the beginning of the subsequent sessions the usefulness of these approaches was discussed with the patients together with any problems with their implementation. Problem solving exercises were employed to aid the implementation of techniques if this was proving difficult.

Reading, mental arithmetic and mental games
(Margo *et al.*, 1981; Gallagher *et al.*, 1994; James, 1983; Nelson *et al.*, 1991).

These approaches were introduced in subsequent weeks. Patients were required to select reading material and to set aside time each day to record how much the reading distracted them from their voices. The reading phase was planned in two stages: the first involved reading to oneself and the second involved reading out loud. Mental arithmetic tasks were also set in consultation with the patient so that techniques appropriate to their functioning could be chosen. Mental games were also chosen by the patient. These involved mental imagery tasks, word games or naming objects in a room. Some patients also chose to use written puzzles such as crosswords or puzzle books. Again, patients were asked to record how effective the techniques were at distracting them from their voices on a scale from zero to ten.

Activity scheduling

Using records from the hallucination diary, individual programmes were developed to increase the patients' range of behaviours which most distracted them from their voices. Recording sheets similar to those traditionally used for activity scheduling with depressed patients (Williams, 1992) were used to plan activities and to rate the degree of distraction they provided. In this way, patients could fine tune their schedules to increase those things which they found gave most relief from their hallucinations. In this phase, time was sometimes spent on helping patients to do activities which they found distracting but which they also found anxiety provoking. Programmes designed to desensitise people to these situations were also devised. By the end of the distraction treatment it was hoped that patients would have a repertoire of behaviours which they knew would distract them from their voices. Patients were then encouraged to use a combination of techniques which were most appropriate to their lives. (E.g. one patient used reading aloud as a method of distraction, but when he was outside in the street he used his personal stereo, as this was more socially acceptable and allowed him to get on with other activities. Another patient found that planning a range of activities using activity scheduling was most effective.) The final sessions were spent reviewing progress and planning for the future. Emphasis was placed on continued use of the procedures employed. Time was spent on planning how they could continue to incorporate these into their lives, and how the person could continue to develop and improve upon their distraction techniques. If possible, links were made with other professionals involved in the patients' care so that they could encourage and reinforce continued use of the techniques (see case study one below for a description of a patient treated using a distraction approach).

Focusing approach

This approach has been briefly described elsewhere (Haddock et al., 1993; Bentall et al., 1994). The emphasis of this approach involved a powerful requirement for the patients to focus on their voices. The approach was a combination of some of the techniques mentioned in the literature and other focusing approaches newly developed for this study. In this approach the amount of time spent on particular strategies varied from patient to patient depending on how comfortable they felt. Patients gradually exposed themselves to the content, meanings, related thoughts and beliefs about their voices. A graded approach was planned so that desensitisation to the anxiety caused by the voices could take place. For some patients, the anxiety associated with their voices was greater than for others so there was therefore no set time for moving on to a later stage. The stages outlined below were worked on with all patients.

Physical characteristics of the voices

This involved focusing on, and discussing, the physical characteristics of the voices, such as: the number of voices, their loudness, their tone, their accent, their sex and their location. Patients were asked to focus on their voices concurrently, by spending time within the session specifically on this. For example, patients were asked to focus on the location of the voice or voices for one minute. If there was more than one voice they were asked to focus on only one at a time. A record of the nature of the voices was then kept during sessions, especially relating to changes in their phenomenology between or within sessions. Patients were also asked to identify a particular time at home when they could do a focusing exercise and write down characteristics of the voice on a particular occasion. This was then reviewed and discussed at the start of the next session.

Content of the voices

When patients became comfortable with focusing on the physical characteristics of the voices, they were asked to focus during and between sessions on the content of the voice. This involved recording exactly what was said, usually aided by shadowing the voice. In sessions the patient either concurrently recorded the content of the voice or repeated it out loud for the therapist to record. The rest of the session was then spent on examining the content.

Related thoughts

This phase followed on quite closely from focusing on the content of the voices. The relationship of a person's thoughts to the content of the voices was examined (i.e. which thoughts resulted from experience of a voice and which might precede a voice). This also involved examining any related emotions such as depression, anxiety, anger or fear. In some cases, monitoring of these related thoughts and feelings was introduced using a combination of voice and thought diaries. Patients were encouraged to change and examine their antecedent or resulting thoughts and feelings to assess the effect on their voices.

Meaning of the voices

This phase involved an attempt to attribute some meaning to the content or the experience of the voice. This would necessarily involve identifying a patient's belief system relating to the voice and helping them to modify these if necessary.

During progression through these stages, a formulation of the meaning and function of the voices was developed using data from all the monitoring exercises. For some patients the actual process of doing this was therapeutic in itself, whereas for others it allowed the identification of areas where changes could be made. For example, some patients became aware that it was not the voices themselves which were most intrinsically distressing, but rather it was the feelings and thoughts which resulted from the voice which caused the distress. This enabled the patients to address these more appropriate areas in therapy. For others it was useful to treat the voices themselves as intrusive thoughts and to introduce techniques aimed at alleviating these. Alternatively, some patients were able to identify aspects of their environment which contributed to the distress caused by the voices. For example, some recognised that the content of their voices reflected the worries they had in general life and that the content could be used to indicate where changes were necessary. One patient recognised that her voices increased following a row with her husband; focusing on the content helped her to become aware that her voices were saying the things which she was feeling and thinking about her husband but which she was at the time not able to express. Identification of this as a problem helped her to decide to intervene by attempting to improve the communication between her and her husband and to resolve some of the issues which were causing bad feeling. In some cases a formulation included the reattribution of the voices to self, i.e. the process of concurrent self-monitoring and focusing allowed patients to correctly identify the voices as originating from themselves. Before this interpretation was presented to a patient, the potential effect on their mental state was assessed by the therapist. For example, if reattribution of voices to self would have been resisted or would have been detrimental to the therapeutic relationship, a slightly different rationale was given. This rationale involved allowing the patient to accept the voices as being externally generated but acknowledged that the antecedent and resulting thoughts and feelings were internally generated and that the individual could exert control and change over these. In the example described above, of a woman whose voices reflected conflict with her husband, she did not accept that the voices were internally generated. She continued to believe that the voices originated from the Devil but was able to acknowledge that her reactions to this and the content of the voices were closely related to her current worries and concerns. She was able to acknowledge that if she could change her thoughts and feelings in response to the voices, this would have a positive effect on their content. In other cases, patients were able to reattribute the voices to themselves (see case study two, showing the progress of focusing therapy, and also Haddock *et al.*, 1993).

The final sessions were treated as a review and plan for the future. Patients were encouraged to take records of the work which they had completed in therapy and to use them to help plan continued work in the future. The emphasis, as with the distraction approach, was that for the benefits to continue, focusing on the voices and their meaning also had to continue. If appropriate, meetings were set up with referrers and other key workers involved with the patient so that the rationale and progress made could be reinforced.

Waiting list control group

Patients allocated to the waiting list control group were assessed using the same pre-assessments as the clinical groups. When these patients were referred for treatment they were asked if they would wish to be considered for treatment after the end of the main study. All control patients requested this, therefore no follow-up data was collected for this group.

Post-treatment assessment

Following therapy, and between six and nine months of ending therapy, patients were reassessed by a blind rater on the same measures as at the beginning of the study (Present State Examination, Hallucination Interview Schedule and the Rosenberg Self-esteem Scale). Patients were also asked to complete diary sheets for seven days, a HAD and the PQRST scale. (Control patients were asked to complete the same assessments with the exception of the HAD and Rosenberg scale approximately four to six months after the pre-assessment, i.e. when treatment would have been completed had it been undertaken. Unfortunately it was not practical to collect further follow-up data from these patients.)

Intervention outcome

Sixty-three referrals were received and, of these, fifty-six people were assessed using the test battery outlined in the method section. Seven people were excluded for the following reasons: one person was no longer hallucinating at the time of the appointment, three patients' voices were pleasant and they did not wish to lose them, two people refused to take part in assessment and one person died between the time of referral and assessment. Thirty-three patients were allocated to a treatment or control group following assessment. Twenty-three patients were not assigned to a group for the following reasons: voices were pleasant or not thought to be a problem, frequency of voices did not reach criteria for study, patient was unwilling to take part, patient was not able to complete assessment.

Of the twenty-six patients who were assigned to a treatment group, six discontinued during treatment (three distracters and three focusers). The following reasons for discontinuation were observed: physical ill health (one focuser), worsening of symptoms (one distracter, one focuser), perceived the approach was not helping (one focuser), unable to complete forms and successfully take part in sessions due to other psychotic phenomena (one distracter), unexplained (one distracter). Of the eight control patients, two were withdrawn from the study because their Consultant Psychiatrist changed their medication to Clozapine between pre- and post-assessment, one patient did not wish to be contacted for post-assessment and one was unable to complete the assessments.

All patients who were assigned to treatment or control groups had a DSM-III-R (APA, 1987) diagnosis of schizophrenia as confirmed by referring or responsible psychiatrists and by classification based on their PSE data (Wing *et al.*, 1974). Patients were both inpatients and out-patients. Of the focusers, eight were men and three were women, and of the distracters, six were men and three were women. Control patients were all men.

The average age of the focusing group was 36 years with an average length of voice history of 15 years. The average age of the distraction group was 46 years with an average length of voice history of 15 years. The average age of the control group was 35 years with an average length of voice history of 11 years. There were no significant differences between the groups for these variables.

Effect of treatment intervention

Collection of follow-up data for this study has yet to be completed, and therefore only preliminary observations can be reported here. Figures 3.1 and 3.2 summarise these data from the three groups. Figure 3.1 shows the mean PQRST ratings for the amount to which the voices have occurred, disruption caused by the voices, distress caused by the voices and the amount to which the voices were believed to be thoughts at pre- and post-treatment and follow-up. Note that a downward slant of the graph for the first three measures illustrates a decrease in the frequency, distress and disruption of voices and an upward slant of the attributions graph illustrates an increase in belief that the voices are thoughts. Figure 3.2 shows mean HAD scores of anxiety and depression at pre- and post-treatment points and Rosenberg self-esteem scores at pre- and post-treatment.

As can be seen from Figure 3.1 showing PQRST ratings, patients taking part in both treatment conditions showed a reduction in frequency of voices, disruption to life and distress caused by the voices at post-assessment and at follow-up (focusers, n = 11; distracters, n = 8; one distracter was not included as she was not able to complete the necessary forms satisfactorily). Only the differences between pre- and post-treatment scores for the amount of time spent hallucinating and disruption to life were significant (F[1,17] = 10.73, p = 0.04; F[1,17] = 7.62, p = 0.013). There

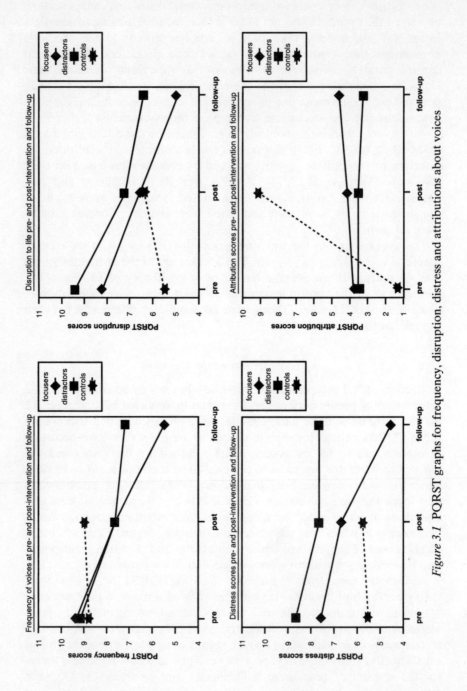

Figure 3.1 PQRST graphs for frequency, disruption, distress and attributions about voices

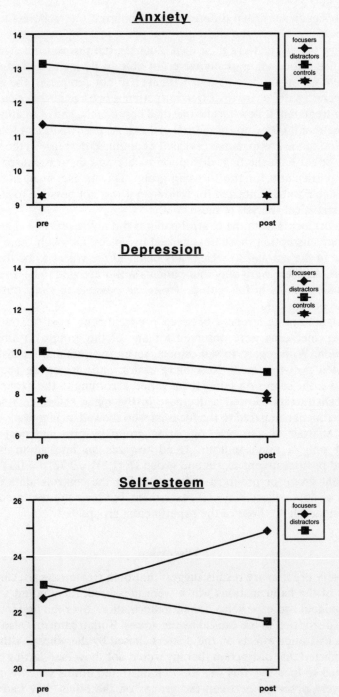

Figure 3.2 HAD and self-esteem scores at pre- and post-treatment

were no significant group differences or significant interactions for any of the variables. There was a slight increase in the focusing patients' tendency to believe the voices were their own thoughts, but this was not significant. Some of the focusing patients were not able to be included in the post-treatment follow-up data as four patients had not completed the relevant assessments. With regard to distraction patients, two had not been contacted for post-treatment follow-up and one died between the end of treatment and post-treatment follow-up (of natural causes). At post-treatment follow-up, inspection of the group means revealed a continued decrease in the amount of time spent hallucinating, disruption to life and distress caused by the voices, particularly for the focusing group. Due to the small number of patients able to be contacted for follow-up it was not possible to carry out formal statistical analysis of these data.

Measurements from the control patients did not reveal any changes for frequency, disruption or distress caused by voices, although there was an increase in the amount to which they believed the voices to be their own thoughts. As there were only four patients who were able to be assessed at four to six months in this group, it was not possible to carry out formal statistics on this data.

No significant differences between pre-treatment, post-treatment and follow-up measures were observed for any of the groups on anxiety or depression. With regard to self-esteem, seven focusers and six distracters completed post-treatment Rosenberg scales, and, as can be seen from Figure 3.2, the scores on self-esteem varied according to the experimental group. Distracters showed a decrease in the mean self-esteem score at post-treatment compared to the focusers who showed an increase. A multi-variate analysis of variance comparing group by pre- and post- scores showed only a non-significant trend towards an interaction between pre- and post-treatment scores and group (F $[1,11]$ = 2.72, p = 0.1) and no significant group or pre-/post- difference. For the controls, data on self-esteem was not collected at post-assessment, but their pre-treatment mean was comparable to those of the experimental groups.

Discussion

These very preliminary results suggest that both treatments affected some aspects of the hallucinations which were measured: the amount to which the individual had experienced their hallucinations over the previous week and the disruption to life caused by the voices. Both treatments also appear to have had some effects on the distress caused by the voices. Although it was predicted that distraction therapy would not show long-lasting benefits compared to focusing, this was not demonstrated in this study. No differences were observed between the groups on the effect they had on the hallucinations, and the benefits were maintained at the short follow-up for those patients for whom data was collected. Much attention was paid in this study to helping the individual to incorporate the most useful distraction techniques into their life, hence attempting to increase the generalisability of the approaches. It could be speculated that perhaps it is this attention to the application of techniques which has contributed to the maintenance of the benefits from this approach.

An interesting preliminary result from this study was that the treatments had different effects on self-esteem as measured by the Rosenberg Self-esteem Scale (Rosenberg, 1965). Self-esteem increased slightly in the focusing group compared to the distraction group. It is not clear what this difference can be attributed to. One speculative account could relate to the process of therapy. An important part of the focusing approach is to help the individual to explore the content of their experiences and to attempt to relate it to their current thoughts, concerns and life situation. In distraction the message which is given to the individual is that the content of the voices should not be attended to and that the more they distract themselves or ignore the voices the better. As a result of this study, it has become clear that the content of the voices is important and relates quite closely to the individual's concerns and worries. It is possible that distraction treatments, with their failure to acknowledge this, make patients feel as though their concerns have not been attended to or that their concerns are unimportant. This may contribute towards a feeling of low self-esteem. In a group of patients who tend to have low self-esteem, any reduction produced by treatment should be viewed as significant, especially as low self-esteem is common in depression which in turn is a risk factor for suicide. (Suicide has been shown to be more common for individuals experiencing persistent psychotic symptoms than in the normal population; Falloon and Talbot, 1981.) Although the distraction approach in this study included strategies which are commonly used as a treatment for depression (activity scheduling), this treatment did not produce a significant decrease in the depression reported by patients in this study. This suggests that, despite the benefits shown, distraction approaches alone may not be useful psychological techniques in the way in which they were utilised in this study.

As outlined in the descriptions of both approaches, the two treatments differed fundamentally in their theoretical approaches. Focusing included a requirement to concentrate on the content and meaning of the voices and to accept voices as being part of, or related to, the individual's own mind. Distraction required the individual to ignore the voices and to concentrate on engaging in activities which made it more difficult to attend to the content and meaning of the voices. It could be hypothesised that focusing would increase the amount to which the individual believed the voices to be their own thoughts, although this was not the case as measured by the PQRST for either the focusing group or the distraction group. Interestingly the mean scores on this measure for the control group indicated that they increased their beliefs regarding an internal origin for their voices, and this was the case for all of the control patients. Although it is not possible to speculate accurately for such a small number of patients, it is possible that measuring attributions regarding the origin of voices in this way is not appropriate. Alternatively it could be argued that attributions regarding the origin of voices are extremely variable and fluctuate widely.

A further limitation of this study is also worth noting. As all the patients in this study had been hearing voices for a large number of years it is possible that more positive results would have been achieved if they had been offered a psychological treatment earlier in their voice history, when their beliefs about the origins and nature of their voices were presumably less systematised and less resistant to change. This is also a common limitation of other studies which have attempted to assess the effectiveness of psychological treatments for psychotic symptoms. This perhaps reflects the current state of treatment for psychosis which usually involves neuro-leptic medication as the first line treatment. Psychological treatments are usually considered only as secondary treatments following the failure of medication to reduce or remove the psychotic symptoms. Further research is needed to establish whether psychological treatments are more effective if delivered shortly after the onset of symptoms and to establish whether they can be offered as an alternative to medication for some patients.

Despite the limitations and the small number of subjects who were involved in this study, it is clear from these results that psychological treatments for people experiencing auditory hallucinations, who have a diagnosis of schizophrenia and who are taking maintenance neuroleptic medication may be helpful in a number of ways. Psychological treatment, using both approaches, was demonstrated to produce significant effects on the duration of time the person hallucinates and the disruption to life caused by them, which was maintained during the short follow-up time during which data was collected. It is also clear that there were benefits on the distress caused by the voices. Longer follow-up is needed to reveal whether the benefits are maintained for both of the approaches, or whether one approach will show more superior long-term effects. As a result of these factors, it is not possible to recommend that only one of the two approaches should be used with all patients. It is possible that different patients may benefit from one of the two approaches, but, as yet, we have not been able to examine the individual factors which will predict this. It is also possible that a combination of focusing and distraction is the most appropriate therapeutic strategy, where an overall focusing approach is taken to explore the content, beliefs and meaning attached to the voices, but that systematic use of distraction techniques is also encouraged to provide patients with some control over their symptoms.

CASE STUDIES

FL: A case study of distraction therapy

FL was a 47-year-old man who lived alone. He was first admitted to hospital in 1974 suffering from depression and was given a diagnosis of schizophrenia in 1977. He had been experiencing auditory hallucinations for fifteen years when he was assessed for treatment. His hallucinations had become more severe in the two years prior to his referral following the death of his mother. FL was unemployed and lived in a flat with his brother, who was also unemployed. FL was prescribed, and reported that he complied with, neuroleptic medication.

Prior to treatment, FL was assessed using the Present State Examination (Wing *et al.*, 1974) and the HIS. He also completed a Rosenberg Self-esteem Questionnaire (Rosenberg, 1965). Assessment revealed that he experienced hallucinations in the auditory and visual modality. His voices were experienced as originating from outside his head and occurred almost continually. He occasionally experienced visual hallucinations from which his voices originated. The content of his voices was both positive and negative, and he was able to describe four voices, one of which was good and three of which were bad. The good voice he called 'Sam' and FL saw a clear image of Sam several times a day. The voices did not occur at any particular time of day and became worse when he was alone and when he was tired or upset. The voices spoke to him directly, commented about his actions, described what he was doing and sometimes talked to each other. He was unsure about the cause of his voices, although he believed that 'Sam' was part of himself and originated from God. The other voices were related to a conspiracy and usually upset him. 'Sam' spoke to him in a pleasant supportive voice, while the negative voices encouraged him to harm himself, criticised him and tried to mislead him. Although he valued his positive voice, he said he would prefer to have no voices as he considered them to be unnatural.

FL was treated over twenty sessions by the first author using a distraction approach as described above. He was asked to complete a weekly PQRST (Mulhall, 1978) and HAD (Zigmond and Snaith, 1983) at the start of every session. This usually took him approximately ten minutes. He was also asked to complete a daily hallucination diary before going to bed each night.

FL accepted the rationale for the approach and was keen to attempt the distraction techniques. Initially FL was asked to use a personal stereo to distract himself by listening to music. After the first week he reported that while using the personal stereo the severity of his voices reduced and he then progressed to listening to talking programmes on the radio. He was asked to identify specific talking programmes during the sessions which he would listen to between sessions. He was asked to rate out of ten how effective the personal stereo was at distracting him from his voices. FL also reported that he had not gone to bed on two nights during the week because the voices frightened him at night. It was suggested that he use his personal stereo when in bed until he dropped off to sleep. He thought this was a good idea and came up with the idea of connecting his personal stereo to the mains electricity supply (rather than using the usual batteries) so that if he dropped off to sleep and left the personal stereo switched on, the batteries would not run out. He continued to gain some benefit while listening to his personal stereo but found that the talking programmes were boring and distracted him less well than listening to music. For the following week he agreed to listen to a number of plays on the radio which he enjoyed, and at other times to listen to music.

During this time FL came up with a number of activities which he wished to begin. He bought an exercise bike and started to exercise daily and found that this, in conjunction with his personal stereo, helped him to get to sleep at night. He also expressed a wish to begin birdwatching, particularly on Saturday, as this was a difficult day of the week. He reported feeling anxious much of the time and decided to cut out caffeine from his diet in order to control this. At this point, FL requested further help with regard to his anxiety, therefore he was instructed in relaxation and breathing techniques and provided with a tape which he could use with his personal stereo.

Later sessions focused on encouraging FL to continue to use the strategies which had been successful at reducing the severity of his voices and introducing new distraction techniques to implement. In session six, mental arithmetic was introduced as a distraction technique and FL came up with the strategy of counting in threes and sevens. He also continued to find exercise a good strategy and took up swimming several times a week. At this point FL's voices had reduced in severity. He reported that the good voice had become more pleasant and the bad voices had become more neutral in their content and occurred less frequently. During this period he continued to implement all of the above techniques and added reading to self and out loud. He exercised daily and carried out relaxation exercises as well as using the specific distraction techniques. Following session eleven, when he missed two appointments, his voices suddenly became much more severe. This was just before Christmas and was a time he had found difficult since the death of his mother (this was only the second Christmas since her death). He reported feeling very depressed and that the voices were encouraging him to harm himself. He did not wish to kill himself but was frightened that the voices would push him into it (FL had previously made several attempts to harm himself following instructions from his voices). He acknowledged that it had been a difficult time for him and was able to link the increase in his voices and depression to the time of year and the death of his mother. During this time he discontinued all his new activities and distraction techniques. Although he did not feel optimistic about returning

60

to therapy, he was willing to return to all the activities he had found useful before Christmas. After three sessions, where he gradually built up his repertoire of distraction techniques and increased those activities which were most effective at reducing the severity of his voices, FL's voices began to be less severe again. He rated swimming and his personal stereo as distracting himself as five out of ten (with zero being no distraction at all and ten being complete elimination). He continued to use these techniques although he became depressed again quite soon. He took an overdose and was admitted to hospital. Examination of the circumstances surrounding this revealed that it was partly in response to his brother getting a girlfriend which resulted in FL being alone for long periods. In the final two sessions, which took place after he was discharged from hospital following the over-dose, the time was spent reviewing the progress he had undoubtedly made and planning how the strategies he had learned could be implemented into his life. He restarted his exercise regimes, started practising relaxation and reduced his caffeine intake again. The following summarise the benefits which FL and the therapist had observed during treatment: Reading, and reading out loud, blocked out voices and helped to pass the time. Listening to music either through a personal stereo or on music videos blocked out voices particularly at night, passed time and helped to relax him. Swimming helped primarily to pass time but also helped to relax him and did block out his voices to a degree. Holidays, and thinking about possible holidays, helped him to think more positively about the future, passed time and helped to relax him. On the basis of these observations the following plans were made for his continued implementation:

1. To swim three to four times per week.
2. To read out loud at specific times when voices were most distressing.
3. To use the personal stereo and watch music videos when voices were distressing.
4. To continue with relaxation and breathing techniques in order to control anxiety.
5. To continue drinking decaffeinated coffee and tea.
6. To take part in trips and holidays organised by the Day Hospital.
7. To practise going on buses with a view to trips to the countryside.

FL undoubtedly found benefits from a distraction approach. There was a reduction in all aspects of his voices and anxiety and depression during the phase when he was using a range of the techniques. Despite this, there were periods when the frequency of his voices and the associated distress became so severe that he required a short spell in hospital. It appears that these incidents were related to stressful events in his life, and following a degree of resolution of these he was able to resume his coping strategies and achieve a further reduction in the frequency and severity of his voices. As can be seen from Figure 3.3, PQRST scores in the final sessions of

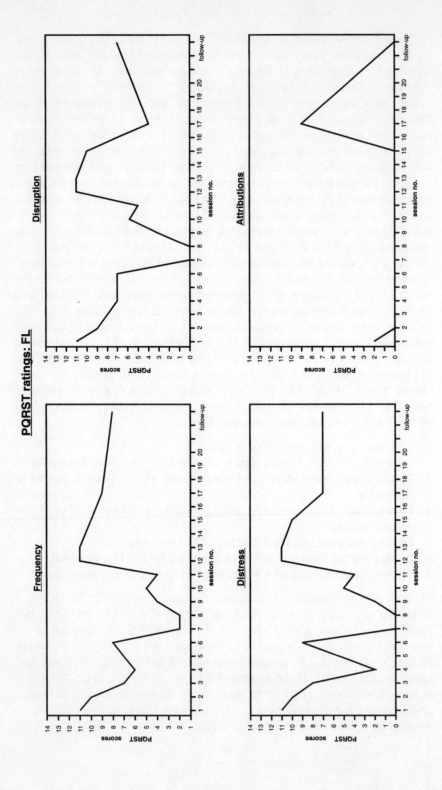

PQRST ratings: FL

Frequency

Disruption

Distress

Attributions

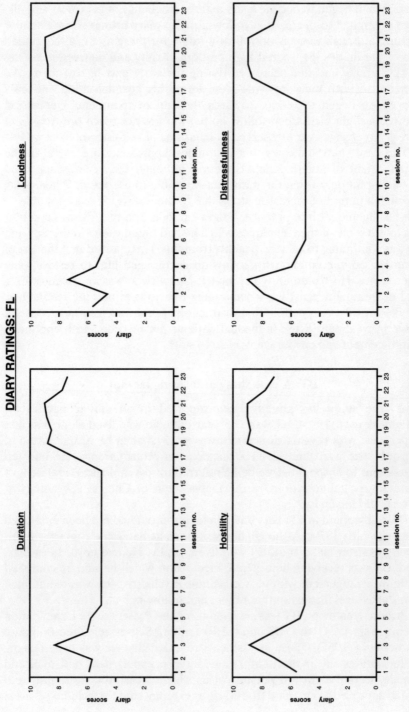

Figure 3.3 Weekly PQRST and average diary ratings for FL

therapy had begun to decline again and the frequency of his voices and distress continued to decrease at follow-up. The diary ratings show a similar picture, although there is no follow-up data for these as FL discontinued use of the diaries. FL scored high on both anxiety and depression on the HAD initially and this decreased during the early part of treatment. An increase in both measures was seen during his hospitalisation and only depression began to reduce towards the end of treatment. Depression showed a slight increase at follow-up but this did not reach pre-treatment levels. No changes were observed in measures of self-esteem.

This case study indicates that distraction approaches are useful in the management of auditory hallucinations, although the benefits appeared to be helpful only when the individual was able to use them. When going through a period of increased stress due to life events, FL was not able to put his techniques into practice. Follow-up indicated that FL was continuing to use some of the techniques which he had found useful in therapy and he was continuing to achieve benefits from this. He reported that the cue of receiving an appointment for follow-up encouraged him to restart some approaches. His Community Psychiatric Nurse (who was informed of FL's end of treatment plan) was encouraging him to continue the techniques. In view of this it is possible that distraction approaches may have a useful place in treatment if the individual patients are provided with continued reinforcement and encouragement from staff.

BT: A case study of focusing therapy

This case study has already been reported in an earlier publication (Haddock *et al.*, 1993). BT was a 45-year-old man who lived alone. His first experience with psychiatric services was in 1972 when he was admitted to a psychiatric ward and given a diagnosis of schizophrenia. He had ten admissions to hospital before being referred for psychological treatment of his auditory hallucinations to the Department of Clinical Psychology at Liverpool University.

BT had worked in a bakery and as a labourer but had not been employed since the early 1970s. Although he lived alone he had some contact with his family (a sister and a brother) who lived locally. He had never been married. BT was receiving neuroleptic medication which he said he complied with; by arrangement with his Consultant Psychiatrist this was maintained at a stable level throughout treatment and follow-up.

Prior to treatment, BT was assessed using the Present State Examination (Wing *et al.*, 1974), the HIS and the Rosenberg Self-esteem Questionnaire (Rosenberg, 1965). These assessments revealed that he was experiencing hallucinations only in the auditory modality. He experienced both male and female, second and third person voices which occurred continuously and which appeared to emanate from various external sources including passers by, television, radio, running water, cars and other machinery. The voices were worst when he was with other people, when it was noisy and when he was feeling depressed. The content of the voices was both positive (e.g. "You're okay, you'll be all right") and negative (e.g. "You're a bastard, we want you dead"). BT was unsure about the cause of his voices. He sometimes believed that they were caused by other people who were conspiring against him but at other times he believed that they were the result of bad experiences from his past. He was particularly concerned with an incident during early adulthood when he had had sexual intercourse with a 14-year-old girl. He felt extremely guilty about this incident and often believed that the voices were caused by people who wished to punish him for it.

BT was treated over twenty sessions by the first author using a focusing approach as described above. He was asked to complete a weekly PQRST (Mulhall, 1978) and HAD (Zigmond and Snaith, 1983) at the start of every session. This usually took him approximately ten minutes. He was also asked to complete a daily hallucination diary before going to bed each night.

By recording the voices between sessions and focusing in detail on them during sessions, the therapist was able to clarify BT's experiences. It became apparent that the voices varied and tended to divide into three distinct types: external voices which originated from no particular source, external voices which originated from people or machinery, and finally voices which originated from inside his head which he reattributed as being negative thoughts. Clarifying these distinctions allowed BT to record the characteristics of each of these separately and allowed him, in conjunction with the therapist, to explore their meaning and function. The external voices which did not appear to originate from a particular source were usually quiet and seemed to come from far away. As can be seen from Figure 3.4, the duration of these voices, reflected in weekly averages of daily diary ratings and PQRST scores, decreased during treatment. In addition, the content of these voices was initially mostly hostile but this changed to exclusively pleasant or neutral voices in the latter part of treatment, as rated by the diary scores.

The second type of voices were those which originated from people or machinery. When asked to focus on these experiences during sessions it became clear that BT was actually hearing something real when these occurred. This was often mumbled voices from adjacent rooms or noise coming from machinery, such as a lawn mower which sometimes went past the window where therapy was taking place. BT was often unclear about the content of these experiences. For example, he would report that "I thought I heard them say 'fuck off'." It became apparent that most of his reports of voices originating from people or machinery were preceded by "I think they said ... ". It was hypothesised, therefore, that these phenomena reflected BT's misinterpretation of actual auditory events. In

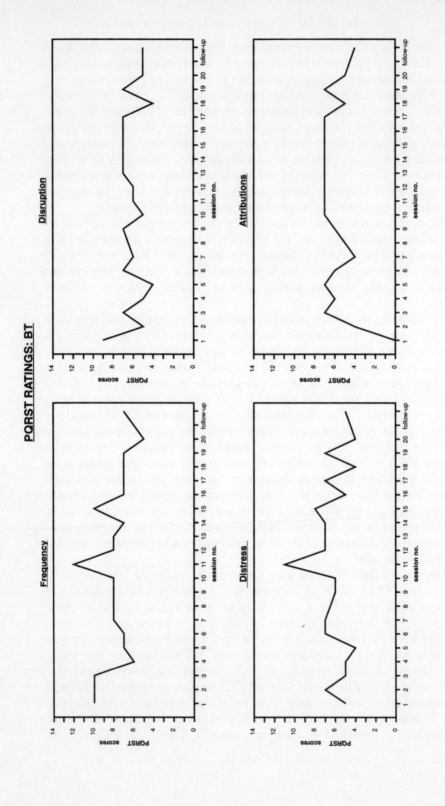

DIARY RATINGS: BT

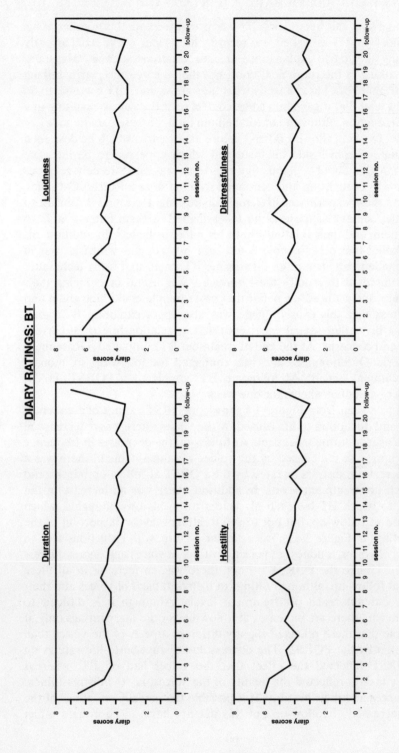

Figure 3.4 Weekly PQRST and average diary ratings for BT

order to test out this hypothesis, BT was presented with this account of his experiences and was asked to record the voices while concurrently generating alternative explanations or interpretations, such as "There are people talking in the room next door, but they are not necessarily talking about me, and I can't hear exactly what they are saying". BT was able to do this and found that it gave him some control over the voices, resulting in a gradual reduction, although not total elimination, of these experiences.

Finally, focusing allowed BT to explore experiences which he described as originating from inside his head and which appeared to be intrusive sexual thoughts about religious figures. As he was an extremely religious man (he was brought up and continued to practise as a Roman Catholic), BT found these experiences extremely distressing. He found it difficult to record the content of these as he felt ashamed of them but was able to discuss them and their relationship to his religious beliefs. In addition, his partial belief that other people could hear his thoughts whilst he was in church made them even more distressing. BT found that using techniques which attempted to modify these thoughts was useful in reducing their occurrence and reduced his belief that other people could hear them and the distress that this caused. Time was also spent exploring BT's guilt regarding his earlier sexual experience and its relationship to his current worries and concerns. At the end of treatment BT completed a Rosenberg Self-esteem Questionnaire and was contacted for follow-up six months after treatment ended. At follow-up BT completed a PQRST, HAD, Rosenberg and diary sheets for one week.

As can be seen from Figure 3.4 showing PQRST ratings of frequency, distress and disruption to life caused by the voices, there was a decrease in these measures during treatment. At follow-up the decreases in frequency and disruption to life caused by the voices were maintained. There was a slight increase in distress as rated by the PQRST at follow-up but this did not reach pre-treatment levels. In addition, there was an increase in the amount to which BT believed his voices to be his own thoughts, which decreased at follow-up, but not to pre-treatment levels. Inspection of the diary ratings in Figure 3.4 shows a similar picture, with reductions seen in duration of voices, loudness of voices, hostility of voices and distressfulness of voices. Unlike the PQRST ratings, there was an increase in all these ratings at follow-up, although ratings of distressfulness of voices and their hostility did not reach pre-treatment levels. Although it is difficult to speculate why there are increases at follow-up for the diary ratings only, it is possible that these reflected slightly different aspects of the voices than those rated by the PQRST. The distress and disruption to life ratings on the PQRST reflected the effect that the voices had on BT, whereas the diary ratings reflected the quality of the voices, i.e. the distressfulness of the voices and their hostility. It is possible that negative qualities of the voices increased at follow-up but this did not have an equivalent effect on BT's response to them. Anxiety and depression both decreased during treatment and although there was a slight increase in depression at follow-up (which did not exceed pre-treatment levels) the reduction in anxiety was maintained. Self-esteem ratings were taken before the start of treatment, at the end of treatment and at follow-up. During treatment there was an increase in self-esteem, although at follow-up there was a decrease in self-esteem to the pre-treatment level. This may be related to the slight increase in depression which was also seen.

This case study highlights the variability in the auditory hallucinations experienced by patients. By focusing on the voices, it is possible to identify the nature of the experiences and to allow reattribution of the experiences to self, if this is appropriate. In the case of BT, he was able correctly to identify the source of his intrusive sexual thoughts and the 'voices' which he believed to be originating from external sources. This resulted in a decrease in the severity of the voices and a reduction in his anxiety and depression. Although all these benefits were not maintained at follow-up, it is clear that for a patient who had previously found no significant effects from traditional approaches to the management of his hallucinations, important changes were achieved. It is likely that BT would have benefited from continued support and reinforcement of the progress made during therapy in order to maintain the benefits he achieved. BT had little contact with other services, apart from a rare appointment with his Consultant Psychiatrist, and therefore he had no one who could help him to continue with the techniques. A longer follow-up would indicate how much the benefits have been maintained.

REFERENCES

American Psychiatric Association (1987) *Diagnostic and Statistical Manual of Mental Disorders* (3rd, revised ed.), Washington DC: APA.

Bentall, R. P. (1990) 'The illusion of reality: A review and integration of psychological research on hallucinations', *Psychological Bulletin* 107: 82–95.

Bentall, R. P., Haddock, G. and Slade, P. D. (1994) 'Psychological treatment for auditory hallucinations: from theory to therapy', *Behavior Therapy* 25: 51–66.

Chadwick, P. and Birchwood, M. (1994) 'The omnipotence of voices. A cognitive approach to auditory hallucinations', *British Journal of Psychiatry* 164: 190–201.

Falloon, I. R. H. and Talbot, R. E. (1981) 'Persistent auditory hallucinations: Coping mechanisms and implications for management', *Psychological Medicine* 11: 329–39.

Feder, R. (1982) 'Auditory hallucinations treated by radio headphones', *American Journal of Psychiatry* 139: 1188–90.

Fowler, D. (1992) 'Cognitive–behaviour therapy in the management of patients with schizophrenia: preliminary studies', in A. Werbart and J. Cullberg (eds) *Psychotherapy of Schizophrenia: Facilitating and Obstructive Factors*, Oslo: Scandinavian University Press.

Frith, C. D. (1992) *The Cognitive Neuropsychology of Schizophrenia*, Hove: Lawrence Erlbaum Associates.

Gallagher, A. G., Dinan, T. G. and Baker, L. J. V. (1994) 'The effects of varying auditory input on schizophrenic hallucinations: A replication', *British Journal of Medical Psychology* 67: 67–76.

Haddock, G., Bentall, R. P. and Slade, P. D. (1993) 'Psychological treatment of auditory hallucinations: two case studies', *Behavioural and Cognitive Psychotherapy* 21: 335–46.

James, D. A. E. (1983) 'The experimental treatment of two cases of auditory hallucinations', *British Journal of Psychiatry* 143: 515–16.

Kingdon, D. G. and Turkington, D. (1991) 'The use of cognitive–behaviour therapy with a normalising rationale in schizophrenia', *Journal of Nervous and Mental Disease* 179: 207–11.

—— (1994) *Cognitive–behavioural Treatment of Schizophrenia*, Hove: Lawrence Erlbaum Associates.

Margo, A., Hemsley, D. R. and Slade, P. D. (1981) 'The effects of varying auditory input on schizophrenic hallucinations', *British Journal of Psychiatry* 139: 122–7.

Morley, S. (1987) 'Modification of auditory hallucinations: experimental studies of headphones and earplugs', *Behavioural Psychotherapy* 15: 252–71.

Mulhall, D. J. (1978) *Manual for the Personal Questionnaire Rapid Scaling Technique*, Windsor: NFER Publishing Company.

Nelson, H. E., Thrasher, S. and Barnes, T. R. E. (1991) 'Practical ways of alleviating auditory hallucinations', *British Medical Journal* 302: 307.

Rosenberg, M. (1965) *Society and the Adolescent Self-image*, Princeton, NJ: Princeton University Press.

Slade, P. D. and Bentall, R. P. (1988) *Sensory Deception: A Scientific Analysis of Hallucination*, London: Croom Helm.

Tarrier, N. (1987) 'An investigation of residual psychotic symptoms in discharged schizophrenic patients', *British Journal of Clinical Psychology* 26: 141–3.

Tarrier, N., Beckett, R., Harwood, S., Baker, A., Yusupoff, L. and Ugarteburu, I. (1993) 'A trial of two cognitive–behavioural methods of treating drug resistant residual psychotic symptoms in schizophrenic patients: I. Outcome', *British Journal of Psychiatry* 162, 524–32.

Werbart, A. and Culberg, J. (eds) (1992) *Psychotherapy of Schizophrenia: Facilitating and Obstructive Factors*, Oslo: Scandinavian University Press.

Williams, J. M. G. (1992) *Psychological Treatment of Depression*, London: Routledge.

Wing, J. K., Cooper, J. E. and Sartorius, N. (1974) *Measurement and Classification of Psychiatric Symptoms*, Cambridge: Cambridge University Press.

Young, H. F., Bentall, R. P., Slade, P. D. and Dewey, M. E. (1987) 'The role of brief instructions and suggestibility in the elicitation of auditory and visual hallucinations in normal and psychiatric subjects', *Journal of Nervous and Mental Disease* 175: 41–8.

Zigmond, A. S. and Snaith, R. P. (1983) 'The hospital anxiety and depression scale', *Acta Psychiatrica Scandinavica* 67: 361–70.

4

COGNITIVE THERAPY FOR VOICES

Paul Chadwick and Max Birchwood

THE COGNITIVE ASSESSMENT OF VOICES

Auditory hallucinations are traditionally associated with a diagnosis of schizophrenia. In the World Health Organization's *International Pilot Study of Schizophrenia* (WHO, 1973) auditory hallucinations were reported by 73 per cent of people diagnosed as having an acute episode of schizophrenia, yet they can be reported by individuals who have been sexually abused, or suffered a bereavement, as well as by individuals diagnosed as having a manic depressive illness or an affective psychosis. Indeed, because they feature in many different disorders, the diagnostic importance of auditory hallucinations has been doubted (Asaad and Shapiro, 1986).

In addition, it appears that auditory hallucinations are not restricted to clinical groups. Auditory hallucinations can be reported by individuals who, whilst showing signs of a specific clinical disorder, display insufficient evidence for a firm diagnosis to be made (Cochrane, 1983). Again, it appears that under laboratory conditions many ordinary people display a propensity to report hearing sounds which are not there, prompting researchers to speculate that proneness to hallucinate may be a predisposition spread across the general population (Slade and Bentall, 1988). Current opinion in psychology veers towards accepting the possibility that hallucinations lie on a continuum with normality (Strauss, 1969).

The auditory hallucination itself can be a noise, music, single words, a brief phrase, or a whole conversation. The present chapter is concerned only with voices, that is, hallucinations which are experienced as someone talking. The experience of hearing voices is a powerful one that demands a reaction. However, the experience is also very personal. Whilst it is known that a common first reaction to voices is puzzlement (Maher, 1988), individuals evolve different ways of interacting with their voices. Certain people, for example, experience voices as immensely distressing and frightening and will shout and swear at them. In contrast, other individuals might find their voices reassuring and amusing and actually seek contact. Again, in the case of imperative voices, many individuals desperately resist the

71

commands, and comply only at times of great pressure, whilst others comply willingly and fully.

Viewing voices from a cognitive perspective

This diversity in the way in which individuals relate to their voices illustrates the point that voices are not necessarily a problem to the individual concerned; indeed, it is fairly common for individuals to believe their voices to be a solution to a problem. This in turn draws attention to the point that the serious disturbance associated with voices, as with so many other symptoms, tends to be located in the way in which an individual feels and behaves. People who hear voices are typically referred to our service because they are desperate, depressed, angry, suicidal, helpless, harming themselves, isolated, violent, etc. This point is implicit in traditional treatment approaches, which have usually been directed at easing distress and altering behaviour (e.g. methods of anxiety reduction, punishment procedures) as well as at eliminating the hallucinatory experience (medication, earplugs, headphones). Such treatments were based on the premise that a particular individual's coping behaviour and affect followed necessarily from the nature of his or her hallucination:

> If the voice attacks the patient he or she is depressed and suicidal. If the voice tells the patient to kill others, then, if the patient loses self-control, murderous attacks on others are likely. If the voice tells the patient he or she is wonderful and powerful, grandiose and manic behaviours appear. . . . In other words, the content of the hallucination is directly responsible for the salient and anomalous behaviours associated with schizophrenia.
>
> (Benjamin, 1989, p. 293)

However, this explanation may be too simple. Research has shown how voices with similar contents may evoke different coping behaviour (Tarrier, 1992). Also, an ingenious study by Romme and Escher (1989; also see Chapter 8) has revealed how voices frequently do not evoke a sufficiently strong reaction to bring the individual to the attention of services, even when the content is extremely serious. It would appear that the nature and strength of an individual's response to voices is mediated by psychological processes.

Research on ordinary people indicates the likely extent of this mediation. For example, in Milgram's famous studies, whether subjects could be persuaded to administer what they believed to be a lethal electric shock to other subjects was strongly influenced by their beliefs about the experimenter's authority and power, their own degree of control, and the presumed consequences of disobedience (Milgram, 1974). Likewise, it is possible that the degree of fear, acceptance and compliance shown to voices might be mediated by *beliefs* about the voices' power and authority, the consequences of disobedience, and so on. For example, an individual who believes his voice to come from a powerful and vengeful spirit may be terrified of the voice and comply with its commands to harm others; if the same voice were believed to be self-generated, however, terror and compliance would be unlikely.

In other words, voices might be viewed from a cognitive perspective. The defining feature of the cognitive model within clinical psychology is the premise that people's feelings and behaviour are mediated by their beliefs, and therefore are not inevitable consequences of antecedent events.

Applicability of the cognitive model to voices

If the cognitive perspective is to be applicable to voices, two hypotheses must be supported. One is that the cognitive model will make sense of why individuals respond in such different ways to their voices; specifically, diverse affective and behavioural responses must be understandable by reference to differences in the beliefs individuals hold about their voices. Second, the cognitive model needs to add to our understanding of voices. That is to say, if differences in voice content accounted fully for people's diverse behaviour and feelings, then from an explanatory point of view the cognitive model would be superfluous (although it could still have important strategic implications for treatment).

In a recent experiment (Chadwick and Birchwood, 1994), we found support for both hypotheses. We interviewed twenty-six people who had heard voices for at least two years in order to assess their behavioural, cognitive and affective responses to persistent voices. All participants met DSM-III-R criteria for schizophrenia or schizoaffective disorder (APA, 1987). All except one were receiving depot neuroleptic medication at All Saints Hospital, Birmingham; one was in hospital and the remainder were outpatients. Participants volunteered for the study and there were no refusals.

Information was gathered using a semi-structured interview. This covered: formal properties of the voices, including content; beliefs about the voices' identity, power and purpose, and about the consequences of compliance; collateral symptoms that were regarded as supporting the beliefs; other confirmatory evidence; and influence over the voice. Confirmatory evidence referred to actual occurrences that were perceived to support a belief; for example, the belief that voices give good advice would be strengthened if complying with a command led to a desired outcome. Influence concerned whether the individual could determine the onset and offset of the voice, and could direct what it said. Also, the behavioural and affective responses were elicited. It usually took more than one interview to collect all relevant information.

73

Beliefs about voices: omnipotence, malevolence and benevolence

All voices were believed to be extraordinarily powerful, or omnipotent, and this belief seemed to be supported by four types of evidence. First, nineteen individuals (73 per cent) reported collateral symptoms that contributed to the sense of omnipotence. One man, for example, was commanded by his voice to kill his daughter; he recalled one occasion when she was standing by an open window and he experienced his body being moved towards her. A second man heard a voice telling him that he was the son of Noah, and occasionally when he heard his voice he experienced concurrent visual hallucinations in which he was dressed in a white robe and walked on water. Second, eleven people (42 per cent) gave examples of how they attributed events to their voices, and then cited the events as proof of the voices' great power. Thus, although two individuals cut their wrists under their own volition, both subsequently deduced that the voices had somehow made them do it. Similarly, one man attributed responsibility for having sworn out loud in church to his satanic voices. Third, twenty-one people (81 per cent) were unable to influence either the onset and offset of their voices or what was said, once again suggestive of the voices' power.

Finally, all voices gave the impression of knowing all about people's past histories, their present thoughts, feelings and actions, and what the future held. Frequently voices would refer to behaviour and thoughts of a highly personal and emotive nature, such as a criminal act or personal weakness, which the individual feared others knowing. Perhaps because of this lack of privacy, individuals would often attribute more knowledge to the voice than the content actually displayed; for instance, general statements like "We know all about you" were thought to refer to specific actions. Understandably, this appearance of omniscience left many individuals feeling exposed and vulnerable.

However, because in our sample a belief in omnipotence was ubiquitous, it would not account for differences in behaviour and affect. On the basis of their beliefs about the voices' identity and purpose, people saw individual voices as being either *malevolent* or *benevolent*. Thirteen people believed their voice or voices to be malevolent. Beliefs about malevolence took one of two forms: either that the voice was a punishment for a bad deed, or that it was an undeserved persecution. For example, one man believed he was being punished by the Devil for having committed a murder, and another man believed he was being persecuted without good reason by an ex-employer. Six people believed their voices to be benevolent. For example, one woman believed that she heard the voice of a prophet who was helping her become a better mother and wife, and one man believed that the voices were from God and there to help develop a special power. Four people believed they heard a mixture of benevolent and malevolent voices; para-digmatic of this group was a man who was tormented by a group of evil

74

space travellers on the one hand and yet protected and nurtured by a guardian angel on the other.

Three people were uncertain about their voices because of an inconsistency or incongruity in what was said. *Uncertainty* was defined as having a strong doubt about the voices' identity, meaning or power, where this doubt was the result of the person's deduction. For example, one man was certain that his voices wanted to help, but observed that they had got things wrong: they wanted him to kill himself and move on to the next and better life, yet his religion told him that suicide is a sin and those who commit it go to hell.

Connection between beliefs, coping behaviour and affect

The behavioural responses to voices were organised into three categories:

Engagement was defined as elective listening, willing compliance, and doing things to bring on the voices (e.g. watching television, being alone, calling up voices).

Resistance was defined as arguing and shouting (overt and covert), non-compliance or reluctant compliance when pressure is extreme, avoidance of cues that trigger voices, and distraction.

Indifference was defined as not engaging with the voice.

Without fail, those people who believed their voices to be benevolent engaged with them and those people who believed their voices to be malevolent resisted them. Those people who were uncertain about their voices displayed no clear pattern between beliefs and behaviour.

Affective responses to voices corresponded very closely to behavioural responses. All seventeen 'malevolent' voices habitually provoked a combination of negative emotions (anger, fear, depression, anxiety). Ten of the eleven 'benevolent' voices habitually provoked positive emotions (amusement, reassurance, calm, happiness) when they spoke; the one exception was a voice which issued warnings about impending danger and provoked anxiety. All three people who were uncertain about their voices experienced negative affect when these voices spoke.

In order to establish the reliability and validity of these concepts, we have developed a thirty-item Beliefs About Voices Questionnaire (BAVQ; see Appendix 4.1) to measure malevolence (six items), benevolence (six items), resistance (nine items), engagement (eight items) and power (one item). A statistical analysis conducted on a preliminary sample of sixty completed questionnaires has shown the BAVQ to be both reliable and valid (for details see Chadwick and Birchwood, 1995), and has established provisional scoring guidelines to define malevolence (a score of four or more), benevolence (three or more), engagement (five or more) and resistance (six

75

or more). Data from this study strongly supported our proposed connections between, on the one hand, malevolence, distress, positive affect and resistance, and on the other, benevolence and engagement (see Table 4.1).

There is currently much debate about the connection between paranoid thinking and depression. Zigler and Glick (1988) have proposed that paranoia might be a defence against low self-esteem and that certain forms of paranoid schizophrenia might be a defended depression. In this respect we were struck by our finding that voices construed as persecutory (i.e. malevolent) appeared to provoke more depressive reactions than voices construed as benevolent. Therefore, those individuals who completed the BAVQ also completed the Beck Depression Inventory (Beck and Greer, 1987). The results were a striking confirmation of our earlier interview data. Taking a score of fifteen or more to be indicative of clinical levels of depressive symptomatology, and a cut off of three items or more on the subscales of malevolence and benevolence, we found that 'depression' was indeed much more common and severe with malevolent, not benevolent, voices (see Table 4.2). Thus, it might well be that paranoia defends against low self-esteem, but it appears not to defend against depression (Chadwick and Lowe, 1994).

Table 4.1 Connections between malevolence, benevolence, engagement and resistance

	Resistance	Engagement	Neither	Both
Malevolent (n=24)	17 (66%)	2 (8%)	3 (11%)	4 (15%)
Benevolent (n=17)	0	13 (76%)	3 (18%)	1 (6%)
Neutral (n=16)	3 (19%)	4 (25%)	8 (50%)	1 (6%)

Table 4.2 Connection between meaning attributed to voices and depressive symptomatology

	Depressed (BDI >15)	Mean BDI score
Malevolent (n=26)	17 (65%)	23 (s.d. = 11.9)
Benevolent (n=17)	6 (35%)	15.6 (s.d. = 11.3)
Neutral (n=16)	7 (44%)	14.9 (s.d. = 9.9)

Connection between malevolence, benevolence, and voice content

Having found that differences in coping behaviour and distress were rendered understandable by reference to beliefs about malevolence and benevolence, it remained to be shown that voice content could not account for these differences with equal clarity. In other words, the distinction between malevolence and benevolence needed to say something about the maintenance of voices which could not be said by inspecting voice content alone.

It is clear that there is a link between voice content and the person's associated feelings and behaviour, and therefore that in many cases resistance and engagement might have been predicted on the basis of content. However, the class of belief was not always understandable in light of voice content alone; that is, in eight cases (31 per cent) the beliefs appeared to be at odds with what the voice said. Two voices of benign content were believed to be malevolent; for instance, one of these voices simply urged the individual to 'take care', 'mind his step', and 'watch how he went', yet he believed these words to have been spoken by evil witches intent on driving him mad. The reverse was also true; two voices commanded the hearers to commit suicide, yet both were believed to be benevolent. Three voices commanded the hearers to commit murder (in two instances, of immediate family members), and yet again were believed to be benevolent. Perhaps most strikingly, one woman's voice identified itself as God and yet she disregarded this and believed it to be an evil force.

Weakness of the cognitive model

The explanatory power of the cognitive model was weakest in relation to compliance. In our group the severity of the command, and not beliefs, was the single most important determinant of compliance; there was no compliance with life threatening commands and compliance with mild commands was commonplace. This might be because the relationship with a voice is regulated by wider considerations such as protecting self-esteem and maintaining involvement with others (Strauss, 1989). Certainly, research on ordinary individuals has shown that compliance is affected by the social acceptability of the behaviour in question (Fishbein and Ajzen, 1975). At present we are interviewing people who have acted on serious commands to investigate if such compliance is associated with factors specific to the hallucinatory experience (e.g. total certainty in the beliefs) or more general predictors of violence (e.g. previous history).

Summary

Thus, it appears that individuals' beliefs about voices have an important bearing on how these symptoms are maintained. In our research, the meaning individuals attached to their voices rendered their coping behaviour and affect understandable, when without recourse to the beliefs many responses would have seemed perplexing or incongruous (see also Strauss, 1991). One advantage of the cognitive approach is that it gives individuals time to describe their belief systems, and then uses these descriptions as the starting point for cognitive therapy.

COGNITIVE THERAPY FOR VOICES

The cognitive approach within clinical psychology (e.g. Trower *et al.*, 1988) is based on two premises. The major premise states that extreme feelings and behaviour (e.g. depression and suicide) are consequences of particular beliefs (e.g. 'I am worthless') rather than events (e.g. divorce). The minor premise states that if these beliefs can be weakened using cognitive therapy, then the associated distress and behaviour will diminish.

Cognitive therapy (CT) is now well established as a treatment for a number of non-psychotic disorders (Hawton *et al.*, 1988); for example, using CT to weaken core depressive beliefs seems to be as effective a treatment of depression as prescribing medication (Hollon *et al.*, 1991). More recent evidence has shown its potential in the management of schizophrenia (see Birchwood and Tarrier, 1992 and Chapters 3, 5, 6, and 7). For example, there is growing evidence that some secondary delusions may be weakened using cognitive therapy (see Chadwick and Lowe, 1990).

Traditional treatments for voices have been directly aimed at reducing either the hallucinatory experience (e.g. medication, earplug therapy) or their consequences (e.g. anxiety reduction methods, punishment procedures). The purpose of using CT for voices is to ease distress and problem behaviour by weakening target beliefs about omnipotence, malevolence or benevolence, and compliance. The possible importance of this new approach is considerable because even the most effective treatment for voices – neuroleptic medication – leaves many voices unchanged (Slade and Bentall, 1988).

The CT we use for people who hear voices draws very heavily on the work of Beck (Beck *et al.*, 1979; Hole *et al.*, 1979; and Ellis, 1962), although we have found it necessary to adapt and develop traditional CT in order to work collaboratively and effectively with individuals who hear voices.

We have found it can be difficult to engage people in CT for voices, because of their powerful beliefs and emotions about their voices. Therefore we have developed a number of strategies to promote engagement and trust. One such strategy is to use our understanding of the connections between malevolence, benevolence, resistance and engagement to anticipate how an individual is likely to feel, think and behave in relation to the voice. This understanding seems to bring individuals a sense of relief. Also, we always inform clients that they may withdraw from therapy at any point without penalty, and this may also reduce anxiety and facilitate engagement. Again, people can meet other hallucinators and watch a video of individuals who have completed therapy successfully discussing their experience; the discovery that others have similar problems, 'universality' (Yalom, 1970), is an important therapeutic process.

The central beliefs are defined early on, together with the evidence used to support them, and we discuss how any distress and disruption attributed to the voices is actually a consequence of the beliefs the individual holds. We emphasise that individuals are free to continue holding their beliefs, and may drop out of therapy at any time; the atmosphere is one of 'collaborative empiricism' (Beck *et al.*, 1979) in which beliefs are considered as possibilities that may or may not be reasonable.

Disputing a belief's veracity involves the use of standard cognitive techniques (see Chadwick and Lowe, 1990). At first the evidence for each belief is challenged; this process begins with the piece of evidence the individual rates as least important and progresses to that rated most important. Next the therapist challenges the belief directly. This involves first pointing out examples of inconsistency and irrationality, and second, offering an alternative explanation of events. This alternative is always that the beliefs are an understandable reaction to, and attempt to make sense of, the voices. In our experience this leaves the person searching to understand the meaning of the hallucinations. We conceptualise the voices as self-generated, and try to explore the possible connection, or personal significance, between the voice content and the individual's history.

We use two approaches to test beliefs empirically. On the one hand, we have a set procedure for testing the universal belief 'I cannot control my voices'. First, it is reframed as 'I cannot turn my voices on and off'. The therapist then engineers situations to increase and then decrease the probability of hearing voices. An initial thorough cognitive assessment should identify the cues that provoke voices, and one technique with a high likelihood of eliminating voices for its duration is concurrent verbalisation (Birchwood, 1986). The person rouses and quells the voices several times to provide a complete test.

With all other beliefs the empirical test was negotiated by the client and therapist. It is essential to examine beforehand the implications of the test not bearing out the belief: if the belief will be modified or adapted, or whether the patient has a ready explanation for the outcome that leaves the belief untouched.

A case example

DD was a 41-year-old single unemployed economics graduate with a ten year psychiatric history. For the last three years she had heard voices in half hour bursts, usually in the morning and at bed time. The content was invariably to do with economics, such as 'Infinitely power the rise in inflation', 'Negatively power productivity a million, trillion times'. These and similar statements were usually perceived as commands and occasionally as predictions. DD also held a delusional belief that she could transmit her thoughts using telepathy. Therapy lasted thirteen sessions spaced over six months. Meetings lasted one to two hours.

DD believed the voice to come from the Devil, and that he was using her telepathic power to destroy the British economy. Specifically, the Devil would give a command that in economic terms was disastrous. DD would be compelled to repeat this command and in so doing would unwittingly transmit it telepathically to the Prime Minister, who would act upon it. She believed that if she resisted, then the economy would be saved, but the voice would continue to torment her. In practice, each time the voice began she would resist by saying exactly the opposite of the command, until she finally weakened and repeated the Devil's command, when the voice would stop. She monitored the economy religiously and felt guilt, anger and depression when it dipped.

Two hypothetical contradictions were put to DD. First, she was asked if her beliefs would be altered if she met with the Prime Minister and he assured her that he did not hear her messages. Second, she was asked if her beliefs would be altered if she went out of her way to *comply* with the commands and the economy was unaffected. DD thought that both these events would weaken her conviction that the beliefs were true.

Whenever the economic news was poor, DD would feel depressed and guilty, inferring 'It is my fault', and she would take the news to be evidence for her beliefs. DD was encouraged to generate and examine an alternative view of events, which was that the main economic indices went up and down regularly and bore no particular relationship to her transmission of messages. This exercise led her not only to question critical evidence for her beliefs, but also to recognise how beliefs influence behaviour and feelings, and are possibly mistaken.

The most obvious inconsistency in DD's beliefs was that on most days she did reluctantly repeat the Devil's commands, and yet the predicted economic disaster had not ensued. Also, there were certain puzzling features in the account; for example, how was the Prime Minister to know that he was to act on the commands, and even should he know this, what does 'infinitely power' require? Again, why should the Devil, an omnipotent being, need to work through DD, as opposed to communicating with the Prime Minister directly?

Following Maher (1988), the alternative explanation offered to DD was that her beliefs arose in response to, and as a way of making sense of, her voice. The beliefs were not labelled as delusions, but were discussed as being a reasonable and reasoned attempt to understand what was a puzzling and alarming experience.

DD first tested the belief that she could not control the voice. She found that by successively reading about economic affairs for five minutes, and then reading aloud material unrelated to economics for five minutes (i.e. concurrent verbalisation), she was able first to increase and then to decrease voice activity. In other words, simple changes in her own behaviour appeared to influence the voice, and this led her to doubt the belief that she could not control it.

In order to test her beliefs about compliance and meaning DD agreed to stop saying the opposite to the voice, and instead, to repeat the commands many times. This process began with comparatively innocuous commands (increasing bus fares and the price of milk) and progressed to the most central (taxation levels and interest rates). Also, with any one command, the principles of systematic desensitisation were applied to reduce DD's anxiety; thus DD would repeat the chosen command several times, rate her degree of distress, relax for a few minutes, and then repeat the procedure again until her distress was negligible. It was agreed that if her beliefs were true then the effects of the tests would appear within two weeks and would be significant, that is, for the belief to be supported bus fares, for instance, would need to double. In all cases the test had no effect and this appeared to weaken DD's beliefs about the consequences of compliance and about the meaning she attached to her voice.

Initially CT worked well for DD. Conviction in all four beliefs about the voice fell significantly and she reported being less fearful, guilty and depressed, and hearing reduced voice activity (see Chadwick and Birchwood, 1994 for full details of this and other cases). By follow-up the extraordinary economic events in Britain in the summer of 1992, including a 5 per cent rise and fall in interest rates in one day, appeared to have undone some of this progress! DD was agitated and her conviction in three beliefs had risen sharply. Since then, earlier gains have been recovered; conviction has once again fallen sharply, DD's voice activity is now far less frequent and, perhaps most importantly, DD is no longer resisting the voice by saying the opposite to the commands.

Personal significance of voices

In our experience, a critical component of CT for voices is often that of drawing out the personal significance of the voices, that is, tentatively making a connection between voice content and beliefs on the one hand, and the individual's history on the other. Indeed, in this chapter we have argued that voices are a powerful experience, one which individuals feel compelled to try and understand. Beliefs about voices are the result of this endeavour and they carry the psychological force of relieving a sense of puzzlement and unease. It has been our experience that whilst many individuals are able to recognise that all or some of their beliefs about voices are mistaken, this can leave them once again struggling to understand the fact that they experience hallucinations.

One possible response open to the therapist is to label the voice a sign of 'illness'. However, there are reasons for not doing this. First, concepts like schizophrenia are of uncertain scientific validity (Bentall *et al.*, 1988) and patients who accept such labels have been found to have a higher incidence of secondary depression (Birchwood *et al.*, 1993). Second, and perhaps of most importance, attributing voices to illness is such an impersonal explanation that it rarely satisfies people. What individuals seem to value is tentatively connecting the content of their own voices to their own histories. For example, in the case of DD, it was suggested that the voice might give a clue as to underlying depressive concerns. The speculation was that DD's childhood experience established a strong need to achieve and earn respect and that as an adult she had experienced a growing sense of failure and inadequacy; indeed, prior to the onset of psychotic symptoms, she had experienced a clinical depression. One effect of her voice was to propel DD into saving the British economy, at great personal cost, and this might be interpreted as both reflecting and offsetting the underlying depressive concerns. As regards this point, DD did experience a drop in mood following the rejection of her beliefs about the voice's identity and purpose; this served to emphasise these depressive beliefs, which were addressed using cognitive therapy.

With other individuals, where there have been grounds to do so, we have made tentative links between voice content and early experience, such as sexual abuse or loss. However, such a link has also been made with more recent experience, such as guilt surrounding abortion. In some instances we have been unable to interpret the significance of the voices.

It is our experience that as beliefs about voices are weakened, underlying themes sometimes emerge spontaneously. We do not interpret this as a reason not to do CT for voices, but rather conclude that certain individuals may require more than symptom-based therapy; however, it is important that such individuals are given the option to address these further issues, with either the same therapist or a new one.

CONCLUSIONS

We have argued that viewing voices from a cognitive perspective increases our understanding of the maintenance of voices, and reveals a new treatment approach of considerable promise. However, our research has thrown up puzzling questions to replace those with which we began. For example, if content does not determine whether voices are believed to be malevolent or benevolent, then what does? Also, the cognitive therapy has not been formally evaluated and the limits of its usefulness are unknown. Nonetheless we feel sure that the cognitive model offers clinicians a useful psychological approach to voices, one which will enable them to work collaboratively and effectively to reduce distress and disturbance associated with voices.

REFERENCES

American Psychiatric Association (1987) *Diagnostic and Statistical Manual of Mental Disorders*, revised 3rd edition, Washington, DC: APA.

Asaad, G. and Shapiro, M. D. (1986) 'Hallucinations: Theoretical and clinical overview', *American Journal of Psychiatry* 143: 1088–97.

Beck, A. T. and Greer, R. (1987) *Beck Depression Inventory Scoring Manual*, The Psychological Corporation, New York: Harcourt Brace Jovanovich.

Beck, A. T., Rush, A. J., Shaw, B. F. and Emery, G. (1979) *Cognitive Therapy of Depression*, New York: Guildford Press.

Benjamin, L. S. (1989) 'Is chronicity a function of the relationship between the person and the auditory hallucination?', *Schizophrenia Bulletin* 15: 291–330.

Bentall, R. P., Jackson, H. F. and Pilgrim, D. (1988) 'Abandoning the concept of schizophrenia: Some implications of validity arguments for psychological research into psychotic phenomena', *British Journal of Clinical Psychology* 27: 303–24.

Birchwood, M. J. (1986) 'Control of auditory hallucinations through occlusion of monoaural auditory input', *British Journal of Psychiatry* 149: 104–7.

Birchwood, M. J. and Tarrier, N. (1992) *Innovations in the Psychological Management of Schizophrenia*, Chichester: Wiley.

Birchwood, M. J., Mason, R., McMillan, F. and Healy, J. (1993) 'Depression, demoralization and control over illness: A comparison of depressed and non-depressed patients with a chronic psychosis', *Psychological Medicine* 23: 387–95.

Chadwick, P. D. J. and Birchwood, M. J. (1994) 'Challenging the omnipotence of voices: A cognitive approach to auditory hallucinations', *British Journal of Psychiatry* 164: 190–201.

—— (1995) 'The omnipotence of voices II: The beliefs about voices questionnaire', *British Journal of Psychiatry* 165, 773–6.

Chadwick, P. D. J. and Lowe, C. F. (1990) 'Measurement and modification of delusional beliefs', *Journal of Consulting and Clinical Psychology*, 58: 225–32.

—— (1994) 'A cognitive approach to measuring and modifying delusions', *Behaviour, Research and Therapy* 32: 355–67.

Cochrane, R. (1983) *The Social Creation of Mental Illness*, Essex: Longman.

Ellis, A. (1962) *Reason and Emotion in Psychotherapy*, New York: Lyle Stuart.

Fishbein, M. and Ajzen, I. (1975) *Belief, Attitude, Intention and Behaviour: An Introduction to Theory and Research*, Massachusetts: Addison-Wesley.

Hawton, K., Salkovskis, P., Kirk, J. and Clark, D. M. (eds) (1988) *Cognitive–behavioural Therapy for Psychiatric Problems*, Oxford: Oxford University Press.

Hole, R. W., Rush, A. J. and Beck, A. T. (1979) 'A cognitive investigation of schizophrenic delusions', *Psychiatry* 42: 312–19.

Hollon, S. D., Shelton, R. C. and Loosen, P. T. (1991) 'Cognitive therapy and pharmacotherapy for depression', *Journal of Consulting and Clinical Psychology* 59: 88–99.

Maher, B. A. (1988) 'Anomalous experience and delusional thinking: The logic of explanation', in T. F. Oltmanns and B. A. Maher (eds) *Delusional Beliefs*, New York: Wiley.

Milgram, S. (1974) *Obedience to Authority*, New York: Harper and Row.

Oltmanns, T. F. and Maher, B. A. (eds) (1988) *Delusional Beliefs*, New York: Wiley.

Romme, M. A. R. and Escher, A.D.M.A.C. (1989) 'Hearing voices', *Schizophrenia Bulletin* 15: 209–16.

Slade, P. D. and Bentall, R. P. (1988) *Sensory Deception: A Scientific Analysis of Hallucination*, London: Croom Helm.

Strauss, J. S. (1969) 'Hallucinations and delusions as points on continua function', *Archives of General Psychiatry* 21: 581–6.

—— (1989) 'Subjective experience of schizophrenia', *Schizophrenia Bulletin* 15: 179–85.

—— (1991) 'The person with delusions', *British Journal of Psychiatry* 159: 57–62.

Tarrier, N. (1992) 'Management and modification of residual positive pschotic symptoms', in M. Birchwood and N. Tarrier (eds) *Innovations in the Psychological Management of Schizophrenia*, Chichester: Wiley.

Trower, P., Casey, A. and Dryden, W. (1988) *Cognitive–behavioural Counselling in Action*, Bristol: Sage.

World Health Organization (1973) *International Pilot Study of Schizophrenia*, Geneva: WHO.

Yalom, I. (1970) *The Theory and Practice of Group Psychotherapy*, New York: Basic Books.

Zigler, E. and Glick, M. (1988) 'Is paranoid schizophrenia really camouflaged depression?', *American Psychologist* 43: 284–90.

APPENDIX 4.1
BAVQ ITEMS

1. My voice is punishing me for something I have done.
2. My voice wants to help me.
3. My voice is persecuting me for no good reason.
4. My voice wants to protect me.
5. My voice is evil.
6. My voice is helping to keep me sane.
7. My voice wants to harm me.
8. My voice is helping me to develop my special powers or abilities.
9. My voice wants me to do bad things.
10. My voice is helping me to achieve my goal in life.
11. My voice is trying to corrupt or destroy me.
12. I am grateful for my voice.
13. My voice is very powerful.
14. My voice reassures me.
15. My voice frightens me.
16. My voice makes me happy.
17. My voice makes me feel down.
18. My voice makes me feel angry.
19. My voice makes me feel calm.
20. My voice makes me feel anxious.
21. My voice makes me feel confident.

WHEN I HEAR MY VOICE, *USUALLY* . . .

22. I tell it to leave me alone.
23. I try and take my mind off it.
24. I try and stop it.
25. I do things to prevent it talking.
26. I am reluctant to obey it.
27. I listen to it because I want to.
28. I willingly follow what my voice tells me to do.
29. I have done things to start to get in contact with my voice.
30. I seek the advice of my voice.

5

COPING STRATEGY ENHANCEMENT FOR PERSISTENT HALLUCINATIONS AND DELUSIONS

Lawrence Yusupoff and Nicholas Tarrier

INTRODUCTION

The Coping Strategy Enhancement (CSE) approach for persistent hallucinations and delusions is characterised by its emphasis on an individually formulated training programme to enhance symptom self-management skills. In practice, however, a range of cognitive–behavioural methods are applied flexibly to match the diversity of clinical presentations of individuals who experience these psychotic phenomena. This chapter begins with a brief background to the approach and basic conceptual model, followed by a summary of research findings from an initial controlled trial of CSE and a description of a second, larger scale investigation currently ongoing. Specific therapeutic methods and mechanisms are described with some illustrative case material.

BACKGROUND

Experience of persistent positive psychotic symptoms is often associated with marked psychological distress, as indexed by measures of anxiety and depression (Breier and Strauss, 1983; Tarrier, 1987; Hustig and Hafner, 1990). By implication, one might expect that the presence of such negative affective states would give rise to the development of naturalistic coping strategies amongst these individuals. Coping in this sense refers to the active self-generation of cognitive and behavioural procedures either to impact on the symptom directly or to minimise the resultant distress. A series of studies confirm that the majority of patients (range: 67–100 per cent) do indeed use active coping strategies with varying degrees of success (Falloon and Talbot, 1981; Breier and Strauss, 1983; Cohen and Berk, 1985; Tarrier, 1987; Carr, 1988).

In the Tarrier (1987) study, twenty-five patients were identified who were experiencing hallucinations and/or delusions during a nine month period after discharge, from a population of eighty-five patients with a diagnosis of schizophrenia. All patients were maintained on neuroleptic medication. Using a detailed semi-structured interview, the Antecedent and Coping Interview (ACI; Tarrier, 1992), the individual's subjective account of their psychotic experiences was elicited as were the conditions under which these were experienced and their idiosyncratic emotional reaction and subsequent use of coping strategies. Seventeen patients (68 per cent) experienced true hallucinations, two (6 per cent) experienced pseudo-hallucinations and nineteen (76 per cent) experienced coherently expressed delusions. Thirteen patients (32 per cent) were able to identify antecedents to either symptom onset or symptom exacerbation. These varied from specific stimuli (e.g. traffic noise, television; 16 per cent), social situations (20 per cent), internal states (e.g. feeling anxious; 4 per cent), being unoccupied or alone (24 per cent), or to specific times of day (16 per cent). All patients were able to identify symptom consequences, although two patients explained that they no longer experienced the severe anxiety that previously accompanied their symptoms. Seventy-two per cent reported that they experienced distress and 36 per cent that the experience of symptoms disrupted ongoing behaviour, with 12 per cent disclosing severe social changes such as arrest or attempted suicide.

Eighteen patients (72 per cent) were able to describe symptom-related coping strategies. Cognitive strategies were used by 40 per cent, which included distraction (12 per cent), attention narrowing (12 per cent) and self-instruction (16 per cent). Thirty-six per cent used behavioural strategies, 16 per cent increased or initiated social interactions, 8 per cent used an increase in solitary activity, and 12 per cent withdrew from social interaction. Sixteen per cent reported coping by increasing sensory stimulation such as turning on the radio to drown out voices. The use of relaxation or breathing exercises were used by 8 per cent to decrease levels of physiological arousal. Of the patients who used active coping strategies, 72 per cent reported at least one of them as being moderately successful or better in controlling symptoms and 75 per cent of all strategies used were rated as being at least moderately successful. Eight patients (32 per cent) reported multiple strategy use which was significantly associated with strategy effectiveness.

On the basis of these findings, Tarrier (1987) concluded that using programmes to train patients in appropriate and effective coping skills was a viable proposition, given that determinants of these symptoms could be identified. It was envisaged that such an approach would utilise and extend coping methods already established in the patient's behavioural repertoire and would thus have high face validity which would facilitate a collaborative therapeutic alliance. Furthermore, the assessment procedure itself, with its emphasis on accurate and detailed cognitive–behavioural analyses of symptoms, would contribute to the psychological reattribution process and also generate additional therapeutic interventions to modify beliefs, which would result in reduced distress. Coping strategies would be practised in vivo where possible and this would be achieved by encouraging the patient to simulate or actually activate the symptom during sessions and to practise coping strategies as homework by entering situations in which symptoms are likely to occur. Finally, training in coping would not be restricted to the application of a single technique, but would include combinations or sequences of individual strategies.

CONCEPTUAL FRAMEWORK

Basic model

The CSE approach is a pragmatic one and a theoretical position regarding symptom origins, biological or otherwise, is not crucial to effective clinical practice. The model is one of symptom maintenance. Hallucinations and delusional beliefs occur in subjective and social contexts and thus symptoms assume significance and meaning only when there is an accompanying emotional reaction (with cognitive, physiological, behavioural and affective components). A psychotic phenomenon is unlikely to develop to a clinically significant degree without the support of these psychological parameters, i.e. a (persistent) symptom cannot exist in isolation from normal evaluative and motivational processes. The emotional reaction both defines the symptom and at the same time creates conditions which result in its maintenance. For example, a powerful physiological reaction may represent confirmation of a delusional belief and the threat associated with it. Even minor changes in behaviour, such as stooping in response to unpleasant voices, may provide additional grounding of the beliefs associated with them; for example, a patient's post hoc rationalisation of his behaviour following symptom onset might include a statement such as "My body stoops, therefore the voices must be more powerful than me and dangerous."

Thus, the CSE approach relies on eliciting a detailed account of the components of the emotional reaction and their reciprocal relationships. These can then be manipulated with the patient, on a collaborative basis, by way of traditional cognitive change methods, including behavioural experiments, reality testing tasks and verbal techniques.

Where coping strategies are present an analysis of their effectiveness, consistency of use and limitations can then be conducted and a systematic training provided to be applied in such a way that is consistent with the cognitive–behavioural formulation developed jointly with the patient. These strategies might include the relabelling of the symptom as self-generated, attentional strategies, changing activity levels, or physiological self-regulation. Some naturalistic strategies may be ostensibly effective but may inadvertently result in long-term symptom maintenance. A maladaptive strategy is defined as one which is used by the individual as a protection from imminent danger or unacceptable personal risk. In other words, the symptom is resisted at all costs and therefore the patient is never in a position to assess the true risk. A patient who always shouts back at his voices, as if their accusations and directives have true potential to threaten his psychological integrity or cause real physical harm, may experience temporary relief by counter-attacking in this way, especially if his response is associated with the symptom stopping. The therapeutic intervention might involve encouragement and training of non-responding to facilitate reality testing, an approach which parallels cognitive-behavioural therapy for obsessive-compulsive patients (Salkovskis, 1989). Other maladaptive strategies which would be targeted for change would include substance abuse and medication misuse to control symptoms.

Symptom content

The basic model described above provides a framework for clinical intervention, but does not address the specificity of individuals' experiences. There are essentially two positions with regard to symptom content relevance. First, one might argue that psychotic experiences are by definition discontinuous with reality agreed by consensus (unlike the neurotic disorders which are merely exaggerated normal responses) and therefore the content of hallucinations and delusions are not amenable to meaningful psychological analysis. Second, symptom content is not arbitrary and may represent personally significant material. Thus, taking the first position, it does not matter that an individual is deluded about his brother organising a plot to kill him versus some impersonal secret organisation trying to do the same; both beliefs would be labelled as a persecutory delusion. Alternatively, one might hypothesise that the relationship with his brother may well be pertinent. The CSE approach does not necessarily argue for the primacy of psychological events as ultimately causing psychoses, but that there may well be therapeutic advantages for acknowledging the potential meaning of symptoms. Clinical experience suggests that therapeutic change is indeed facilitated by acknowledging the psychological relevance of psychotic symptoms by linking them with key aspects of the patient's historical narrative. The more powerful the psychological formulation for the patient, the greater the likelihood of therapeutic compliance; the degree of conviction with which a patient may hold a delusional belief may be such that shifting away from his view of reality will be too threatening unless legitimised in some way. Kingdon and Turkington (see Chapter 6) provide such a legitimisation by using a normalising rationale, and Haddock, Bentall and Slade (see Chapter 3) offer hallucinating patients an opportunity to compare the content of their voices with the content of their own thought processes/current concerns to reconsider their misattributions. Romme and Escher (see Chapter 8) also detail and differentiate between different types of meaning that the voice content may represent.

The CSE approach to symptom content is perhaps best illustrated by a case example. A patient, in his late fifties, frequently experienced the belief that strangers were talking about him. He believed that they were aware of his schizophrenia diagnosis and in particular that he was a 'dangerous schizophrenic' and that they were likely to persecute him because of this. During the first cognitive–behavioural interview the dangerousness issue was examined further and cognitively he disclosed a strong association with a past event; the key historical link was his account of the onset of his psychosis thirty years previously, when in the Navy. He described having violently assaulted a colleague because he thought the man had hinted that he had had an affair with the patient's girlfriend; the seriousness of the offence was such that he was subsequently admitted for psychiatric care and discharged from the Navy. The dangerousness had continued to be an important issue for him, as he had always remained unclear about his potential to lose control in such a way again. Going back even further he recalled the terror of living with a violent father who would frequently accuse his mother of having affairs and would attack her physically. These links facilitated rapid clinical changes thereafter such that the patient was more than willing to engage in reality testing tasks to establish to what extent his interpretation of interpersonal events may have been influenced by memories of past events being reactivated. Another symptom for this patient was the daily experience of non-verbal Morse code hallucinations. His associations were again illuminating; he had assumed that his success-ful brother who had remained in the Navy was sending coded messages to undermine him. Towards the end of therapy, he disclosed that he had always resented his brother for abandoning the family and escaping to the Navy. He also accepted that the Morse was a daily reminder of his regret and sadness of a lost career.

Motivation

The third element of the current CSE model is that of motivation and its role in modulating therapeutic engagement and outcome. Motivation, in this case, does not refer to the amotivational state associated with the negative symptoms of schizophrenia, but rather whether there is sufficient incentive to achieve therapeutic goals. Motivational considerations are pertinent to therapeutic interventions for any clinical problem, although there may be specific issues with regard to the loss or change of persistent hallucinations and delusions.

The experience of distress in itself may not be a sufficient condition for therapeutic engagement. There may be both perceived advantages and disadvantages associated with psychotic phenomena, which will be reflected in individuals' mixed attitudes. Miller *et al.* (1993) investigated the relationship between the attitudes of fifty psychiatric inpatients towards their hallucinations and the outcome at discharge. The majority of subjects (98 per cent) confirmed that their hallucinations were associated with undesirable effects, but 52 per cent reported that their hallucinations were beneficial in some way. Advantages included feelings of relaxation, a sense of companionship, protective functions and self-concept enhancement. Inpatient treatment involved a combination of pharmacotherapy and a range of psychosocial interventions. Patients who had disclosed some symptom benefit were significantly more likely to continue hallucinating post-treatment. The implication of the study was that symptoms persisted because they were valued, but as the authors themselves note, positive attitudes towards symptoms may represent an adaptive response, rationalising the experience of chronic therapy resistant phenomena. The CSE approach supports the view that attitudes to symptoms should be clarified at the outset of therapy where possible and addressed where appropriate.

A separate, but related, issue involves patients' expectations regarding the potential loss or change of symptoms. There may be feared practical consequences, for example the loss of social security payments, which if unaddressed may compromise outcome. A change of symptom status may be associated with an alteration of role; an example here would be the individual who believed that the supportive network provided by psychiatric services would be available only to patients who were clearly symptomatic. Also, the chronicity of some individuals' persistent symptoms may be such that a life without them cannot be imagined; assisting the patient to consider and rehearse the potential positive effects of a change in symptoms may be useful at a preliminary stage, to generate sufficient incentive to remain engaged in the therapeutic process.

The motivational factors described above may be readily accessible by the use of appropriate questioning. It is, however, also possible that symptom change may be associated with consequences that are not immediately apparent, but operate at an implicational level to undermine good outcome. Cognitive–behavioural methods are potentially powerful and rapid clinical change may be seen after a short number of sessions, even with psychotic patients (Tarrier *et al.*, 1990). The potentially sudden realisation that one's experiences may not have a basis in reality may have deleterious effects such as the patient disempowering the therapist (and his cognitive–behavioural logic) by including him in the delusional system, especially where the implications of symptom loss are threatening. Psychological reattribution, for example, may result in individuals becoming acutely aware of their 'lost years' spent as a psychiatric patient, with regrets about disrupted career and relationship goals. The shift in locus of responsibility for past events might also result in the experience of guilt feelings for actions/behaviours which were consistent with the delusional material at the time, but not acceptable in retrospect. What may be required is a relegitimisation of the individual's psychotic experiences, by enabling the patient to appreciate that he or she was not in a position to choose their earlier history and other factors which may have contributed to the development and maintenance of the psychosis.

Perhaps the clearest example of disadvantages associated with symptom loss is with individuals whose symptoms are enmeshed with beliefs about the self. Religious and grandiose delusions potentially fall in this category. There is some evidence that individuals with chronic, systematised delusions of this type have higher levels of perceived purpose and meaning in life and lower levels of depression and suicidal ideas compared to individuals who have 'recovered' from their delusional beliefs (Roberts, 1991). This would suggest that it may be more appropriate to assist these patients by working within the delusional framework to enhance coping strategy effectiveness, rather than attempting to change the delusional beliefs themselves.

Although some of the notions described above regarding motivation are speculative, and based mainly on clinical experience, the application of the CSE approach may require sensitive modifications during therapy to maximise good outcomes.

CSE STUDY 1

The first controlled trial was conducted with patients with a diagnosis of schizophrenia, living in the community, who continued to experience hallucinations and delusions despite anti-psychotic medication (Tarrier *et al.*, 1993a). The CSE approach was compared with a problem solving (PS) therapy which was selected as a control treatment since this is an established cognitive–behavioural treatment method (D'Zurilla and Gold-fried, 1971; Hawton and Kirk, 1989) with wide applicability and was considered to be a credible control treatment with potential benefits in terms of increased social functioning. It was predicted that a reduction in hallucinations and delusions would be obtained only amongst those patients allocated to the CSE condition, and that these patients would also improve in their social functioning, as a byproduct of decreased impairment resulting from the experience of the positive psychotic symptoms. Forty-nine suitable referrals were received for the project, but the attrition rate was high; 45 per cent either refused to participate or dropped out prior to the start of treatment. Twenty-seven continued through treatment and twenty-three were assessed at six month follow-up. Methodologically, the difficulties in recruiting and retaining subjects may have biased outcomes in favour of positive results, given the potentially self-selected population of treatment acceptors. Given the heterogeneity of individuals who receive a diagnosis of schizophrenia, much stands to be gained from careful descriptions of populations, methods of recruitment and details of attrition amongst published studies of cognitive–behavioural treatments for hallucinations and delusions.

Subjects were randomly allocated to one of the two treatment conditions, both of which involved attending for ten one hour sessions. Approximately half of the patients were assigned to a waiting list control group. Overall, the results demonstrated that patients in both treatment conditions obtained significant improvements in positive psychotic symptoms compared to subjects in the waiting list control group, who did not demonstrate any change in symptom severity scores. Comparing the results of the CSE and PS therapy was less clear-cut. Significant improvements were obtained from inclusion in either condition and there was some evidence that CSE was superior in terms of reducing delusional beliefs. Treatment gains were maintained at six month follow-up. To establish whether improvements were at a clinically significant level, a criterion of a 50 per cent or greater decrease in hallucinations and/or delusions was used. Sixty per cent of the CSE patients and 25 per cent of those who received PS achieved this criterion at post-treatment assessment; the difference between the groups approached significance. At six months, these figures fell to 42 per cent and 36 per cent respectively. Overall, at this stage, five patients (22 per cent of the follow-up sample) were completely free of positive psychotic symptoms. Significant changes were not noted for negative symptoms and social functioning in either of the conditions.

Pre- and post-treatment coping and problem solving skills were also assessed; these data were rated blind to both treatment condition and time of assessment (Tarrier et al., 1993b). Multiple strategy use was associated with increased efficacy, as had been found previously. There appeared to be a linear relationship between the number of coping strategies used and the rated efficacy of each strategy. Subjects who received CSE significantly improved their coping skills and improvements in coping were significantly related to decreases in hallucinations and delusions. Conversely, patients who received PS did not show improvements in coping skills. All patients improved their problem solving skills, whether they received CSE or PS. Improvements in problem solving skills, unlike improvements in coping skills, were not related to symptomatic improvement.

CSE STUDY 2

The CSE approach is currently being investigated further, in a second, larger scale treatment trial funded by the Wellcome Trust over five years. The first study demonstrated that the severity of positive psychotic symptoms could be reduced by a clinically significant margin with ten sessions of therapy and that these changes were maintained at six months. Using coping skills as a process measure was suggestive of the therapeutic specificity of the clinical procedures employed, however, the unexpected positive outcomes obtained with PS highlighted the possibility that changes were a function of non-specific factors or at least hitherto unspecified mechanisms. An extended package has been developed for the present study, which combines both the coping strategy and problem solving procedures and formal relapse prevention training has also been introduced. Subjects are seen for a total of twenty sessions, over a ten week period, followed by four, monthly booster sessions. This cognitive–behavioural treatment is being compared to a supportive counselling condition (thus controlling for therapist contact factors) and a routine psychiatric care condition. Individuals are followed up at one and two years and the impact of the interventions on the long-term course of psychotic illness, including relapse rates, can thus be assessed. Subjects are now also independently assessed, the rater being blind to allocation, which was not the case in the first study. The random allocation process includes stratification for gender and symptom severity scores, since a more favourable prognosis has been noted for women with a diagnosis of schizophrenia (Shepherd *et al.*, 1989) and symptomatic improvement following therapy may be a function of higher initial severity scores (Tarrier *et al.*, 1993a).

In the first study, symptomatic subjects were recruited from a community population who had been free of an acute episode for at least six months; this is also the case with the current study, but recruitment is now being extended to acute episode patients, who have been stabilised on medication and are due for discharge, but continue to experience hallucinations and/or delusions. Favourable outcomes for this latter group would support the future provision of psychological intervention, on a routine basis, to those whose recovery from an acute episode is incomplete. Improvements in social functioning were not noted in the first study; the brevity of the interventions and the abrupt cessation of therapy after ten sessions may have accounted for this. The assessment procedure in the present investigation includes the selection of six deficits perceived by the patient as personally significant; these are operationally defined (for a range of good and poor outcomes) and three are selected randomly as goals to be addressed with the therapist during the problem solving component of treatment. Outcomes will be compared to the three functioning deficits not selected as goals, thus assessing for treatment generalisation.

A wide range of pre-treatment measures have been included to access the potentially diverse factors associated with differential therapy response and drop-out. These include illness attributions, cognitive deficit measures, current and pre-morbid intellect estimates, expectation of the positive and negative impact of symptom loss, suspiciousness, affect, hopelessness, negative symptomatology, sociodemographic and other illness variables.

Subjective reasons for non-continuation of therapy will be assessed by means of a drop-out questionnaire.

SPECIFIC THERAPEUTIC METHODS

The following account represents a selection of therapeutic methods as opposed to a comprehensive treatment protocol.

The cognitive–behavioural interview and engagement

Prior to cognitive–behavioural interviewing, a systematic assessment of all positive psychotic symptoms is desirable, using the Present State Examination (Wing *et al.*, 1974), or a similarly reliable equivalent. Establishing the presence of other non-psychotic symptoms is also recommended; the presence of these may well affect clinical decision making. A recent case may highlight this point. A man with a lengthy history of persistent auditory hallucinations and thought echo, also described frequent episodes of distressing, vivid, intrusive imagery, the contents of which appeared to support the nature and content of his voices. This phenomenon was given clinical priority and successful intervention secondarily resulted in a reduction in the frequency and severity of the voices, without directly addressing these. Cognitive–behavioural analyses of each psychotic symptom then follows and for this purpose the Antecedent and Coping Interview (Tarrier, 1992) is used as the basic format to determine symptom contexts, emotional reactions, symptom-related beliefs and meanings as well as adaptive and maladaptive coping.

Usually, a disproportionate amount of time is spent obtaining a detailed phenomenological account of each symptom. Even at this stage, where sufficient rapport between therapist and patient has been established, information gathering is a highly interactive process, such that statements made by the individual about their beliefs or experiences are not taken at face value and recorded, but are enquired about beyond what is usually available to clinicians and perhaps the patient himself. For example, where the patient describes a plot against him, the therapist may ask about the organisation's motivations, the reasons why the persecutory agents have failed to date, their source of funding, power hierarchies within the organisation, mechanisms by which unusual skills are achieved by the group, etc. This process can be conducted respectfully, and is designed to disrupt the patient's habitual processing of the delusional material, to determine the rules which govern what is possible and not possible in the patient's alternative reality and to access the patient's 'free behaviours' (Brehm, 1976) which might be of use therapeutically. Asking the patient to come up with new material in such a way, thus extending the number of descriptive statements, is potentially useful later on in therapy when reviewing the evidence for and against beliefs, and eventually highlighting inconsistencies within the account (Lowe and Chadwick, 1990).

In order to elicit the emotional reactions which accompany symptoms, the patient is asked to generate the phenomenon in vivo, and where this is not possible, the therapist may use guided imagery, symbolically reactivating a recent symptom occurrence. Under such circumstances, 'hot cognitions' are more readily available and also the therapist is in a position to 'track' the patient's affective state, observable physiological changes and minor behavioural and postural alterations. At this stage in the interviewing, initial hypotheses about the personal significance and meanings associated with symptom content might guide subsequent questioning.

There may well be good opportunities in the initial interview(s) to conduct brief behavioural experiments as part of the engagement process. This would involve the manipulation of any or all aspects of the emotional reaction in relation to the experience of the symptom (see case study at the end of this chapter).

At some point during initial sessions symptom attitudes and expectations regarding symptom change or loss should be established and addressed. It may also be pertinent to enquire about the patient's perceptions of the likely reaction of significant others in the event of a change in symptoms and the implications for therapy.

Treatment methods

These vary considerably and are dependent on whether the phenomena are delusional, hallucinatory (or both) and whether the therapeutic goal is purely to reduce distress or to change fundamental aspects of the symptom and its maintaining factors. There may well be a range of delusional beliefs and hallucinations in a number of modalities, but target symptom selection can usually be achieved relatively easily by establishing the degree of distress experienced, the discreteness of occurrence and a jointly agreed account about the relationship (or non-relationship) between symptoms. A coping strategy or other intervention is selected initially on the basis that there is a high probability of demonstrating, even temporarily, a successful reduction in distress.

The intervention, whether this involves coping strategy training, manipulation of the emotional reaction or response prevention is conducted under salient training conditions. This might involve requesting that symptoms are elicited by the patient during sessions, especially where auditory hallucinations are experienced (Fowler and Morley, 1989). An alternative method involves symptom simulations; for example, once an account is obtained of the typical content of voices and their physical characteristics these can be recorded onto a cassette tape (by either patient or therapist or both) and played back for a more detailed assessment or to experiment with and rehearse alternative responses. The benefit of this method is that different parameters can be manipulated (such as voice location in three-dimensional space and loudness) as part of a graded approach with regard to task difficulty, as the patient progresses. Additionally, the role-playing of symptoms, for example, the therapist taking the part of typical auditory hallucinations or presenting a summary statement reflecting delusional beliefs (and related cognitions), is a method which can be applied flexibly with roles reversed as necessary. Often, even under such simulated conditions, emotional reactions may be powerful and the modelling of alternative responses may be insufficient to disrupt the automaticity of the patient's response. One solution would be to request that the patient exaggerates his response in a dramatic fashion, a technique adapted from Gestalt Therapy (Van De Riet *et al.*, 1985) and repeating this several times, to bring the reaction under conscious control which may temporarily change the meanings ascribed to symptoms, thus allowing further training to take place.

The development of a shared psychological formulation is a key aspect of this approach. The degree of complexity, the timing with regard to communicating this to the patient, or whether the account is developed jointly will also vary depending on the nature of the case. In general, a formulation might include an individualised cognitive–behavioural model of maintenance and educational aspects regarding psychological processes such as the 'confirmatory bias' (Chadwick, 1992). A further component might be to offer symptom explanations consistent with the patient's historical narrative, such as previous relationship conflicts, psychological traumas, bereavement and significant life events around the time of the first onset of psychosis. Symptom maintenance can also be defined in terms of what the symptom may represent with regard to the future functioning and quality of life of the individual compared to prior life goals; the symptom may be associated with fleeting imagery of the individual finally being overcome by the symptom some time in the future, and, by implication, life having become meaningless.

CASE STUDY

Mrs M, a 48-year-old married woman, was a subject in the first CSE investigation. She was referred to the project nine months following her first psychotic episode. Her core delusional belief was that a malevolent sex machine had invaded her abdomen and was forcing her to have sexual intercourse with it. She was convinced that other individuals were similarly afflicted, but did not admit to the experience. During her previous inpatient admission a high dose of neuroleptic was used, but had little impact on her delusional beliefs; she was discharged back to the family home and continued to take anti-psychotic medication.

97

Independent pre-treatment assessment revealed the presence of five psychotic symptoms, which included a delusion of thoughts being read, delusional misinterpretation, delusion of grandiose ability, delusional explanation, and the sexual delusion. Thematically, all the symptoms were related. She scored maximally on measures of delusional conviction, pre-occupation and interference. She was also assessed with regard to her cognitive adaptability in relation to her abnormal beliefs; this test is known as the Reaction to Hypothetical Contradiction (Brett-Jones et al., 1987); this involves presenting the subject with a hypothetical scenario which would represent powerful evidence against the abnormal beliefs being true, and in Mrs M's case she indicated that she would reject the evidence and would continue to be thoroughly convinced of her material.

Despite her initial reluctance to pursue therapy, given the degree of her distress and her severely curtailed functioning, she agreed to attend. The first session was spent obtaining a more detailed account of her symptoms. She believed that a group of individuals, several miles away, operated a computer to control powerful vibrations produced by the sex machine and that they had designed the apparatus such that she had been wired up to a video which recorded her responses. She explained that communication between the group and herself occurred telepathically, by thought waves, and that they were able to read her thoughts at any time. She was similarly aware of their intentions, although she was not able to hear what was being said. When asked about the individuals' motivation she said that four of them were annoyed with her, because of her refusal to have sex with them, but one of the group tended to support her. At this point in the interview, some of her associations were elicited. She admitted that she had always wondered what sex would be like with other men as she had only been intimate with her husband. A historical link was established fairly quickly, she recalled that her parents divorced when she was 15 years of age and she described having been distressed at the time and was aware that both her parents were having affairs.

Physically, she described the sex machine as 'something like a magnet' but that at other times it took the form of a penis. More often than not, however, it took the form of sensations, rather than an object. When the machine was active, she experienced somatic hallucinations in her arms, abdomen, vagina and lower back. She explained that actual intercourse with the machine was less common now, but that she continued to spon-taneously climax, frequently during the day (up to fifteen times per day), whenever the 'vibrations' were present. She found this aspect particularly embarrassing, from a social point of view, although she did admit to enjoying the experience. Mrs M pointed to her abdomen at one stage during the interview to indicate when the vibrations had started and these were indeed clearly visible. She reported that these occurred with very high frequency, every few minutes, throughout the day, although she admitted to

98

some variability in intensity (and preoccupation) when she was able to keep herself busy.

In terms of her emotional reaction, a good account was obtained during the session as she was clearly experiencing her symptoms at the time; she was agitated, being unable to sit down for more than a few minutes and experienced a range of autonomic symptoms of anxiety as well as marked muscular tension. When she experienced the involuntary movements of her abdomen, she either crossed her arms over her abdomen or attempted to 'force the machine out' or at least suppress the sensations by voluntarily tensing her abdominal muscles. During such an episode, the other delusional material was also activated but her attention was largely taken up by her sensations. She believed that she had no control over the experience and 'wished it would go away'.

In terms of her coping strategies, she described a partially effective strategy for her delusion of thoughts being read, for which she used attention switching 50 per cent of the time, although her strategies for the sexual vibrations were largely non-effective.

The long-term consequences and impact of symptoms on her life included increased sexual contact with her husband (because of the general increase in her sexual arousal), significant social anxiety, especially with groups of men, such that she was unable to pursue her usual leisure activities out of the home and most of her household chores could not be completed. She had been unable to return to work and she was realistically concerned about being made redundant.

The misattribution of somatic sensations, i.e. 'the vibrations', suggested that Mrs M would require a powerful face valid alternative explanation and that this might be available from her medical history. She recalled her 'sterilisation' following a biopsy at the age of 37 or 38; it was noted that she used the term sterilisation as opposed to 'hysterectomy' and she confirmed that she was unhappy with her loss. She received a course of hormone replacement tablets at the time. She was also diagnosed as having arthritis of the lower back, the first symptoms being noted approximately eight years prior to therapy. She was also asked whether she had a history of bowel problems. She confirmed this and described a series of investigations for rectal bleeding. She also reported that she had been advised to start a high fibre diet approximately six years ago, but had stopped this two to three years ago. She currently complained of diarrhoea alternating with normal bowel habit and she was asked whether she had every received a diagnosis of 'irritable bowel syndrome' and she recalled that the term had indeed been used. Her medical notes were subsequently checked to confirm her account.

Towards the end of the first session a number of simple trial interventions were attempted. She was asked, non-confrontationally, whether her vibrations could possibly be misinterpreted symptoms of irritable

99

bowel syndrome. She was dubious of this explanation, but agreed that it would be worthwhile, as an experiment, to return to a high fibre diet. Also, a brief behavioural experiment was conducted by asking her to reverse her protective behaviours (i.e. crossing her arms over her abdomen and the voluntary tension of her abdominal muscles) as well as the manipulation of her attention from her abdomen to external stimuli. Ratings of preoccupation and distress were obtained during this experiment and when directed to behave as she normally did in response to the vibrations. Significant reductions in the levels of preoccupation and distress were demonstrated and she expressed relief that some control was available to her. She agreed to try the strategies as homework prior to the next session and symptom self-monitoring was also started.

At the second session, she indicated that her ability to cope with her experiences had been enhanced by reversing her habitual responses and 'keeping busy'. She had been compliant with her high fibre diet and experienced less abdominal discomfort. By session three, she reported continued improvement and had noted that the vibrations were less frequent. There had been an associated reduction in preoccupation, and she had stopped seeking reassurance from her family about the delusion, at the therapist's request. She remained deluded, but her conviction rating had reduced such that she was beginning to accept the possibility of an alternative explanation. A full psychological formulation was introduced at this point incorporating notions of misattribution of somatic sensations, a physiological arousal-attentional vicious cycle mechanism and the role of behavioural maintaining factors such as her protective behaviours and reassurance seeking. The sexual content of the delusions were explained in terms of the historical context of her parents' extra-marital affairs coupled with aspects of her own sexual relationship with her husband, prior to the onset of her psychosis. Some explanation was also offered for the timing of her first onset of psychosis and included a number of key stressors, such as the death of her mother two years prior to onset, the start of heavy alcohol use associated with the bereavement and also a relationship 'crisis' with her own daughters around this period. Symptoms were also legitimised by engaging the patient in a discussion about the 'complexity of the human mind' and how unusual phenomena could be accounted for in psychological terms, such as vivid dreams, visual illusions and hypnotically induced analgesia. A significant shift in her conviction rating was noted such that her symptoms were now a 'mystery' to her and this change was consolidated by further verbal cognitive therapy techniques. She continued to experience some muscular tension and autonomic symptoms of anxiety when sensations were present and these were addressed by introducing formal progressive muscle relaxation training. As therapy progressed, further reductions in conviction and preoccupation were noted and a series of behavioural targets were introduced to improve her ability to complete daily chores and reinstigate her leisure pursuits which she had dropped because of her abnormal beliefs. She also received training to employ covert self-instructional statements to activate her coping behaviours whenever the sensations and/or beliefs were experienced.

At session ten, a belief conviction rating of 5 per cent was noted for the sexual delusion and her other related delusions had dissipated completely. At the start of therapy, her self-monitoring data suggested that she had experienced vibrations for several hours per day and by the tenth session this had reduced to approximately forty-five minutes per day. Her husband confirmed that she had improved significantly, in terms of her level of agitation and daily functioning, but that she was still relatively amotivated compared to her pre-morbid state.

At six month follow-up, Mrs M was asymptomatic with regard to her positive symptoms. She declined an offer of a formal interview at thirty month follow-up because she wanted to minimise her contact with services, but agreed to a brief assessment over the telephone. She reported that there had not been a recurrence of her sexual (or other) delusions and that she had continued to pursue an active social life. She admitted to the experience of occasional auditory hallucinations (which had been intermittently present in the past), which she described as a faint voice, approximately once or twice per month for a few seconds, to which she paid little attention.

REFERENCES

Birchwood, M. and Tarrier, N. (eds) (1992) *Innovations in the Psychological Management of Schizophrenia*, Chichester: Wiley.

Brehm, S. S. (1976) *The Application of Social Psychology to Clinical Practice*, New York: Wiley.

Breier, A. and Strauss, J. S. (1983) 'Self-control in psychotic disorders', *Archives of General Psychiatry* 40: 1141–5.

Brett-Jones, J., Garety, P. A. and Hemsley, D. R. (1987) 'Measuring delusional experiences: A method and its application', *British Journal of Clinical Psychology* 26: 257–65.

Carr, V. (1988) 'Patients' techniques for coping with schizophrenia: An exploratory study', *British Journal of Medical Psychology* 61: 339–52.

Chadwick, P. (1992) *Borderline: A Psychological Study of Paranoia and Delusional Thinking*, London: Routledge.

Cohen, C. I. and Berk, B. S. (1985) 'Personal coping styles of schizophrenic out-patients', *Hospital and Community Medicine* 36: 407–10.

D'Zurilla, T. J. and Goldfried, M. (1971) 'Problem solving and behaviour modification', *Journal of Abnormal Psychology* 78: 107–26.

Falloon, I. R. H. and Talbot, R. E. (1981) 'Persistent auditory hallucinations: Coping mechanisms and implications for management', *Psychological Medicine* 11: 329–39.

Fowler, D. and Morley, S. (1989) 'The cognitive–behavioural treatment of hallucinations and delusions: A preliminary study', *Behavioural Psychotherapy* 17: 267–82.

Hawton, K. and Kirk, J. (1989) 'Problem solving', in K. Hawton, P. M. Salkovskis,

J. Kirk, and D. Clark (eds) *Cognitive Behaviour Therapy for Psychiatric Problems*, Oxford: Oxford Medical Publications.

Hawton, K., Salkovskis, P. M., Kirk, J. and Clark, D. (eds) (1989) *Cognitive Behaviour Therapy for Psychiatric Problems*, Oxford: Oxford Medical Publications.

Hustig, H. H. and Hafner, J. (1990) 'Persistent auditory hallucinations and their relationship to delusions and mood', *The Journal of Nervous and Mental Disease* 178: 264–7.

Lowe, C. F. and Chadwick, P. D. J. (1990) 'Verbal control of delusions', *Behaviour Therapy*, 21: 461–79.

Miller, L. J., O'Connor, E. and DiPasquale, T. (1993) 'Patients' attitudes toward hallucinations', *American Journal of Psychiatry* 150: 584–8.

Roberts, G. (1991) 'Delusional belief systems and meaning in life: A preferred reality?', *British Journal of Psychiatry* 159 (supplement 14): 19–28.

Salkovskis, P. M. (1989) 'Obsessions and compulsions', in J. Scott, J. M. G. Williams and A. T. Beck (eds) *Cognitive Therapy in Clinical Practice: An Illustrative Casebook*, London: Routledge.

Scott, J., Williams, J. M. G. and Beck, A. T. (eds) (1989) *Cognitive Therapy in Clinical Practice: An Illustrative Casebook*, London: Routledge.

Shepherd, M., Watt, D., Falloon, I. and Smeeton, N. (1989) 'The natural history of schizophrenia: A five-year follow-up study of outcome and prediction in a representative sample of schizophrenics', *Psychological Medicine*, Monograph Supplement 15: 1–46.

Tarrier, N. (1987) 'An investigation of residual psychotic symptoms in discharged schizophrenic patients', *British Journal of Clinical Psychology* 26: 141–3.

—— (1992) 'Management and modification of residual psychotic symptoms', in M. Birchwood and N. Tarrier (eds) *Innovations in the Psychological Management of Schizophrenia*, Chichester: Wiley.

Tarrier, N., Harwood, S., Yusupoff, L., Beckett, R. and Baker, A. (1990) 'Coping strategy enhancement (CSE): A method of treating residual schizophrenic symptoms', *Behavioural Psychotherapy* 18: 283–93.

Tarrier, N., Beckett, R., Harwood, S., Baker, A., Yusupoff, L. and Ugarteburu, I. (1993a) 'A trial of two cognitive–behavioural methods of treating drug-resistant residual psychotic symptoms in schizophrenic patients: I. Outcome', *British Journal of Psychiatry* 162: 524–32.

Tarrier, N., Sharpe, L., Beckett, R., Harwood, S., Baker, A. and Yusupoff, L. (1993b) 'A trial of two cognitive–behavioural methods of treating drug-resistant residual psychotic symptoms in schizophrenic patients: II. Treatment specific changes in coping and problem-solving skills', *Social Psychiatry & Psychiatric Epidemiology* 28: 5–10.

Van De Riet, V., Korb, M. P. and Gorrel, J. J. (1985) *Gestalt Therapy: An Introduction*, New York: Pergamon Press.

Wing, J. K., Cooper, J. E. and Sartorius, N. (1974) *Measurement and Classification of Psychiatric Symptoms: An Instruction Manual for the PSE and Catego Programme*, Cambridge: Cambridge University Press.

6

USING A NORMALISING RATIONALE IN THE TREATMENT OF SCHIZOPHRENIC PATIENTS

Douglas Turkington and David Kingdon

An integrated treatment strategy with a community key worker is the backbone of community management of patients with schizophrenia. A range of accommodation options after discharge from mental hospital (Kingdon *et al.*, 1991), befriending schemes (Kingdon *et al.*, 1989) and crisis intervention accommodation (Turkington *et al.*, 1991) complement neuroleptics, standard rehabilitative and family therapies. However, whether the patient will be able to engage in such an integrated strategy will depend on his or her own level of insight and attitudes to the symptomatology, as well as the attitudes of the psychiatrist and the community mental health team. The issues of engaging the psychotic patient in discussion about their symptoms is therefore fundamental to issues of recovery, relapse, compliance and coping. The classical psychiatric teaching that discussing psychotic symptoms with a patient is at best useless and at worst an exacerbating factor (Scharfetter, 1980) has percolated throughout psychiatry and psychiatric nursing. This has led to a stand-off approach to those psychotic symptoms which are most distressing to the patient, for example persistent voices or passivity phenomena. As a result of this approach, patients have often drawn catastrophic conclusions of madness and untreatability. Cascades of negative cognition, dysfunctional affect and disordered behaviour often follow with lack of treatment compliance and deteriorating social function. There is the need to address the key area of what we say to the schizophrenic patient and how to say it in order that they might be engaged as active agents in their own treatment. To this end, we felt that engaging the patient in the collaborative production of an explanatory normalising rationale/model of symptom emergence was a crucial first step in the relationship with the patient (Kingdon and Turkington, 1991). With the patient 'on board' a variety of techniques can then be used to reduce distress and improve compliance. It is only really in the last twenty years that an accumulating body of research evidence has started to indicate that such

103

an approach is safe and feasible (Kingdon *et al.*, 1994). Our study (Kingdon and Turkington, 1991), of sixty-four patients with schizophrenia treated with cognitive–behaviour therapy (CBT) revealed high acceptability and a low readmission rate with no suicides or homicides over a seven year period. More recently we have performed a study of CBT versus befriending in the treatment of schizophrenia on the basis of random allocation (Kingdon *et al.*, in press). This study shows that while cognitive therapy and befriending are both useful in acute psychosis the cognitive therapy was much more beneficial, and to a statistically significant degree, with those patients with chronic drug-resistant symptomatology. The cognitive–behavioural repertoire continues to expand into a diversity of therapeutic modalities including coping skills enhancement (Tarrier *et al.*, 1993; see Chapter 11), cognitive remediation (Green, 1993) and early intervention (Birchwood *et al.*, 1989; see Chapter 10).

This chapter covers the rapidly growing area of cognitive–behavioural therapy in schizophrenia (Kingdon and Turkington, 1994). Our approach stresses the use of developing a rationale with patients to explain symptom emergence and decatastrophise the psychiatric diagnosis of schizophrenia.

ENGAGING AND RAPPORT BUILDING

It is worthwhile outlining the stages of therapy which are gone through with a schizophrenic patient when CBT is being used. The rate-limited step for all future progress is, of course, the initial one of engaging and building up rapport. This is worth exploring in some detail as, if the therapy gets off on the wrong foot, it can become increasingly difficult to test out the reality of psychotic symptoms. The following would seem to be the key points.

1. *Empathy, warmth, genuineness and unconditional acceptance*; these are features of all good psychotherapists and apply equally to psychosis as to neurosis.
2. *The experience of interacting* with psychotic patients and knowledge of the typical modalities of psychotic expression (for example thought disorder, hallucinosis, delusional perception, systematisation of delusions, etc.). There is no substitute in this regard to spending many hours dealing with the problems of the severely mentally ill.
3. *Word perfect accuracy and consistency*. When building up a relationship with a patient with schizophrenia it is vital not to do anything either verbally or non-verbally to invalidate their experience. Confrontation of a delusional belief, for example, leads only to invalidation of the patient's account, weakening of the therapeutic alliance and often entrenchment of the delusion. If a patient reports that their house is bugged, the appropriate response is not to say that this is not so, but to acknowledge that this would be possible, but very unlikely, unless the patient has been involved in

espionage or intelligence activities. The next step would be to collaboratively investigate the matter further using diaries and planned homework
tasks. The tightrope between non-confrontation and collaborative reality
testing needs to be walked in each treatment session.

4. *Agreement to differ*. At times patients who are very preoccupied will
continue to attempt to persuade the therapist of the reality of, for example,
their telepathic powers. This can become counter-productive and at times
the therapist has to accept their right to their own opinion. This again
should not be seen as confrontation, merely as an individual's right to
express an alternative point of view. The following therapy extract
illustrates this (the patient was very preoccupied with beliefs about his
telepathic powers).

Patient: I need to know, do you believe in telepathy or not?

Therapist: The research position on this is that the possibility exists that
                some people under certain conditions of extreme emotion
                or stress may be able to pass feelings or images to a close
                relative but that it is not a viable method of communicating
                thoughts on a day to day basis. The homework from this
                session is for you to go up to the library and look up the
                research on this subject on reported occurrences of spon-
                taneous telepathic phenomena. Once we have read this
                together we can then work on your own experiences.
                [Patient was given a brief reading list and an article on the
                subject.]

5. *Tactical withdrawal*. If your patient is becoming distressed by any
particular approach or subject then this should be noted and appropriate
support given. The subject matter may be very important and can be
tentatively returned to later in therapy.

6. *Allowing the waves of psychosis to roll over you*. Therapists are very
often put off by the large quantity of seemingly incomprehensible psychotic
material produced by patients in the early sessions. This will gradually
become comprehensible in light of the patient's life history, personal
schemas and misinterpretations of normal phenomena. The cognitive
therapist, through the engaging phase, is gradually working toward an
early formulation of psychotic symptom emergence which will allow the
mobilisation of specific techniques and must be able to tolerate a period
when much of the data will be incomprehensible.

7. *Teaching the cognitive model*. This is done with the help of some reading
material, numerous case examples and often personal disclosure of how
the therapist has tackled one of his or her own problems using cognitive
therapy, for example public speaking anxiety. The model describes how
thoughts can cause feelings and behaviour. Thoughts may be amenable
to change and can be tackled with a superficial emotion, for example anger

at a member of staff or carer may be reduced to annoyance using less demanding rational responses.

A NORMALISING RATIONALE

The next phase after engaging is to provide an explanation of puzzling and distressing symptoms and to deal with catastrophic cognitions concerning insanity and possible treatment methods. Often patients with schizophrenia are not given the diagnosis themselves due to the clinician's 'catastrophisation'. The patient may learn of the diagnosis from a carer, work it out for themselves or recognise the symptoms from an article or television programme. The conclusions that the patients draw from not being told the diagnosis are inevitably catastrophic. Typical cognitions which we have had reported include the following: "I am mad", "I will be locked up", "I will be beaten and tortured in an asylum", "there is no hope", "they will strap me down and give me electric shocks", "I will turn into a vegetable" and "they will give me very strong drugs and I will be a zombie". These cognitions are culture syntonic and reflect typical views of schizophrenia given in the media. Jack Nicholson's portrayal of psychiatric treatment in *One Flew Over the Cuckoo's Nest* contains many of the anxiogenic images which dominate a patient's thinking when they draw the conclusion that they must have schizophrenia. These cognitions are future orientated and catastrophic. They also contain some truth but are mostly anachronistic and terrifying images of treatment and outcome in schizophrenia which cause marked hyperarousal and anxiety. There is certainly evidence that such an emotional state can exacerbate psychotic symptoms (Slade, 1973). Depressive cognitions of hopelessness cause lowering of mood, withdrawal and suicidal ideation. The combination of hyperarousal and depression often leads to poor compliance with neuroleptic drugs and day care. The anxiogenic-depressive cognitive set can therefore become a self-fulfilling prophecy leading to maintenance of psychotic symptoms and a poor outcome. The rationale which is discussed with the patient describes the typical symptoms and possible genetic predisposition to respond in that way. The vulnerability-stress hypothesis (Zubin, 1987) is explained in detail to the patient in relation to the stressor or accumulation of stressors which preceded the emergence of symptoms. The patient is led towards an understanding that there is probably a discernible reason or reasons why the symptoms have occurred and the possibility that anyone stressed in certain ways could become psychotic. If there is a family predisposition to respond in this way this can be fully explored to help the patient to feel less different and isolated. It is often useful to itemise the types of stressors which can typically produce psychotic symptoms in 'you' or 'I'.

1. *Sleep deprivation.* There is evidence that lack of sleep can lead to illusions, hallucinations and paranoid ideation (Oswald, 1974); as an

example, medical staff working without sleep for prolonged periods have been reported to behave in bizarre and irrational ways. Again this is often best backed up with appropriate literature and given to the patient. As psychotic patients have often been sleep deprived at the time of symptom onset this can be taken as part of the explanation of what has been happening. This may lead to a reduction in anxiety and improved compliance with neuroleptics.

2. *Post-traumatic stress disorder*. As very significant life events often precede the development of psychosis it is useful to discuss the types of psychological reactions which people can have to extreme stress. Again the patient is given the literature showing that hallucinations were very common amongst veterans of the Vietnam war (Wilcox *et al.*, 1991). This again can help patients to feel less alienated by their symptoms.

3. *Sensory deprivation*. Bed rest in a darkened room and water tank immersion can both lead to the development of simple and eventually complex hallucinations. The latter more intensive experimental situation is by far the more powerful of the two in inducing hallucinosis. Often patients show interest in reading this material (Slade, 1984) as they may identify their long-term isolation, albeit much less intense, with such short-term sensory deprivation.

4. *Hostage situations*. This work is described by Siegel (1984), and patients often find it helpful to discuss this material. In particular the communication problems and isolation of the hostage are often identified with by the schizophrenic patient.

5. *Solitary confinement*. Grassian (1983) describes the emergence of psychotic symptoms in prisoners kept for prolonged periods without contact with others. Schizophrenic patients often describe similar periods of isolation prior to psychotic breakdown.

6. *Sexual abuse*. Recent work has shown that hallucinosis is surprisingly common in those patients who have undergone repeated or particular brutal sexual abuse (Ensink, 1992). Most patients will not be ready to disclose such traumatic events early in treatment but when they eventually do, explaining that there is a possible connection between symptoms of psychosis and such treatment can help to explain symptom development.

This can improve the therapeutic alliance, help the patient feel more 'normal' and less alienated and allow work on non-threatening and explanatory areas prior to tackling the patient's own personal symptomatology. Therapist and patient can begin to work out collaboratively a formulation of how the symptoms may have emerged and also to decatastrophise the term schizophrenia, which is a descriptive term for those patients suffering from certain of these symptoms. The importance of rationale has been well described by Romme and Escher (1989, and see also Chapter 8). They showed that many people who do not have schizophrenia hear voices and those who cope well with them may be those who have developed clear rationales to explain them. The most useful rationales included mystical, parapsychological, Freudian and Jungian explanations. Biological rationales were not strongly favoured and indeed it is our experience that patients are loathe to accept biological rationales early on although they may adopt them later in treatment.

EXAMINING THE ANTECEDENTS

In developing a rationale, a close examination of the antecedents of psychotic breakdown may be necessary. The importance of this was shown as far back as the early 1950s (Beck, 1952). The crucial period leading up to the psychotic breakdown should be worked through most often with inductive questioning. Other useful techniques for exploring this period include imagery and role play. Key cognitions can be detected from this period pointing to underlying schemas concerning achievement, approval and control. Sessions around this stage of the therapy can be very rich with important material. If the patient does not have paranoid delusions it is often helpful to tape record sessions for playback as homework. Care is needed as inductive questioning performed in relation to the immediate pre-psychotic period can hit upon sensitive and painful material. It may be necessary in some cases to tactically withdraw if this occurs. It is our experience that in perhaps 70 per cent of cases this stage of therapy is viewed as being integrative and emotionally helpful. In the other 30 per cent there can be some degree of flare-up of psychotic symptoms. However, we have always found this to be containable using a variety of supportive techniques. It is also worthwhile stating that informal follow-up has not detected any suicides or homicides in our schizophrenia cohort over a nine-year period. This is an important stage of therapy which needs to be handled sensitively.

TREATMENT OF ANXIETY AND DEPRESSION

This would generally be the next stage of therapy and its importance lies in the fact that affective symptoms often seem to be delusionally misinterpreted and can also lead to poor compliance with psychosocial and biological treatments. Anxiety symptoms should have reduced with the collaborative production of a normalising rationale. Some persist, however, as illustrated below.

Patient: Planes that pass over my house have the power to move my intestines. There are communist agents on board working a ray gun that causes this.

Therapist: Let's keep a diary of exactly how often this happens in the next week and exactly what it feels like for you.

Patient: [next session] This has happened at least five or six times each day but the diary shows that the planes could be linked to two or maybe three episodes in total.

Therapist: What does the diary show was the cause of the other episodes?

Patient: Doors banging, dogs barking and loud music.

Therapist: I am going to give you a handout describing the main anxiety symptoms. Can you recognise any of these in yourself?

The patient identified sensitivity to sound, abdominal churning, tension, worry, irritability and episodic palpitations as being symptoms which he himself suffered from. As he began to learn about anxiety and practice progressive muscular relaxation on a daily basis the particular delusional misinterpretation concerning the planes and communists was dropped. In relation to depression, mild and reactive forms are best tackled cognitively. However, antidepressant drug treatment is sometimes required to complement CBT at this point in treatment. Propanolol can also be a useful adjunct to relaxation for somatic anxiety symptoms.

CBT TECHNIQUES FOR NEUROLEPTIC-RESISTANT POSITIVE PSYCHOTIC SYMPTOMS

The appropriate techniques can be listed in relation to the main symptom groups, i.e. delusions, hallucinations and thought disorder.

Delusions

These are defined as false beliefs held in spite of evidence to the contrary and out of keeping with the patient's social, cultural and educational background. Whilst it is certainly true that a patient cannot be argued out of a delusion (confrontation generally leading to entrenchment), the effectiveness of collaborative gathering and assessment of evidence in relation to the delusion has not yet been fully tested. Pioneering early work in this area (Watts *et al.*, 1973) did show that delusional beliefs could be modified by psychological intervention (see Chapter 2 for a review of this work). This classical definition of delusion cannot therefore be regarded as scientifically evaluated. Strauss's analysis of schizophrenic delusions showed them to be points on continua of function (Strauss, 1969). He believed that this spectrum extended from normal belief through overvalued ideas to delusions. Delusions may then be regarded as fluid structures which, given the appropriate therapist strategies and attitudes, are amenable to gradual weakening. Those delusions which are held most rigidly frequently involve high investment of self-esteem. The following CBT techniques may be used in working with schizophrenic delusions.

1. *Peripheral questioning*. This is a technique for sensitively helping the patient to draw his own conclusions about some of the inconsistencies surrounding the delusion. It is important not to start questioning at the heart of the delusion as this may be too threatening unless these are the key issues that the patient wishes to discuss. Initially the approach is to gather as much pertinent information as possible. Peripheral questioning can then proceed on to some of the 'nuts and bolts' of the delusion. Socratic questioning can then be sensitively used in relation to the implications of the delusion. Peripheral questioning is illustrated by the following therapy examples.

Patient:	My house is bugged and this interview room is too.
Therapist:	What would the bugs look like? Let's try and find them.
Patient:	They are set inside the concrete of the walls.
Therapist:	What kind of bugs can hear through concrete?
Patient:	I don't know.
Therapist:	But I understand bugs to be like small microphones, they need to be out in the open or at least only superficially hidden. Will we look for them here and then perhaps we can check out at home? [Homework – reality testing with diary.]

This excerpt from a therapy session reveals the kind of deficit in real world knowledge, i.e. understanding of microphones, often exhibited in relation to delusional thinking.

Patient:	I am being followed everywhere I go.
Therapist:	What kind of people are normally followed in this way?
Patient:	People that are being terrorised by someone.
Therapist:	Think about films that you have seen and books you have read. What kind of people get followed?
Patient:	Spies, terrorists, politicians, royal family, pop stars.
Therapist:	You are not any of those sorts of person are you?
Patient:	No, but I felt like royalty when I was younger as my twin sister was always with me and we did everything together.
Therapist:	Perhaps this thing about being followed has in some way arisen from your separation from your twin sister. What we really need to know is whether it is a feeling of being followed or whether there are actually people there. Will you record the exact appearance of the followers (what they are wearing, facial expressions, etc.) and circumstances of each episode in which you feel you are being followed and record it in a diary on a day to day basis [reality testing homework].

The tactics here are to work in a non-challenging and gradual way from the periphery of the delusion towards the centre.

110

2. *Reality testing*. As above, tests of specific delusions need to be set up in a collaborative way. It should not be done in an abstract way, but with a firm record kept of findings. In the early stages it is often useful to involve a community key worker to go with the patient on these reality testing exercises and to help him or her to record the findings. In analysing the findings a 'guided discovery' mode is used and the patient helped to generate possible explanations for the findings. This kind of work is normally enjoyed by patients and can be applied to many situations and beliefs.

3. *Working through the emotional investment of a delusion*. Delusions of persecution are often invested with fear or anger. Similarly, grandiose delusions are often invested with elation, and delusions of control with anger and depression. If it is proving difficult to tackle a delusion in the ways outlined above, a cognitive therapy approach aimed at reducing the emotional investment may be effective. Techniques used are those which have been well described elsewhere, as in the treatment of anxiety and depression (Blackburn and Davidson, 1990). Once the emotional investment has been reduced it is possible to proceed with reality testing.

4. *Using schema level CBT with delusions*. The pertinent schemas are often detected at the time of examining the antecedents. Other techniques include identifying common themes in cognitions, examining meanings of specific events and use of the downward arrow technique (this allows the therapist to follow a distorted automatic thought down to the underlying belief which generated it). It often seems to be the case that delusions emerge at times of invalidation of key personal schemas. A delusion would then be regarded as a distorted schema which serves the function within the psyche of protecting against devastating loss of self-esteem. Where this is the case, schema work could be expected to help patients gradually weaken the intensity with which a delusion is held, or start to behave in a less restricted way. This may, however, be at the expense of precipitating depressive symptoms. Whilst this does not occur in all cases it should be watched for and may require appropriate support in terms of structured activities, supportive counselling and the use of antidepressant drugs. Standard techniques for schema level CBT are described elsewhere, for example Beck *et al*. (1979).

Hallucinations

It is surprising how often voices are accepted in schizophrenia without the development of a rationale to explain them or research to identify their exact location. A vital stage in the treatment of hallucination is to help the patient do exactly this. The activation of appropriate coping strategies often follows. A critical collaborative analysis of the voices begins by generating hypotheses about their origin. Very often patients will have no immediate answer as to what the voices might be, but using a guided discovery modality,

111

possibilities can be generated, percentage belief allocated and then home-work devised to test out the options. This usually leads to a reduction in belief that the voices actually exist in the external world and may lead to an increased belief that the voices could be of mystical and parapsychological origin. Consequently patients may start to accept, particularly when consid-ering the content of the voices, that they might in fact be the product of their own mind manifested in an unusual way, due to severe stress. If either a variable external rationale or a belief that the voices could be internally produced can be tentatively accepted, then patients are often more enthu-siastic at pursuing coping strategies (Falloon and Talbot, 1981). In relation to the voice content, this is best dealt with either by considering the voices as automatic thoughts or by acting directly in contradiction to them. In the former approach the patient records (often with key worker help) the main statements made by the voices. The truthfulness of these statements is then considered and rational responses generated. These responses can then be recorded onto an audio tape for the patient to listen to when the voices are active. Behavioural homework experiments, e.g. acting against the voices, has a similar effect to taped rational responses. The voices may initially become more severe, but generally, after a period, fade into the background. This would appear to be a phenomenon related to cognitive dissonance. Patients need to be warned that voices may become a bit worse before improving. The following case relates to a young lady with neuroleptic resis-tant hallucinosis who had come to believe that she was a witch because the voices told her so, and dressed accordingly in long black gowns etc.

Therapist: Our work on the voices seems to show that we are unsure where they are coming from.
Patient: I think they are either ghosts [50 per cent belief] or thoughts [50 per cent]. I think they might be thoughts because quite often I hear my mother's voice and she is still alive.
Therapist: Have you tested out whether it could be your mother?
Patient: Yes, she denies it and my friend couldn't hear them either.
Therapist: If they are your own thoughts then maybe they aren't so scary and maybe you don't need to believe them if they are unreasonable.

Rational responses were formulated and used with a measured reduction in voice frequency and intensity. The next stage was the behavioural home-work of dressing in her normal clothes and wearing make-up etc. Voices initially flared up and then further settled.

Thought disorder

One of the main CBT techniques involved in treating schizophrenic thought disorder is thought linkage. In this technique the patient is repeatedly asked to clarify the links between disconnected fragments of speech. Neologisms are not accepted and the patient is asked to explain where the word comes from and what it means. Video/audio taping of 'incomprehensible' interviews can be extremely helpful in case formulation. Often the main themes, including stressors, can be disentangled and addressed individually with more focus leading to increased comprehensibility (Turkington and Kingdon, 1991).

NEGATIVE SYMPTOMS

The maintaining factors for negative symptomatology are frequently preoccupation with positive symptoms, neuroleptic side effects and depression. The process of therapy is described in tandem with the use of low dose medication and standard behavioural rehabilitation approaches. This may allow negative symptoms to gradually improve as positive symptoms ameliorate and motivation improves. However, the absence of a range of community psychiatric facilities and support options makes attempts to alleviate negative symptoms much more difficult (see Chapter 9 for an account of negative symptom management).

RELAPSE PREVENTION

CBT booster sessions and delineation of the specific relapse prodrome for individual patients do much to arm the patient against the possibility of future relapse. A list of telephone numbers to access staff and other response options needs to be formulated.

CONCLUSIONS

The use of cognitive–behaviour therapy with a normalising rationale in schizophrenia is currently being scientifically evaluated. Studies have been designed and funded to measure compliance with neuroleptics and outcome, and to measure efficacy on an 'intention to treat' basis. The techniques described would appear to be safe and acceptable to schizophrenic patients. This form of treatment cannot, however, be maximally beneficial without the full support of a comprehensive community psychiatric service including sensitive neuroleptic prescribing and monitoring, drop-in and day care facilities and a full range of accommodation options.

REFERENCES

Beck, A. T. (1952) 'Successful out-patient psychotherapy of a chronic schizophrenic with a delusion based on borrowed guilt', *Psychiatry* 15: 305–12.
Beck, A. T., Rush, A. J., Shaw, B. F. and Emery, G. (1979) *Cognitive Therapy of Depression*, Chichester: John Wiley.

Birchwood, M., Smith, J., Macmillan, F., Hogg, B., Prasad, R., Harvey C. and Bering S. (1989) 'Predicting relapse in schizophrenia: the development and implementation of an early signs monitoring system using patients and families as observers', *Psychological Medicine* 19: 649–56.

Blackburn, I. M. and Davidson, K. (1990) *Cognitive Therapy for Depression and Anxiety*, Oxford: Blackwell.

Ensink, B. J. (1992) *Confusing Realities: a Study on Child Sexual Abuse and Psychiatric Symptoms*, Amsterdam: Free University Press.

Falloon, I. R. H. and Talbot, R. E. (1981) 'Persistent auditory hallucinations: coping mechanisms and implications for management', *Psychological Medicine* 11: 329–39.

Grassian, G. (1983) 'Psychopathology of solitary confinement', *American Journal of Psychiatry* 140: 1450–4.

Green, M. F. (1993) 'Cognitive remediation in schizophrenia: is it time yet?', *American Journal of Psychiatry* 150: 178–87.

Kingdon, D.G. and Turkington, D. (1991) 'The use of cognitive behaviour therapy with a normalising rationale in schizophrenia', *Journal of Nervous and Mental Disease* 179: 207–211.

—— (1994) *Cognitive Behaviour Therapy of Schizophrenia*, New York: Guildford Press.

Kingdon, D. G., Turkington, D. and John, C. (1994) 'Cognitive behaviour therapy of schizophrenia. The amenability of delusions and hallucinations to reasoning', *British Journal of Psychiatry*, (editorial) 164: 581–7.

Kingdon, D. G., Turkington, D. and Judd, M. (1989) 'Befriending: cost effective community care', *Psychiatric Bulletin* 13: 350–1.

Kingdon, D. G., Turkington D., Malcolm, K., Szulecka, K. and Larkin, E. (1991) 'Replacing the mental hospital: community provision for a district's chronically psychiatrically disabled in domestic environments', *British Journal of Psychiatry* 158: 113–16.

Kingdon, D. G., Turkington, D., John, C., Rowlands, P. and Hope-Gill, M. (in press) 'A controlled study of cognitive–behavioural therapy vs befriending in the treatment of schizophrenia', *British Journal of Psychiatry*.

Oswald, I. (1974) *Sleep* (3rd edition), Harmondsworth: Penguin.

Romme, M. A. J. and Escher, A.D.M.A.C. (1989) 'Hearing voices', *Schizophrenia Bulletin* 15: 209–16.

Scharfetter, C. (1980) *General Psychopathology* (translated H. Marshall), Cambridge: Cambridge University Press.

Siegel, R. K. (1984) 'Hostage hallucinations', *Journal of Nervous and Mental Disease* 172: 264–71.

Slade, P. D. (1973) 'The psychological investigation and treatment of auditory hallucinations: a second case report', *British Journal of Medical Psychology* 46: 293–6.

—— (1984) 'Sensory deprivation and clinical psychiatry', *British Journal of Hospital Medicine* 32: 256–60.

Strauss, J. S. (1969) 'Hallucinations and delusions as points on continua of function', *Archives of General Psychiatry* 21: 581–6.

Strauss, J. S., Walker, W. and Brenner, H. D. (eds) (1987) *Psychosocial Management of Schizophrenia*, Toronto: Hans Hoober.

Tarrier, N., Beckett, R., Harwood, S., Baker, A., Yusupoff, L. and Ugarteburu, I. (1993) 'A trial of two cognitive–behavioural methods of treating drug resistant residual psychotic symptoms in schizophrenic patients: 1. Outcome', *British Journal of Psychiatry* 162: 524–32.

Turkington, D. and Kingdon, D.G. (1991) 'Ordering thoughts in thought disorder', *British Journal of Psychiatry* 159: 160–1.

Turkington, D., Kingdon, D. G. and Malcolm, K. (1991) 'The use of an unstaffed flat for crisis intervention and rehabilitation', *Psychiatric Bulletin* 15: 13–14.

Watts, F. N., Powell, G. E. and Austin, S. V. (1973) 'Modification of delusional beliefs', *British Journal of Medical Psychology* 46: 359–63.

Wilcox, J., Rionase, D. and Suez, L. (1991) 'Auditory hallucinations, post-traumatic stress disorder and ethnicity', *Comprehensive Psychiatry* 32: 320–3.

Zubin, J. (1987) 'Possible implications of the vulnerability hypothesis for the psychosocial management of schizophrenia', in J. S. Strauss, W. Walker and H. D. Brenner (eds) *Psychosocial Management of Schizophrenia*, Toronto: Hans Hoober.

7

AN OUTCOME STUDY OF COGNITIVE–BEHAVIOURAL TREATMENT FOR PSYCHOSIS

Elizabeth Kuipers, Philippa Garety and David Fowler

INTRODUCTION

One of the aspects of psychotic disorders that is often overlooked is the prevalence of severe depression and its associated problems of lowered self-esteem. While not universal, there is evidence that affective symptoms are found in 25–40 per cent of those with psychosis (Hemsley, 1992; Johnstone *et al.*, 1991). Similarly there is an increased risk of suicide, compared to the general population, of around 10 per cent (Hirsch, 1982; Briera *et al.*, 1991). Even if not severely depressed, in discussion many clients with psychosis mention ongoing feelings of reduced achievement and potential not fulfilled, which can in time develop into ideas of being 'a failure' or 'having a wasted life'. Those clients who live in family settings are likely to be aware to at least some extent of the burden that their care can impose (Noh and Turner, 1987). This may be confirmed by relatives who themselves often feel what amounts to a bereavement reaction to the fact of long term psychotic problems (Kuipers *et al.*, 1992).

Our group (Fowler *et al.*, 1994) has therefore concentrated on an approach to the cognitive–behavioural therapy (CBT) of psychosis which includes an awareness of, and a focus on, affective symptomatology where it exists. Since this is an aspect of our therapy which is relatively less emphasised by other workers, we will describe this work in some detail in this chapter, and also provide two relevant case examples.

A MODEL OF COGNITIVE–BEHAVIOURAL THERAPY (CBT)

Our treatment approach has been developed since the early 1980s. The outcome study to be described below is one of a series of pilots in which a total of thirty-four patients have been offered therapy (Fowler and Morley,

116

1989; Fowler, 1992; Garety *et al.*, 1994). The intervention has been derived from an attempt to use general principles of cognitive–behavioural therapy in an individualised case formulation approach, in an attempt to understand and address the heterogeneity of problems presented by these clients. Over the years, therapy procedures have been tested on a single case basis. For instance, the initial pilot work focused specifically on the management of residual psychotic symptoms, based on Meichenbaum's ideas of stress inoculation training (Meichenbaum, 1977) and on other work developed to help clients cope with particular symptoms of psychosis (Slade and Bentall, 1988). At that stage the aim of therapy was to help clients incorporate such procedures into their own coping repertoire. While this single case study approach was able to show some success in reducing the clinical impact of specific symptoms, and of increasing clients' ability to tolerate the problems, it was also clear that other problems such as adverse affective reactions, loss of hope and poor understanding of difficulties were equally important (Fowler and Morley, 1989).

This led to the development of a more comprehensive therapy to try and encompass the associated difficulties of coping with long term psychosis. Thus a supportive therapy was attempted which aimed to maximise engagement. This included not only a warm, empathic and essentially collaborative therapeutic style, but also an ability to be flexible within sessions and about their timing and location. Particular emphasis was put on reducing 'pressure' or distress within sessions, for instance by changing topic, reducing eye contact, or if necessary by stopping a session early.

A more general strategy for managing disability included giving people information, discussing their understanding of the condition, providing a rationale for medication use and realistic goal setting in both the short and the long term. Strategies for recognising and trying to avoid future relapses were also discussed. At this stage the emotional aspects of disability were examined if this was a feature for the individual.

This more comprehensive approach was piloted on nineteen clients (Fowler, 1992). While there were clear improvements among those with residual positive symptoms and for those with accompanying affective problems, very little change was observed in those with only negative symptoms and non-specific difficulties.

The results of these studies provide a rationale for the therapy offered in this current study. Our aim at this stage was to offer integrated techniques to encompass the wide variety of problems that individuals could present with. We would conceptualise this as a tree with branches; for each individual a therapeutic plan would follow up from the trunk and along the branches to the particular difficulties found, and the technique required for them. For instance, for those with psychosis and affective symptoms, the latter would be seen as equally important and both would be offered the appropriate help. For those with one particularly distressing symptom, poor insight and limited coping skills, the intervention might attempt to branch into sharing information, extending coping skills, and reality testing. For those where depression was a primary feature and residual symptoms were more incidental, or fed into depressive thinking, then cognitive restructuring of negative self-appraisals might be offered as a primary focus. If low self-esteem and depression were not features, however, this branch would not be attempted in therapy.

Our ideas on treatment have been written in a manual (Fowler *et al.*, 1995) but an outline of some of the main strategies can be given here. Our main techniques are adapted from cognitive–behavioural ideas (e.g. Hawton *et al.*, 1989) but directed specifically at psychotic symptoms. They include improving coping responses, psychoeducation and belief modification. All of these have been the subject of a few other studies, which have shown improvements; Chadwick and Lowe (1990) focused on belief modification, Kingdon and Turkington (1991) on normalising and psychoeducation and Tarrier *et al.* (1993) on making coping responses more adaptive. Our model differs from these to the extent that it attempts to offer a range of techniques, depending on individual needs and also in using strategies derived from cognitive therapy in depression (Beck *et al.*, 1979) when affective aspects are a feature. We have found, however, that techniques that might apply for those with severe depression should be applied both flexibly and with creative adaptations for this client group. As well as this, both persistence and an ability to be optimistic over a long time scale, a general feature of work with most long term clients, are necessary therapist attributes. Within these caveats, our therapy is directed at all or any of three main goals.

1. To reduce the distress and interference that arises from the experience of persistent psychotic symptoms.
2. To increase the individual's understanding of psychotic disorders and to foster motivation to engage in self-regulation behaviour.
3. To reduce the occurrence of dysfunctional emotions and self-defeating behaviour arising from feelings of hopelessness, negative self-image or perceived psychological threat.

We aim for a lengthy assessment of four to six sessions. One of the main aims of this is not only to foster therapy engagement and a trusting relationship within which change can occur, but also to model the collaborative therapeutic style which involves clients in their own formulation of problems. Therapy is very much geared to difficulties that clients want to change, and areas that are not identified as causing problems or are already coped with, may well be left alone. Some of the most helpful procedures that we have used are described here.

Cognitive–behavioural coping strategies

These procedures aim to equip the client with a set of adaptive ways of managing the occurrence of psychotic experience. The therapist first carries out a detailed cognitive–behavioural analysis of the situations associated with the patient's experience of particular distressing psychotic symptoms. For example, psychotic symptoms may be triggered by specific situations, such as distressing cognitions, may interfere with a person's ability to enter social situations or to go shopping, or may result in severe distress while alone at home. These analyses are then discussed with the patient and the implications for new ways in which the patient may act or think to reduce frequency of symptom onset, or distress or disability in such situations are discussed. The patient is then encouraged to practise using new coping strategies in vivo and to experiment with a number of different strategies until a useful coping repertoire is developed. Generally the aim is to encourage the client to use one or two strategies consistently rather than rigidly. It is very important if a strategy does not work, that responsibility for 'failure' is focused on the unworkability of the strategy not on the client. It is sensible to abandon a strategy if it cannot be readily used. Examples of specific coping strategies include listing rational alternatives to paranoid ideation or learning to distract attention from hallucinations. Such approaches have been described in more detail by Fowler and Morley (1989) and by Tarrier *et al.* (1990; 1993).

Relabelling and psychoeducation

The aim of these strategies is to help the person to relabel psychotic experiences and to suggest that such experiences are not unique, but have been described by others. The aim is not simply to give information which may or may not be accepted. Valins and Nisbett (1971), Johnson *et al.* (1977) and Kingdon and Turkington (1991) describe similar approaches. Therapy proceeds by first eliciting specific examples of psychotic experience and then, by using careful Socratic questioning, suggesting that there may be rational explanations for the occurrence of such experience. Information is provided to begin to correct maladaptive assumptions concerning the nature of psychotic experience, and to add weight to more adaptive appraisals. This may lead to exploring the implications of the new understanding, in particular the idea that it might be possible to reduce the risk of onset of psychotic experience in the future. Initially the implications for an alternative explanation of symptoms within a general illness framework are not forced. The discussion is descriptive rather than explanatory and the client is left to decide what the implications might be. In this way, careful questioning may lead to the development of rationales for taking neuroleptic medication, or adapting behavioural patterns likely to reduce the risk of relapse.

119

Goal setting and overcoming hopelessness

A number of patients describe being overwhelmed by their life situation as a person with long term mental illness and have little understanding of how to help themselves. Here the aim is to generate hope by highlighting worthwhile short term and long term goals which may be achieved despite continuing disabilities. This may involve discussion of the person's experience of more enduring problems such as continuing cognitive deficits or the social consequences of disability. It may be important to clarify limitations set by such disabilities and to help a client reframe expectations so that a small change is perceived as a success rather than a failure. Once the nature of the problem is clarified, proposals for the self-regulation of disabilities may be discussed, and tasks set that may be achievable.

Modification of delusional beliefs

There is a growing consensus on the effectiveness of psychological approaches to modify strongly held beliefs. (The process has been described in Shapiro and Ravenette, 1959, Watts *et al.*, 1973 and Chadwick and Lowe, 1990). First, the therapist carefully elicits the person's view of the reasons for the development and maintenance of the delusional beliefs, which may involve extensive discussion of the development of beliefs in the past. The therapist then invites the patient to consider alternative interpretations of specific pieces of evidence cited by the patient. Many clients will resist this and the alternatives must be considered in the atmosphere of a trusting and collaborative therapeutic relationship. More peripheral evidence and beliefs are addressed before moving to a re-evaluation of more central beliefs. Any anxiety or unwillingness by the client to discuss more central beliefs is noted and the therapist must be prepared to back track or move material into a future session if the client is not coping with discussing alternatives at a particular point. For some clients with really firm convictions it may be better to aim at altering or loosening beliefs rather than accepting alternatives. A client with an unshakeable belief about controlling voices may be asked to come to a reasonable compromise with them, rather than to reject his or her views. This might mean answering back to the voices, or accepting their validity but separating this from behavioural consequences so that client distress begins to reduce. For instance, it might be possible to suggest that a voice which says "read the newspaper" could be ignored and not acted upon, and once tried it might then be found that no dire consequences actually occur. Separating the voices from a client's action can thus help reduce feelings of powerlessness and control and often will also reduce distress.

Modifying dysfunctional assumptions

A number of patients with continuing psychotic symptoms may hold dysfunctional assumptions about the self which imply worthlessness, uselessness and unlovability. Such assumptions may be associated with self-defeating patterns of thought and behaviour and may be an important cause of the failure of earlier coping strategies. To address such assumptions, the therapist starts by attempting to clarify the nature of the assumptions held. Sometimes it is necessary to offer some guesses; at other times the client may be able to identify them. Most often this is done by a longitudinal assessment (Williams, 1992), a process involving questioning about the origins of assumptions and how they have affected the person's life since the time they started to the present. This may predate the onset of psychosis or be part of the initial or subsequent episodes. By a process of guided discovery the client may begin to realise the implications of dysfunctional assumptions, and then be able to develop a more appropriate and adaptive general view. We have found a life review useful to help clients restructure and re-evaluate negative assumptions into more positive and realistic self appraisals.

RELATIONSHIP ASPECTS OF THERAPY

As mentioned earlier in this chapter, we deliberately offer a long and unpressurised engagement period so that a supportive and trusting relationship with a potential therapist can be formed before any sustained treatment is offered. We have also found, from experience in the earlier pilot studies, that the therapeutic style should be not only supportive, but also flexible and sensitive. Those with continuing positive symptoms require therapist awareness of the possibility of reduced concentration or client discomfort during sessions. Some clients may also suffer enduring cognitive deficits. We have found it essential that a therapist is able to notice these aspects and be prepared to modify or abandon a session if necessary.

Once trust has been built up, we envisage therapy lasting for several months. In our outcome study we were able to offer treatment for only 4–6 months. However, particularly for those with depressive symptoms, therapy duration of up to a year seems more realistic, as it may take the first few months to begin to discuss negative self-assumptions or schemata.

Another aspect that we have felt important and which is not yet stressed by other workers in this area, is the issue of supervision and support for therapists while treatment is being offered. We have found that during therapy sessions some of the material discussed, whether from clients' early experience or from the events leading up to a psychotic breakdown, has been of a particularly distressing nature. In a prodromal phase, a client is likely to be experiencing a variety of distressing and confusing mental phenomena at a time when processing is at its least efficient (Birchwood *et al.*, 1988). Our experience has been not only that ordinary life events are likely to occur and be extremely worrying, but also that for a proportion of clients the life events revealed have been unexpectedly distressing, e.g. being thrown out of parental home, being the initiator of a sexual assault, the victim or initiator of child sexual abuse.

For all of these reasons – the prolonged engagement period, the sensitive and flexible therapeutic style which encourages collaboration in the treatment, therapy contracts of up to a year, and the distressing nature of some of the material revealed in treatment sessions – we have found it necessary to provide support for each other while treatment was in progress. As in the literature on staff dealing with post-traumatic stress syndrome (De Loos, 1990) it seems likely that some opportunity to process and defuse the intensity of therapeutic contact is helpful. At present we do not know definitively that such therapeutic contact is necessarily beneficial, but our results do suggest it. Thus, during the active treatment stage we purposely scheduled monthly peer supervision sessions during which the content of therapy sessions was discussed in detail, making it possible to 'normalise' the emotional impact of sessions. We would recommend this strategy, or something comparable, to others interested in offering these sorts of treatments.

OUTCOME STUDY: PILOT

Details of our pilot study are published elsewhere (Garety *et al.*, 1994) but an outline of our procedures and results will be mentioned here.

Aim

This study was designed to find out if our rather detailed assessments (ibid.) were feasible, if clients could be successfully engaged in therapy over a six month period and if our results might justify proceeding on to a larger project. In the time available (one year) it was not possible to offer more than six months of therapy time as a maximum, and it was also not feasible to look at maintenance effects of treatment. At the beginning of the trial, it was not clear how effective treatment might be and a waiting list control design was used rather than a randomly allocated control design. This meant that eventually all clients referred to the project were both assessed and offered therapy. At the beginning of the project it was also not clear that all clients would benefit from therapy. In view of the literature on the raised suicide rate of this client group, the therapists were extremely cautious in monitoring mental state and offering therapy gradually and at a pace that was acceptable. The trial was based in Fulbourn Hospital, Cambridge, and The Institute of Psychiatry, and Maudsley Hospital, London.

Subjects

Clients were included who had a diagnosis of schizophrenia or schizoaffective disorder, and presented unremitting (of at least six months' duration) drug resistant positive psychotic symptoms, e.g. delusions, hallucinations and passivity phenomena. In the light of earlier clinical work, we also sought clients who expressed some distress as a result of their symptoms and excluded any with only negative symptoms. Clients primarily suffering from alcohol or drug problems or organic disorders were also excluded. Fourteen clients who fulfilled these criteria were referred, and thirteen were successfully assessed on a full package of measures. One person was excluded: a man with a twenty year history of unremitting psychosis whose attention and concentration were too poor to complete the assessment. The control group consisted of seven people subsequently referred for therapy and placed on the waiting list. An eighth person was excluded because of a lack of current positive symptoms. The demographic characteristics of the sample and the controls are given in Table 7.1.

Measures

A battery of measures were used to assess the patients:

Before and after the intervention

Present State Examination (PSE) (ninth edition; Wing *et al.*, 1974)
Maudsley Assessment of Delusions (MADs) (Buchanan *et al.*, 1993)
Insight Measure (David, 1990)
Rosenberg Self-esteem Scale (Rosenberg, 1965)
Attribution Questionnaire (Garety *et al.*, 1994)
A Life Skills Profile (Rosen *et al.*, 1989) was completed by a relative or key worker.

Before and after intervention and monthly during the intervention

The Beck Depression Inventory (BDI) (Beck *et al.*, 1961)
The Social Avoidance and Distress Inventory (Watson and Friend, 1969)
Hustig and Hafner Hallucinations Assessment (Hustig and Hafner, 1990)
Personal Questionnaires to assess key symptoms identified by the PSE (Brett-Jones *et al.*, 1987). For each delusion, intensity of conviction, preoccupation and distress were measured on a 0–5 scale (Garety *et al.*, 1994).
Brief Psychiatric Rating Scale (BPRS) (Overall and Gorham, 1962)
An estimate of cognitive functioning was also made before the intervention using the National Adult Reading Test (Nelson, 1982) and sub-tests of the Wechsler Adult Intelligence Scale, Revised (Wechsler, 1981), and subjects also completed reasoning tasks.

Table 7.1 Subjects who entered the trial – demographic data

	Subjects n = 13		Controls n = 7	
Variable	Mean	Range	Mean	Range
Age	39.6	21–70	37.6	26–53
Duration of illness	16.5	6–30	10.9	5–20
Number of admissions	2.9	1–5	2.0	1–3
Predicted IQ (NART)	108	94–125	112	98–125
Gender	Male n = 12		Male n = 6	
	Female n = 1		Female n = 1	

Therapy

CBT was given at weekly and fortnightly intervals over six months. Clients received an average of sixteen sessions (range 11–22). Thirteen clients commenced therapy, but one dropped out after three sessions after a change in medication and a major relapse. A second person, despite continuing in therapy, became suspicious of the researcher doing assessments and could not be reassessed. Therapy was carried out by the authors, clinical psychologists experienced in working with psychotic clients.

A summary of the results is presented here. A full analysis can be found in Garety *et al.* (1994). There was a striking reduction in the level of conviction with which delusions were held ($p < 0.01$; see Figure 7.1). There were also significant changes in the BPRS ($p < 0.01$) and BDI ($p < 0.05$) scores over the course of treatment, and these are shown in Tables 7.2 and 7.3. There were significant improvements on other aspects of psychotic experience as assessed by the MADs: acting on beliefs ($p < 0.05$), preoccupation ($p < 0.05$), and on an attribution questionnaire assessing the extent to which the client experienced distress ($p < 0.05$) and interference with daily life ($p < 0.05$).

Discussion

It can be seen from the results that even this six monthly intervention was able to show significant clinical improvement in the experimental group in general symptomatology (BPRS), depression (BDI), and a range of specific aspects such as conviction about delusional ideas and preoccupation, distress and interference with daily functioning. There were very few refusals and no adverse effects such as suicide. The considerable success with our treatment approach suggested it was feasible, acceptable to clients and improved outcome.

However, it was not a true randomised case control design, the numbers were relatively small, and although our evaluator was independent, she was

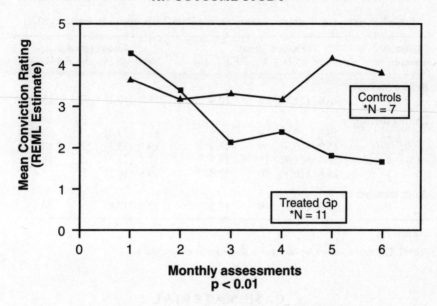

Figure 7.1 Fall in delusional conviction during treatment (*Ratings were obtained for 5 out of 7 in the control group, 10 out of 11 in the treatment group)

Table 7.2 Before and after measures on the Brief Psychiatric Rating Scale (BPRS)

Monthly assessment	Treatment group				Control group			
	Mean	(S.D.)	N	REML Est.	Mean	(S.D.)	N	REML Est.
Before therapy:								
1	34.4	(5.6)	12	34.4	29.9	(6.9)	7	29.8
During therapy:								
2	32.5	(7.1)	9	30.9	31.7	(7.0)	7	31.7
3	30.3	(6.4)	9	30.8	31.4	(7.2)	7	31.4
4	29.5	(6.0)	10	29.2	31.6	(10.0)	5	30.6
5	28.4	(5.1)	10	28.1	32.4	(9.8)	5	31.4
After therapy:								
6	30.2	(10.4)	8	28.5	36.7	(11.0)	3	31.9

$p < 0.01$

REML Estimates: *allows for bias due to dropouts or missing values.*

not blind to the treatment group. In view of these drawbacks, a further trial was indicated which would be larger, allow longer therapy time and be able to focus on maintenance of treatment effects as well as initial changes. This is ongoing.

Table 7.3 Before and after measures on the Beck Depression Inventory (BDI)

Monthly assessment	Treatment group				Control group			
	Mean	(S.D.)	N	REML Est.	Mean	(S.D.)	N	REML Est.
Before therapy:								
1	18.0	(11.5)	13	18.0	15.9	(10.2)	7	15.9
During therapy:								
2	19.6	(9.8)	9	18.9	17.1	(14.8)	7	17.1
3	15.2	(10.8)	9	18.9	19.1	(13.3)	7	19.1
4	12.0	(11.9)	10	13.5	17.4	(13.3)	5	16.0
5	10.8	(10.3)	10	11.8	19.8	(16.5)	5	18.4
After therapy:								
6	15.7	(13.0)	9	15.5	27.0	(15.6)	3	20.5

$p < 0.05$

REML Estimates: *allows for bias due to dropouts or missing values.*

CASE MATERIAL

In order to illustrate more specifically what our CBT approach involves when working with clients who are experiencing psychosis, we have picked out two individuals who both had affective problems and poor self-esteem. Certain details have been changed in order in protect client anonymity.

Case 1: Mr X

Mr X was a 40-year-old man who had lived in a community based hostel for the last nine years. He was divorced and had few friends. He had first become unwell in his early twenties. He was resigned to a poor quality of life and could see no likelihood of improvement occurring. He felt actively suicidal at times and had previously taken several overdoses. He was pessimistic that anyone or anything could help and was not keen to engage in therapy. He agreed reluctantly to attend weekly, initially, at least to come and talk to the therapist.

Initial assessment

1. Cognitive functioning was found to be within the average range:

    National Adult Reading Test error score = 31

    Wechsler Adult Intelligence Scale, Revised:
    Vocabulary   = 8   Block design   = 9
    Comprehension   = 7   Object assembly = 5
    Similarities   = 6

2. Mental state: Present State Examination

Mr X's main delusion was that people could read his thoughts and his mind. He reported that this began in a supermarket when another shopper, a woman, looked at him and said to her friend "I can read his thoughts".

He also heard voices which commented on the thoughts. These reinforced his belief that others read his thoughts. This was a worry, particularly if he felt that others would not 'admit' this capability. He knew that telepathy could be practised and felt that television and radio were a sort of 'pollution' which encouraged this.

He was distressed by others' ability to read his thoughts. He felt that because he knew strangers could read thoughts that this might mean that Mr X would be physically attacked. This worried him and made it hard for him to go out in case he was attacked.

3. Social avoidance

Mr X showed some social avoidance and distress.

4. Self-esteem

This was rated as low. He felt he was a nuisance to others and that, now in his forties, he was no longer attractive to women.

5. Depression

Beck Depression Inventory = 9. Mr X was not depressed when assessed, but had been actively suicidal in the past.

6. Coping

Mr X used avoidance and tried not to think about his problems because this could bring on the voices. He had found smoking to be helpful, as was getting drunk once a week (when he could afford it). He also found it helped to watch television because it was distracting.

7. Insight

He did not believe he was ill but put the onset of his symptoms down to his divorce and a leg operation.

Problems identified after 6 weeks

1. Mr X knew that others could read his mind. This was particularly distressing at night. His own coping responses of getting drunk or asking for reassurance were ineffective. His voices tended to occur every day. Mr X identified this as his main problem and so this was given priority in his treatment.

2. With regard to low self-esteem, as well as feeling he was a nuisance to others Mr X felt useless, that his life had nothing more to offer and that he had already achieved whatever he was going to. He also felt isolated and that his problems were worsening over the years. This was also identified as a main problem with which Mr X wanted some help.

3. Suicidal feelings were acted on once during the assessment/therapy period. Mr X took an overdose, which was discovered because the therapist

127

telephoned him about non-attendance. The overdose led to a brief hospital admission, after which Mr X discharged himself back to his hostel and continued not to take medication.

4. Isolation: it was hard for him to walk down the street, and this made attendance at sessions more difficult.

5. Being ambivalent about help meant that Mr X wanted to attend sessions less often than once a week. He was difficult to engage in therapy because he was pessimistic that anything could change for the better.

Interventions

1. The idea that others could read his mind was tackled in the following ways:

Self-recording

Mr X was asked to keep a diary to specify when this happened, but he was not able to do this for more than a few days and it was discontinued. This is an example of an inappropriate strategy being rapidly abandoned.

Identifying triggers and coping responses

After discussion it emerged that the main triggers were being alone at night, walking down the street and hearing others talk, e.g. outside the hostel, or on the radio. Mr X's own coping had proved ineffective, so the therapist suggested enhancing it, e.g. distraction by listening to music which Mr X himself had found helpful.

Explanation of illness

Several sessions were spent discussing Mr X's understanding of his problems and offering an alternative view. A view that was acceptable to Mr X was that his brain was particularly sensitive to patterns because of having had schizophrenia, and was particularly likely to put meaning into patterns of sound (extraneous sounds or voices such as the radio) that others might not notice. Examples of when he did this, and a possible alternative view, were taken from life where possible, e.g. during a session, people walked past the window while talking and Mr X heard his name spoken. What he heard and how he might have put meaning on to these sounds were discussed and evaluated.

Coping statements

Mr X was given statements to repeat to himself at times of distress. These were discussed and agreed with Mr X before being written down, e.g. he found it helpful to have "it's the pattern" as a coping statement, which he could look at when he felt his name had been spoken.

Reality testing

Mr X agreed to ask others what they were thinking and check if it was about him, e.g. to ask the therapist. He also agreed to ask others at the hostel if they had heard the 'message' that Mr X had just received, or not. Once he started to do this he rapidly found that others did not share his perceptions. This helped reinforce the coping statement "it's the pattern", which meant that his experiences were individual to him and not shared by others.

2. Low self-esteem and suicidal feelings were tackled by a *life review*. Mr X was asked about early experiences and his feelings about himself. It emerged that since he was a teenager he had felt guilty about his behaviour towards a sibling. Re-evaluation of Mr X's life and the reason for his behaviour, plus some alternative views on the accuracy of his assessments were attempted. These re-evaluations, which included emphasis on the positive rather than the negative, particularly of his marriage and the conduct of his divorce, began to help him to reduce hopelessness and active suicidal ideation.

3. For social isolation, increased social activities were encouraged. Mr X began to visit a friend and have a meal with him most evenings. This worked well. He was also encouraged to get out more if he wanted to, and to sit in the lounge downstairs rather than in his room. Both of these began to be more frequent and even enjoyable.

4. Ambivalence about any treatment was obviously related to Mr X's poor self-esteem, feelings of hopelessness and that he was past worrying about. Mr X was reassured that it was pleasant to spend time with him and that at 40 years old his life was not necessarily finished. Sessions were rearranged from weekly to fortnightly, at his request. Mr X was also telephoned and reminded about appointments, which were shifted to his hostel by mutual agreement. This improved his motivation and engagement in treatment because he did not have to walk outside and also because he was being seen on home territory, where he could offer the therapist a cup of tea and show her around the premises.

Outcome

Mr X was seen for a total of thirteen sessions over six months. They ranged from twenty to forty-five minutes, as he was not able to tolerate longer periods. Mr. X began taking medication during this time, something he had previously refused. He had become more aware of triggering factors, such as sitting alone in his room, and his hallucinations were not so persistent or distressing as when first seen. He began to cope by spending more time in the living room of the hostel, felt more in control of the voices and was less upset by them.

He continued to believe his thoughts could be read but felt less convinced that there would be any consequences of this, i.e. he would not be attacked. It helped to separate the beliefs from the possible consequences as Mr X began to agree that it was not likely that he would be attacked as it had never happened.

He still found going out difficult, but would manage it when necessary. He felt content with life. These improvements can be seen in some of the scores in Figure 7.2.

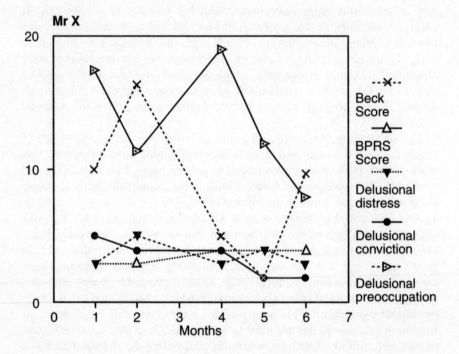

Figure 7.2 Changes in outcome over 6 months of treatment for Mr X

It was obvious when sessions finished that Mr X would miss the social contact of the therapy and the assessments. This was reflected as a raised Beck Depression Inventory score at follow-up assessment. It was recommended that the key worker consistently offer regular contact to counteract this. This was instituted and Mr X has continued to cope and remains reasonably well a year after sessions were discontinued.

Case 2: Mr Y

Mr Y was unusual in being 70 years old when referred, with a forty year history of psychosis. He also lived in a hostel, for over fifteen years, and attended a sheltered workshop for day care. He had some physical problems and found it hard to use public transport. He attended day care facility by using volunteer transport. He was also rather isolated and had high levels of anxiety and tension at times.

Initial assessment

1. Cognitive functioning

Mr Y had a marked verbal-performance discrepancy in his scores.

> Wechsler Adult Intelligence Scale, Revised
> Vocabulary   = 7   Block design   = 2
> Comprehension = 11   Object assembly = 2
> Similarities   = 8
> National Adult Reading Test error score = 10

2. Mental state: Present State Examination

Mr Y had two main beliefs which caused him anxiety and distress. First, he believed over the years that his face and neck had become emaciated. Second, because of this he was convinced that others stared and roared with laughter at him. Because he felt his neck was getting thinner over time, these feelings were worsening. Mr Y frequently checked to see if he was being laughed at and felt he frequently was. The feelings had started many decades earlier and were worse unless he kept his hair long. Because of these feelings he felt constantly tense and anxious and avoided going out.

3. Coping

He tended to avoid people and tried to reassure himself. He kept his hair long to reduce anxiety.

4. Insight

Insight was poor. Mr Y was unable to explain why he had these beliefs but did agree he had a psychiatric illness.

5. Social avoidance and distress

Mr Y rarely went out apart from going to a workshop at a day centre. He frequently felt distressed about his problems.

6. Self-esteem

This was rated as very low. Mr Y felt completely useless, worthless and inferior to others. He felt he was partly to blame for his problems because he had failed to achieve anything with his life. He was angry with himself for not being able to cope better. He felt the length of time he had been like this made everything worse, i.e. he was becoming too old to change.

131

7. Depression
Beck Depression Inventory = 20, mild depression.

Problems identified after assessment

Mr Y was seen weekly for six sessions and four main target problems were
identified with him.
1. Mr Y felt he looked very abnormal: he felt that his head and neck were
very thin and emaciated, "like a coconut on a stick". He had felt this way
on and off for decades and it impeded his socialising because of (2) below.
2. He felt that people were laughing at him.
3. Very low self-esteem. Mr Y had felt inferior to others since he was
11 years old and had failed his exams. He frequently said that his life "feels
like a failure".
4. Tension. This was a result of and a trigger for his delusional thinking
and also led to social avoidance, and keeping his hair long. Mr Y found he
could not go out by himself without effort.

Interventions

1. His fear of his abnormal looks was based on his delusional ideas, which
began during a hospital admission in the 1950s where he had a forcible hair
cut. These ideas were discussed, i.e. how they began and what they were
based on, as part of a re-evaluation of Mr Y's life. Alternative explanations
were given so that many of his responses were understandable and positive
given the circumstances. Mr Y had never considered this and began to
reappraise his reactions at that time.

Reality testing

Mr Y stated at one point that his neck was definitely thinner than the
therapist's which looked normal. After considerable discussion Mr Y
agreed to spend one session measuring necks. Mr Y was subsequently able
to agree that his neck was normal and probably looked normal to others.
This measurement was discussed several times in subsequent sessions. Mr Y
continued to think his face emaciated, but began to call it "an obsession of
mine". After the reality testing Mr Y's beliefs about his appearances began
to be less distressing to him and this itself helped his feelings of worthlessness and tension.
2. Reality testing (above) gave a different focus as to why people should
laugh. Mr Y began to say "there is no reason because my neck looks
normal". Mr Y then began to develop his own *coping statements* such as "I
should mind my own business". He also used *distraction* such as "I should
get on with my job" (at the workshop) and *reappraisal* such as "they are
probably just laughing" (i.e. not at me).

132

3. Treating his low self-esteem involved a re-evaluation of Mr Y's life which took many sessions because of Mr Y's age and history. Alternative views of Mr Y's achievements were balanced with the fact that he had been coping with intractable mental illness problems for many decades. It also emerged that at one stage Mr Y had successfully found a partner and helped her and her children for about ten years. Mr Y began to say "I've been too harsh on myself", and to agree that he did have many positive achievements in his life.

4. Mr Y was very knowledgeable in several areas, and with therapist encouragement began to revive these interests.

5. Because of his frequent feelings of tension, and both night and day sweats, *anxiety management* was instituted. Ways of increasing Mr Y's social activity and coping with the tension that resulted, rather than using avoidance, were discussed. He was encouraged to try out difficult situations and congratulate himself on managing. This reduced the sweating almost immediately. Mr Y increasingly began to do this for himself, by instituting social activities such as another local day centre, and by beginning graded activities such as spending time during lunch breaks sitting with others rather than in the quiet room by himself.

Outcome

Overall, Mr Y attended thirteen sessions, ranging from thirty minutes to one hour. These were usually fortnightly at Mr Y's preference. After the life review and reality testing, most sessions focused on anxiety management, including practising graded tasks of social exposure.

At follow up, a month after therapy sessions finished (not shown on Figure 7.3; point 7) it was reported that Mr Y described people looking and laughing at him as a "silly obsession". He still thought that people looked at him, but felt that he must tackle it himself. He was rational, coped better with his symptoms and appeared less tense and anxious, and scored 13 on the BDI. He was talking more to others and spending more time socialising. His scores on the main measures during therapy can be seen in Figure 7.3.

A year after this follow up Mr Y is still socialising. His ideas about his neck and face remain muted. This has meant that he had managed two hair cuts without feeling too distressed; his previous pattern had been to avoid this for as long as possible.

DISCUSSION

Both of these cases illustrate the importance of working with problems of low self-esteem, if it exists. Feelings of hopelessness and failure for Mr X led to suicidal ideas and attempts, and for Mr Y led to depression and considerable anxiety and tension. As low self-esteem was a feature, both

133

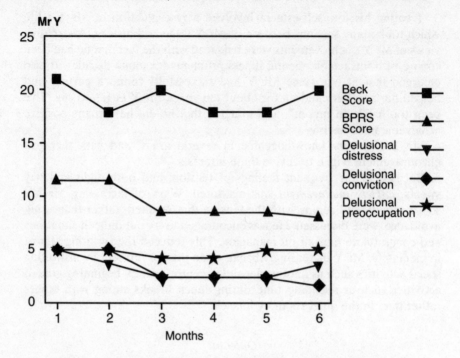

Figure 7.3 Changes in outcome over 6 months of treatment for Mr Y

men were offered intervention that focused specifically on these aspects – the branch of tackling depression and low self-worth was taken for both of them. Once these aspects were focused on, using a life review, reappraisal and alternative explanations, much of the distress of the delusional thinking could then be tackled. Reality testing was important for both men, particularly for Mr Y. Because of their low self-worth neither of them had been motivated by themselves to try this out with any consistency, as 'failure' would have confirmed their poor self-evaluation. However, in a supportive therapeutic context it was possible to use reality testing in a positive way, and this pathway in itself helped bolster more hopeful and realistic self-appraisals.

We have often found that intervention in one area helps improve other problems. This is particularly true of low self-esteem because of its effect of reducing motivation and feeding into depressed mood. We would suggest that the impact of ongoing psychotic problems on self-worth should be routinely assessed, and if it exists this needs to be tackled, both to maximise engagement and to make it more likely that other positive changes can be made.

REFERENCES

Beck, A. T., Rush, A. J., Shaw, B. F. and Emery, G. (1979) *Cognitive Therapy of Depression*, Chichester: John Wiley.

Beck, A. T., Ward, C. H., Mendelson, M., Mock, T. and Erbaugh, J. (1961) 'An inventory for measuring depression', *Archives of General Psychiatry* 4: 561–71.

Birchwood, M., Hallet, S.E. and Preston, M.C. (1988) *Schizophrenia: An Integrated Approach to Research and Treatment*, London and New York: Longmans.

Brett-Jones, J., Garety, P. A. and Hemsley, D. (1987) 'Measuring delusional experiences: a method and its application', *British Journal of Clinical Psychology* 26: 257–65.

Briera, A., Schreiber, J. L., Dyder, J. and Pickard, D. (1991) 'NIMH longitudinal study of chronic schizophrenia: prognosis and predictors of outcome', *Archives of General Psychiatry* 48: 239–46.

Buchanan, A., Reed, A., Wessely, S., Garety, P., Taylor, P., Grubin, D. and Dunn, G. (1993) 'Acting on delusion (2): the phenomenological correlates of acting on delusions', *British Journal of Psychiatry* 163: 77–81.

Chadwick, P. and Lowe, F. (1990) 'The measurement and modification of delusional beliefs', *Journal of Consulting Clinical Psychology* 58: 225–32.

David, A. (1990) 'Insight and psychosis', *British Journal of Psychiatry* 156: 798–808.

De Loos, W.S. (1990) 'Psychosomatic manifestations of chronic post traumatic stress disorder', in M. E. Wolf and A. D. Mosnaim (eds) *Post-traumatic Stress Disorder: Etiology, Phenomenology and Treatment*, Washington DC: American Psychiatric Press.

Fowler, D. (1992) 'Cognitive behaviour therapy in the management of patients with schizophrenia: preliminary studies', in A. Werbart and J. Cullberg (eds) *Psychotherapy of Schizophrenia: Facilitating and Obstructive Factors*, Oslo: Scandinavian University Press.

Fowler, D. and Morley, S. (1989) 'The cognitive behavioural treatment of hallucinations and delusions: a preliminary study', *Behavioural Psychotherapy* 17: 267–82.

Fowler, D., Garety, P. A. and Kuipers, L. (1995) *Cognitive Behaviour Therapy for People with Psychosis: A Clinical Handbook*, Chichester: John Wiley.

Garety, P. A., Kuipers, L., Fowler, D., Chamberlain, F. and Dunn, G. (1994) 'Cognitive Behaviour Therapy for drug resistant psychosis', *British Journal of Medical Psychology* 67, 259–71.

Hawton, K., Salkovskis, P., Kirk, J. and Clark, D. (1989) *Cognitive–behaviour Therapy of Psychiatric Problems*, Oxford: Oxford University Press.

Hemsley, D. R. (1992) 'Anxiety and depression in schizophrenia' (personal communication).

Hirsch, S. R. (1982) 'Depression revealed in schizophrenia', *British Journal of Psychiatry* 140: 421–2.

Hustig, H. H. and Hafner, R. J. (1990) 'Persistent auditory hallucinations and their relationship to delusions and mood', *Journal of Nervous and Mental Disease*, 178: 264–7.

Johnson, W. G., Ross, J. M. and Mastria, M. A. (1977) 'Delusional behaviour: An attributional analysis of development and modification', *Journal of Abnormal Psychology*, 86: 421–6.

Johnstone, E. C., Owens, D. G. C., Frith, C. D. and Leavy, J. (1991) 'Clinical findings: Abnormalities of mental state and their correlates. The Northwick Park follow-up study', *British Journal of Psychiatry* 159, (suppl. 13): 21–5.

Jones, E. E. and Canouse, D. (eds) (1971) *Attribution: Perceiving the Causes of Behaviour*, New Jersey: General Learning Press.

Kingdon, D. G. and Turkington, D. (1991) 'Preliminary report: the use of cognitive behaviour therapy with a normalising rationale in schizophrenia', *Journal of Nervous and Mental Disease*, 179: 207–11.

Kuipers, L., Leff, J. and Lam, D. (1992) *Family Work for Schizophrenia: a Practical Guide*, London: Gaskell.

Meichenbaum, D. (1977) *Cognitive Behaviour Modification*, New York: Plenum.

Nelson, H. E. (1982) *The National Adult Reading Test*, Windsor: NFER/Nelson.

Noh, S. and Turner, R. J. (1987) 'Living with psychiatric patients: implications for the mental health of family members', *Social Science and Medicine* 25: 263–72.

Overall, J. and Gorham, D. (1962) 'The Brief Psychiatric Rating Scale', *Psychological Reports* 10: 799–812.

Rosen, A., Hadzi Pavlovic, D. and Parker, G. (1989) 'The Life Skills Profile: a measure of assessing function and disability in schizophrenia', *Schizophrenia Bulletin* 15: 325–37.

Rosenberg, M. (1965) *Society and Adolescent Self-Image*, Princeton, NJ: Princeton University Press.

Shapiro, M. B. and Ravenette, A. T. (1959) 'A preliminary experiment of paranoid delusions', *Journal of Mental Science* 105: 295–312.

Slade, P. D. and Bentall, R. P. (1988) *Sensory Deception: Towards a Scientific Analysis of Hallucinations*, London: Croom Helm.

Tarrier, N., Harwood, S., Yusupoff, L., Beckett, R. and Baker, A. (1990) 'Coping strategy enhancement (CSE): a method of treating residual schizophrenic symptoms', *Behavioural Psychotherapy* 18: 283–93.

Tarrier, N., Beckett, R., Harwood, S., Baker, A., Yusupoff, L. and Ugarteburu, I. (1993) 'A trial of two cognitive–behavioural methods of treating drug-resistant residual psychotic symptoms in schizophrenic patients: 1 Outcome', *British Journal of Psychiatry* 162: 524–32.

Valins, S. and Nisbett, R. E. (1971) 'Attribution processes in the development and treatment of emotional disorders', in E.E. Jones and D. Canouse (eds) *Attribution: Perceiving the Causes of Behaviour*, New Jersey: General Learning Press.

Watson, D. and Friend, R. (1969) 'The measurement of social evaluative anxiety', *Journal of Consulting and Clinical Psychology* 33: 448–57.

Watts, F. N., Powell, G. E. and Austin, S. V. (1973) 'The modification of abnormal beliefs', *British Journal of Medical Psychology* 46: 359–63.

Wechsler, D. (1981) *Wechsler Adult Intelligence Scale, Revised*, New York: The Psychological Corporation.

Werbart, A. and Cullberg, J. (eds) (1992) *Psychotherapy of Schizophrenia: Facilitating and Obstructive Factors*, Oslo: Scandinavian University Press.

Williams, J. M. G. (1992) *The Psychological Treatment of Depression: a Guide to the Theory and Practice of Cognitive Behaviour Therapy*, London: Routledge.

Wing, J. K., Cooper, J. E. and Sartorius, N. (1974) *The Measurement and Classification of Psychiatric Symptoms*, Cambridge: Cambridge University Press.

Wolf, M. E. and Mosnaim, A. D. (eds) (1990) *Post-traumatic Stress Disorder: Etiology, Phenomenology and Treatment*, Washington, DC: American Psychiatric Press.

8

EMPOWERING PEOPLE
WHO HEAR VOICES

Marius Romme and Sandra Escher

INTRODUCTION

In this chapter we intend to show that people hear voices in the normal population even when there is no evidence of psychiatric disease (Tien, 1991; Eaton *et al.*, 1991) and that the reported presence of verbal hallucinations is not always related to psychopathology (Barret and Etheridge, 1992).

Despite this, hearing voices does occur in specific psychiatric diseases at a much higher percentage than in the normal population. For example, schizophrenia, 53 per cent (Landmark *et al.*, 1990), major affective disorders, 28 per cent (Goodwin and Jamison, 1990) and the normal population, 2.3 per cent (Tien, 1991). Although these two kinds of information appear to be contradictory, there are two possible connections. First, it may be that there is a connection between specific characteristics of hearing voices and the existence of psychiatric illness, or second there may be a connection between hearing voices and problems in the person's life history. In the latter case, it is possible that psychiatric patients may have experienced more problems which they have found difficult to cope with than the average person.

In our own research, we have not found a connection between the characteristics of hearing voices and specific psychiatric illnesses. This led us to question whether hearing voices has a functional role in aiding coping with problems in daily life. In more dramatic terms: is it a survival strategy instead of a symptom of a particular illness? If this is the case, then there should be a connection between hearing voices, life history and living circumstances. To investigate this question further we conducted an experiment where we brought together a large number of people who heard voices. Within this group of voice hearers we compared people who could cope well with their voices with those who felt they could not cope.

The results of this investigation will be presented in this chapter, followed by some short case examples. These examples will demonstrate how the connection between hearing voices, life history and living circumstances manifests itself and how this connection may be handled in learning to cope

137

with hearing voices. These examples may also demonstrate that as long as the phenomenon of hearing voices is viewed as a symptom of a disease, and treatment is focused on this disease, problems in daily life and circumstances as expressed by the voices, will not be solved.

HEARING VOICES IN THE NORMAL POPULATION

At the end of the last century, Sidgewick (1894) showed that the phenomenon of hearing voices appeared in 2 per cent of the normal population. Recently, Tien (1991) replicated this research, with the help of the National Institute of Mental Health Epidemiological (NIMH) catchment area programme using the structured Diagnostic Interview Schedule for auditory hallucinations (D.I.S.; Robins *et al.*, 1981). He found that there was a prevalence rate of 2.3 per cent, in a survey compiled from 15,000 members of the general population. Only one third of these hallucinators reported distress or impairment of functioning (level 5 D.I.S.), meeting the D.I.S. criteria for a psychiatric diagnosis. Eaton *et al.* (1991) selected a sample of 810 individuals from the same NIMH programme. They found a prevalence rate of auditory hallucinations of 4 per cent elicited by psychiatrists using the same D.I.S. Only a small minority of these people (16 per cent) met the D.I.S. criteria for a psychiatric diagnosis.

In the 1980s, Posey and Losch (1983) and Bentall and Slade (1985) developed a questionnaire assessing different aspects of experiencing auditory hallucinations. In both studies the authors found a number of normal students who claimed to have had hallucinatory experiences. More recently, Barret and Etheridge (1992) replicated Posey and Losch's (1983) study using their auditory hallucination questionnaire, and found the same frequencies as those reported by Posey and Losch on all listed items. Subsequently, they conducted a second study where they compared hallucinators and non-hallucinators on tendencies towards psychopathology. They used the Minnesota Multiphasic Personality Inventory (M.M.P.I.) for the ten standard clinical scales (Graham, 1987). They found as many people in the hallucinating group as in the non-hallucinating group with a scale score above seventy which Graham suggests indicates pathology. This result indicates that hearing voices cannot reasonably be explained only as the result of psychopathology.

HEARING VOICES IN PSYCHIATRIC ILLNESS

If hearing voices in itself is not the result of psychopathology, then we may expect that it would not be linked to a specific disease and would appear in a wide variety of psychiatric disorders and that the quality of the voices would not be related to specific diagnoses. In order to research this particular point, the authors made an inventory of a group of patients undergoing treatment at a community health centre in Maastricht, Holland. All patients were asked by their case manager (this being in most cases a Community Psychiatric nurse) to complete a questionnaire that included both open and closed questions that probed for experiences of hallucinations.

The total sample consisted of 288 patients of which 165 (57 per cent) were female. The mean age of the participants was 45 years (plus or minus 13 years), with a median age of 43 years. About one third of the population was diagnosed as having an affective disorder, one fifth with schizophrenia and the third largest diagnostic group was a personality disorder (see Table 8.1).

Twenty-eight percent (n = 81) of the population reported hearing voices over a prolonged period of time. The percentage found for the two major diagnostic groups, 53 per cent in schizophrenia and 28 per cent in affective disorders, were similar to those found by others (Landmark *et al.*, 1990; Goodwin and Jamison, 1990).

In this study, we also compared the quality of perceived hallucinations as related to these two major diagnostic groups. As Table 8.2 indicates,

Table 8.1 Auditory hallucinations per principal diagnosis in the total sample

	Total	No. of subjects who heard voices	
	n		%
Total population	288	81	28
schizophrenia	62	33	53
affective disorder	90	25	28
dissociation disorder	5	4	80
psychotic disorder (N.A.O)	17	7	41
personality disorder	48	6	13
other diagnosis	66	6	9

Table 8.2 A comparison of the quality of the voices between schizophrenia and affective disorder

Quality of voices	Schizophrenia		Affective disorders	
	n	%	n	%
via ears	24	80	16	70
in the head	19	63	15	65
in the body	3	11	1	4
outside the head	15	52	9	39
communicate with	14	47	8	36
from self	7	24	4	17
from outside self	28	93	18	78

there were no significant differences found between those diagnosed with schizophrenia and those with an affective disorder as far as the quality of voices was concerned.

We concluded that hearing voices is present in people with very different kinds of diagnoses and that qualitative characteristics of hallucinations are not specific to a particular psychiatric diagnosis.

COPING WELL AND COPING BADLY

When hearing voices in itself is not the result of psychopathology, nor is it specific in characteristics to any specific psychiatric illness, it is of interest to analyse the differences between people who can cope well with their voices and those who cannot.

In an earlier study the authors brought together a group of people who heard voices (Romme and Escher, 1989). We conducted this study because in our clinical approach we felt quite powerless in our attempts to assist people with auditory hallucinations and we did not feel able to help a number of sufferers sufficiently (a notion already reported as a result of previous research by Falloon and Talbot, 1981). Even when medication helps in diminishing anxiety or chaos, one must then continue to prescribe prophylactic medication, otherwise the voices, together with their accompanying hindrances, will in most cases reoccur. Many of our patients did not know how to cope well with their voices. As a result of these observations we looked round for a television talkshow which would be willing to help us explore the phenomenon more fully. A patient with auditory hallucinations recounted her story on this talkshow and requested that people experiencing hearing voices and who were coping well with them, telephone after the programme, as we were looking for individuals who would be able to help the patient cope better. The result was unexpected as more than 500 people hearing voices responded to our request. We followed this up by sending out a questionnaire in order to obtain more information concerning the characteristics of their voices, their medical history and most important for us, their ability to cope and the methods they used. As a result of this questionnaire we learned that there were quite a number of people who could cope well with their voices, but to our astonishment, we also received questionnaires from people hearing voices, who had never been a psychiatric patient. We were especially interested in exploring the coping methods used by these people. We decided to organise a conference so that people hearing voices could meet and exchange their experiences. This conference was held in Utrecht in 1987, and resulted in the formation of an organisation for people who heard voices. This organisation now has more than 1000 members. By meeting a large number of these people we have had the opportunity to interview both a number of good copers and bad copers about their voice experiences and coping methods. We would like to begin with a report on some of the data accumulated from the questionnaire comparing good and bad copers, and patients and non-patients (Romme *et al.*, 1992).

The questionnaire comprised thirty open-ended questions and was distributed amongst 450 people suffering from chronic auditory hallucinations or hearing voices. Of the 254 replies received, 186 were able to be used for analysis. It was doubtful as to whether thirteen of these respondents were actually experiencing true hallucinations therefore these were excluded. Of the remaining 173 respondents, fifty-eight reported an ability to cope with their voices.

Differences between good and bad copers existed in what we call the power structure between the voices and the person who hears them, as well as in the coping strategies that were used. Table 8.3 compares the power structure between those who said that they were able to cope well with the voices (group A) and the group who said they were not able to cope with the voices (group B).

Table 8.3 shows that those who could cope with their voices (Group A) experienced themselves as significantly stronger than the voices (72 per cent) while those who could not cope experienced the voices as being

Table 8.3 A comparison of power structure between groups A and B

	Group A coping +	Group B coping −
	58 (34%)	*115 (66%)*
Who is stronger?		
self	39 (72%)	40 (38%)
voice	5 (10%)	44 (42%)
otherwise	9 (16%)	20 (19%)
missing	5	11
		p < 0.001
Nature of voices		
positive	16 (30%)	10 (10%)
contradictory	14 (26%)	17 (16%)
negative	23 (43%)	75 (73%)
missing	5	13
		p <0. 001
Imperative hallucinations		
yes	10 (20%)	26 (24%)
no	38 (74%)	41 (38%)
sometimes	3 (6%)	41 (38%)
missing	7	7
		p < 0.001

Total N = 173

stronger. The most important differences between the two groups were:

- Those who could not cope (B) often experienced voices which were stronger than self.
- Those who could not cope (B) often experienced voices in a negative sense.
- Those who could cope (A) experienced less imperative voices.

We also found differences between the good (A) and the bad (B) copers, in the kind of coping strategies that were used. These are illustrated in Table 8.4. Those people who did not cope well with their voices (group B) used different coping strategies to those who could cope with their voices.

We also found differences in social circumstances between patients and non-patients which are shown in Table 8.5. The main differences were:

1. Non-patients were more likely to be married than patients.
2. Non-patients experienced or perceived more support than patients.
3. Non-patients were more likely to discuss their voices with people other than patients.

Table 8.4 Coping strategies comparing copers (A) and non-copers (B)

	Total	%	Group A		Group B	
			coping + total	%	coping – total	%
	173	100%	58	34%	115	66%
Distraction						
yes	42	(24%)	10	(26%)	32	(43%)
no	72	(42%)	9	(74%)	43	(57%)
missing	59	(34%)				
					$p < 0.05$	
Ignoring						
yes	54	(31%)	31	(56%)	23	(25%)
no	57	(33%)	21	(37%)	36	(39%)
sometimes	37	(21%)	4	(7%)	33	(36%)
missing	25	(14%)				
					$p < 0.001$	
Selective listening						
yes	30	(17%)	19	(46%)	11	(14%)
no	87	(50%)	22	(53%)	65	(85%)
missing	56	(33%)				
					$p < 0.001$	
Setting limits						
yes	45	(26%)	19	(48%)	25	(30%)
no	79	(46%)	20	(51%)	59	(70%)
missing	49	(28%)				
					$p < 0.001$	

Table 8.5 Social interactions in patients and non-patients

	Non-patients n = 70	Patients n = 103
Marital status	n = 58	n = 79
single	11 (19%)	30 (38%)
married	35 (60%)	31 (39%)
divorced	11 (19%)	15 (19%)
widowed	1 (2%)	3 (4%)
Perceived support	n = 70	n = 96
no	1 (2%)	47 (49%)
yes	69 (98%)	49 (51%)
Do others know about my voices ?		
	n = 70	n = 101
no	1 (2%)	15 (14%)
yes	69 (98%)	86 (86%)

The following summarises the differences we observed between copers and non-copers.

People who could cope with voices:

- experienced themselves as stronger;
- experienced more positive voices;
- experienced less imperative voices;
- set more limits to the voices;
- listened selectively to the voices;
- communicated more often about their voices.

People who could not cope with voices:

- experienced themselves as weaker;
- experienced more negative voices;
- experienced more imperative voices;
- did not dare to set limits to them;
- tried to escape from the voices by using more distraction techniques.

The most relevant differences between copers and non-copers may be interpreted as relating to feeling 'stronger' not only with respect to the voices, but also with respect to their environment, i.e. feeling less threatened and more supported in the environment.

EMPOWERING PEOPLE

Receiving support and having the opportunity to talk about voices with other people appear to be associated with them being accepted by others.

As a result of the conference in 1987 for people who hear voices, it became clear that all of the people who heard voices experienced problems with the societal taboo factor associated with them. It is difficult to talk about voices with others without being looked at in a strange way, so therefore empowering people who hear voices will have to take place on an individual and societal level.

Our approach addresses both levels. As a way of stimulating societal changes, we organise annual conferences, information meetings in psychiatric hospitals and conduct interviews with patients and non-patients on television and in popular magazines. In the following case studies we have outlined our approaches on an individual level.

CASE STUDIES

We have developed an interview schedule that has allowed us to explore the dynamics of the relationship between the voices and the life history of patients who hear voices. We are currently investigating this relationship more systematically in a study that includes three groups of people hearing voices: those who have a diagnosis of schizophrenia, those who have a diagnosis of dissociative disorder and those who have never received a psychiatric diagnosis, but who hear voices. The results of this comparison are not yet available. In this chapter we will provide a description of some cases to illustrate the dynamics that exist between hearing voices and the life history of the person experiencing them. The following examples illustrate different categories of life influences which we have found to be related to the onset of voices.

1. Intolerable or unsatisfying living situations
2. Recent traumas
3. Aspirations or ideals
4. Childhood trauma
5. Emotional intolerance and control

When discussing these examples, the following areas are of special interest in understanding the dynamics of the interaction between voices and the life history of the person hearing them:

• the identity of the voices
• the characteristics of their communication with the person, e.g. the way of talking, the age of voices and what they say
• what triggers the appearance or disappearance of the voices
• what important change in the individual's life was related to the onset of hearing voices
• the characteristics of a person's upbringing and childhood including any special experiences that occurred in that period.

144

Intolerable or unsatisfying living circumstances

A 16-year-old young woman heard a voice that said unpleasant things to her. It was a male voice who called himself Erichem. In the background she also heard other voices who wanted to help her, but these voices were not very powerful. In addition, she heard voices of relatives that had passed away. She saw them and could communicate with them. They included her grandmother, her grandfather and her uncle. Sometimes she had prophecies and sometimes she saw coloured auras around people.

The young woman had a problem only with the unpleasant voice, which angered her. This voice first appeared when she was 14 and having problems with her father. Her father was very concerned with her performance and wanted to control her life. The voice of Erichem treated her in the same manner as her father. Whenever she was tense the voice appeared, but when she was relaxed or, for example, working at school, the voice would disappear. The voice of Erichem spoke directly to her and also spoke about her. The voices of the family members who had passed away spoke directly to her and gave her advice or offered solutions to existing problems.

The following interpretations were made relating to her voices and life history. The identity of the voice did not mean anything to her. She could not imagine a person around it or link the voice to anyone in particular. The voice was completely identified through the characteristics of its behaviour. This was more or less the same relationship that she had towards her father. The relationship was dominated by his behaviour and did not have the characteristics of a personal relationship like the one she shared with her mother. Erichem's dialogue made her angry. This was also the case with her father, but expressing anger towards him was not possible.

The following provided the starting point for treatment, beginning with the confirmation of the good relationship with her mother, together with increasing her coping strategies towards the anger of Erichem. The mother sometimes advised her on how to cope with Erichem's behaviour, which she achieved, because the mother could cope more easily with the aggression of the father than the daughter. In the next step, it was important to establish, with the help of the mother, a more personal relationship with the father rather than a relationship based on the experiences of her upbringing.

This meant that the father also had to become more personally involved with both women. Additional steps were taken to ensure that the daughter would no longer act as an intermediary in the poor relationship between the mother and father. Direct psychodynamic interpretations did not make a lot of sense in this therapeutic approach. Looking for better ways of dealing with daily living problems was more effective and made more sense. This may be particularly important for young people in their development into adulthood.

145

Recent trauma

Hearing voices following the death of a loved one is not uncommon (Frantz, 1984). One usually hears the voice of that specific person. This can happen for a short period of time or, in some cases, it can linger on. This is mostly dependent upon the problems encountered during the mourning process. It is less commonly known that voices can appear following other kinds of trauma, e.g. divorce or loss of a job. The following is an example:

Monique was a 30-year-old woman who was fired from her job and felt that she had been treated in an unpleasant way. Losing her job left her with a strong feeling of helplessness. She was so ashamed about what had happened to her that this made it difficult for her to talk about it. After some time she began to notice that when she sat in a cafe, for example, she would hear people seated at the table behind her talking about her and discussing what had happened to her.

She heard people say things about her in the exact voice of the person in the cafe. She found this so threatening, that after a brief period she would leave the situation. Her reaction went further than thinking people were talking about her: she clearly heard what they said about her. The identity of the people around her did not change, only the things that they were saying and how they related to her problem.

We made the following interpretation. The identities of the voices were those of people around her. This fitted in with the trauma of losing her job. She had lost her job because people from another firm had been gossiping about her. What the voices said also fitted in with the trauma because they were talking about what had happened to her. The trauma of losing her job was the change in her life which triggered the voices.

The following intervention and strategies were utilised. A direct explanation of the relationship between the voices and the loss of her job did not help and was not accepted by Monique initially. Information was provided regarding the nature of her experiences. While participating in a self-help group she discovered that she was not the only one to have had such experiences. This opened up her interest in her voices and helped to diminish the shame she was experiencing. The main issue in therapy was then to help Monique to get up the nerve to look for a new job. The voices almost completely disappeared when she started to apply for, and finally found, a new job.

Aspirations and ideals

In this category we placed those people who hear voices which are easily related to certain aspirations or ideals. Examples of this are when people use their voices to guide them when they have a difficult decision to make, and also when people strive for ideals that are not possible to achieve, e.g.

146

denying their sexuality. Here we provide an example of somebody whose voices confront him with difficulties in attaining certain desired goals.

This man was married and 27 years old when he came to our rehabilitation department. He had started to hear voices in his head and also sometimes through his ears. The voices were men and women talking to each other. He did not recognise the voices as those of people he knew. His own thoughts were repressed by the voices so that when they were there he could not think. He wanted to get rid of the voices because they mostly consisted of critical comments. The voices mainly occurred in stressful situations. Those situations were specially related to his training for an administrative education. The voices in those situations worsened his own negative thoughts about himself. He had doubts about his possibilities to follow this education and the voices confirmed these doubts in an exaggerated way. The voices were absent when he was alone or with his wife. This was confirmed by a research method called *experience sampling* (de Vries *et al.*, 1990).

The changes in his life situation when he first heard voices were not clear. We made the following interpretation. The voices did not belong to anyone special, they had no clear identity and they destroyed his own thinking. Thus, we made the interpretation that the voices confronted him with his own doubts about his education. The voices may have been right. The voices may have been more realistic than his own ideal to proceed and finish his training successfully.

In therapy this is a difficult dilemma, because it has consequences for the person's professional life and labour possibilities. The therapist dealt with this by stimulating him to formulate his own opinion about the things the voices were telling him. It took some time before the therapist, in discussion with the man, reached the conclusion that his training was too difficult. He improved, i.e. the voices reduced in frequency, after he stopped his training course. At the same time he was offered an unpaid job as a concierge at a school, which he came to like very much. He had to give up his original aspiration, but by doing so the quality of his life was augmented.

Childhood trauma in combination with emotional control

The best known trauma after which hearing voices occurs is the experience of incest. The research of Ensink (1992), showed that 27 per cent of incest victims researched heard voices later in their lives. It was striking that this phenomenom was most likely to occur when the trauma took place before the age of 7. As there are other kinds of childhood traumas associated with hearing voices, we have chosen here to provide an example of development of voices following trauma not specifically related to incest.

A young woman began to hear voices after her fourteenth birthday. When she reached age 23, the voices began to worsen and her behaviour

147

towards the voices began to change. From that time, she began to hear voices that read her mind. This occurred two times a week, sometimes lasted for up to eight hours and took place on Wednesdays and Sundays. While in this state, she was unable to do anything. In the beginning the voices were female. Prior to the moment that the voices began to worsen, she had experienced some problems at a female student club. During her introduction for membership she had been confronted with sexual subjects that disturbed her. Afterwards, she was afraid that she had acted in a ridiculous manner and this resulted in her not returning to the student club. Her sensitivity towards issues of sexuality originated from her earlier life. Her mother had been a psychiatric patient and always expressed herself in a very rude and negative way about sexuality. Thus, as a child the young woman decided never to become sexually involved. Up until the time we saw her she had managed to avoid sexual relationships completely.

We made the following interpretation. The young woman could not say that the voices had any identity. We interpreted the voices as being her own mind telling herself what she was thinking. The onset of voices was connected to her confrontation with sexuality. The first episode of hearing voices occurred when she was around 14, which was also the beginning of her menstruation cycle. The second occurrence, when it began to worsen, was after she was confronted with the sexuality problem at the student club.

For this reason we decided to confront her about her decision not to deal with sexuality as we concluded that the voices were confronting her with this problem anyway. We also made this decision because she was slipping more and more into a patient role. The day after the confrontation she had sex for the first time with a boy she hardly knew. She became psychotic. We supported her, but also continued to confront her. We were able to do this because we had informed all therapists involved. After a few months she decided to change her attitude. Today she is married and she has developed into a much more independent person. She is once again in charge of herself, although every now and then she hears the voices but has developed a much more independent attitude towards them.

CONCLUSIONS

What we have shown with these examples is that the voices know the person with whom they are communicating extremely well; they usually say things that are especially relevant for the person hearing them and usually are related to their problems. The voices usually refer to an unsolved problem in daily life, and/or emotions related to a trauma that has not yet been resolved, or problems that are connected to earlier traumas or unrealised ideals that, in some cases, are impossible to realise.

In treatment, it is not relevant to reject the voices but to stimulate the curiosity of the person hearing the voices about their content. As long as the person hearing the voices reacts only in an emotional way, it will be difficult to stimulate curiosity. This is a difficult process to accomplish. One possibility is the focusing technique, as described by Bentall *et al.* (1994) which is described in more detail in Chapter 3. Besides focusing on characteristics of the voices, the kind of relationship that exists between the person and the voices and the possibilities of changing these relationships, it is also important to work on the problems that the person hearing voices is confronted with in their daily life.

Our experience with people hearing voices is that if the total attention in therapy is focused on treating the psychiatric illness, problems in daily life as expressed by the voices will not be solved. The final objective is not only to influence the methods used in coping with the voices but to change the manner in which he or she copes with their problems.

REFERENCES

Barret, T. R. and Etheridge, J. B. (1992) 'Verbal hallucinations in Normals I: people who hear voices', *Applied Cognitive Psychology* 6: 379–87.

Bentall, R. P., Haddock, G. and Slade, P. D. (1994) 'Cognitive–behaviour therapy for persistent auditory hallucinations: From theory to therapy', *Behavior Therapy* 25: 51–66.

Bentall, R. P. and Slade, P. D. (1985) 'Reliability of a scale measuring disposition towards hallucinations: a brief report', *Personality and Individual Differences* 6: 527–9.

Eaton, W. W., Romanoski, A., Anthony, J. C. and Nestadt, G. (1991) 'Screening for psychosis in the general population with a self-report interview', *Journal of Nervous and Mental Disease* 179: 689–93.

Ensink, B. J. (1992) *Confusing Realities: a Study on Child Sexual Abuse and Psychiatric Symptoms*, Amsterdam: Free University Press.

Falloon, I. R. H. and Talbot, R. E. (1981) 'Persistent auditory hallucination: coping mechanisms and implications for management', *Psychological Medicine 11*: 329–39.

Frantz, T. T. (1984) 'Helping parents whose children have died', *Family Therapy Collections* 8: 11–26.

Goodwin, K. and Jamison, K. R. (1990) *Manic Depressive Illness*, New York: Oxford University Press.

Graham, J. R. (1987) *The MMPI: A Practical Guide*, 2nd edition, New York: Oxford University Press.

Landmark, J., Merkskey, Z., Cernousky, Z. and Helmes, E. (1990) 'The positive trial of schizophrenic symptoms. Its statistical properties and its relationship to thirteen traditional diagnostic systems', *British Journal of Psychiatry* 156: 388–94.

Posey, T. B. and Losch, M. E. (1983) 'Auditory hallucinations of hearing voices in 375 normal subjects', *Imagination, Cognition and Personality* 3: 99–113.

Robins, L. H., Helrer, J. E., Croughan, J. and Ratcliff, K. A. (1981) 'National Institute for Mental Health Diagnostic Interview Schedule: its history, characteristic and validity', *Archives of General Psychiatry* 38: 381–9.

Romme, M. A. J. and Escher, A. D. M. A. C. (1989) 'Hearing voices', *Schizophrenia Bulletin* 15: 209–16.

Romme, M. A. J., Honig, A., Noordhoorn, E. O., Escher, A. D. M. A. C. (1992) 'Coping with hearing voices, an emancipatory approach', *British Journal of Psychiatry* 16: 99–103.

Sidgewick, H. A. (1894) 'Report of the census of hallucinations', *Proceedings of the Society for Psychical Research* 26: 25–6.

Tien, A. Y. (1991) 'Distribution of hallucinations in the population', *Social Psychiatry and Psychiatric Epidemiology* 26: 287–92.

de Vries, M. W., Dijkman-Caes, C. I. M. and Delespaul, P. A. E. G. (1990) *The Sampling of Experience, Comorbidity of Anxiety and Mood Disorders*, Washington DC: Maser and Cloninger.

9

PSYCHOLOGICAL TREATMENTS FOR NEGATIVE SYMPTOMS

Lorna Hogg

THE NATURE OF NEGATIVE SYMPTOMS

Clinicians and researchers have grappled for many years with the puzzle of negative symptoms. Given that the term refers to the absence of normal functioning, they are by definition elusive to identify or measure. The difficulty is neatly illustrated by the exasperated parent struggling to tease apart the effects of negative symptoms, adolescence and emerging adulthood in their child recently diagnosed as having schizophrenia. This begs an age-old question – what is normal functioning? – to which there is no simple response. Unfortunately, negative symptoms have also proven remarkably resistant to pharmacological treatment, and therapeutic pessimism abounds both in individuals debilitated by these very unpleasant symptoms, and in clinicians. Sadly, few areas of functioning are unaffected. Cognitive functioning tends to be markedly impaired, the ability to feel and express emotion diminishes, speech skills deteriorate, and people appear to have no energy or motivation even to carry out activities they previously really enjoyed. It is unusual for people to be affected in only one of these areas. The usual pattern is for some degree of overall impairment. Consideration of the nature of these difficulties quickly enables an appreciation of the devastating impact on the quality of life of the sufferer, and the task facing sufferers, families and clinicians attempting to improve the situation.

A list of the main symptoms and signs usually called 'negative' is given in Table 9.1, but a case description probably gives a better picture of the true nature and awfulness of symptoms.

Susan is a 54-year-old woman with a diagnosis of chronic schizophrenia. She has lived on a long-stay hospital ward for eight years. She usually misses breakfast as she has great difficulty getting out of bed in the morning, despite repeated prompts from staff. Once up, she will often fail to wash, and will dress in the same clothes as the previous day whether or not they are clean. Her day is largely spent

151

sitting on the ward, smoking and staring into space, or lying on top of her bed, if she has access to her room. Her movements are slow, and if spoken to she will either fail to respond at all or respond very briefly and in a monotonic way after a considerable time delay. She seldom expresses any emotion and her face appears blank. She is often incontinent of urine and will sit in wet clothes until noticed by ward staff.

It used to be thought that negative symptoms were by-products of people with schizophrenia being looked after in large-scale, dehumanising institutions. The advent of community care was believed to be the answer to the problem. Unfortunately this has not proved to be the case. Community care has not provided the answer. Many severely disabled patients have simply transferred their problems to group homes and bed and breakfast accommodation. Here, opportunities to take part in community-based activities may, in theory, be more prevalent, but the self-motivation and necessary encouragement are no greater. Creer and Wing (1974), in their survey of the needs of people with schizophrenia living in the community, found that the most frequent needs were for treatment of negative symptoms and social performance difficulties.

Table 9.1 Long-term impairments in schizophrenia

Restricted expression of emotion
Limited range of facial expression; poor eye contact; loss of expressive gestures; lack of inflections of speech; poor emotional responsivity

Speech impairment
Poverty of speech; limited content of speech; blocking; increased latency to respond

Underactivity/apathy
Loss of energy; poor self-care; difficulty persisting with activities; lack of initiative; slowed movements

Loss of pleasure
Loss of interest in sex; abandonment of recreational interests and activities; loss of interest in friendships; loss of intimacy

Attentional impairment
Poor concentration; distractibility

Description of a second case illustrates the pervasive nature of negative symptoms even in a community context. Jason is 32 years of age. He developed schizophrenia while at university at the age of 20 years. Since then he has had three admissions to hospital. Between admissions, he lives in a shared group home, where he has his own bedroom. Despite taking maintenance neuroleptic medication, he continues to experience some residual symptoms, notably persecutory delusions. He believes that people dislike him, and as a result repeatedly snub him or laugh at him. His worst fear is that people so actively dislike him that they will physically attack him. He states that in response to this fear, he spends most of his day in his bedroom, lying on his bed. He avoids using the shared kitchen at times when others might be there and never goes into the sitting room. He has lost his place at a craft centre because of failure to attend. Despite being a sociable person at university, with many friends, he states that he now has great difficulty relating to people. He finds it difficult to think of topics of conversation. He is aware of looking blank when people speak to him and being unable to respond enthusiastically. He tends to listen to others speaking rather than reciprocate but even then his concentration wanes. He no longer finds activities he used to enjoy to be pleasurable and has therefore lost interest in them.

The tenacious nature of these symptoms, even in the face of what would appear to be major environmental change (community care), lent itself to the argument that perhaps negative symptoms are the outward signs of an essentially dementing condition. The belief that schizophrenia is a dementing disorder is certainly not a new contention. However, the failure to find neuronal loss (Crow et al., 1984), increasing ventricle size (Gattaz et al., 1991) or gliosis (Roberts and Bruton, 1990) in the brains of people diagnosed as having schizophrenia would not support this. Also, the discovery of reduced blood flow in the frontal cortex of people with schizophrenia at an early stage in the disorder, and before the commencement of drug therapy, would suggest that the disorder may be developmental rather than the product of dementia. The failure to see improvement in negative symptoms with the move to community living most likely has a much less pathological explanation and that is the continuation of institutional practices in these new environments. Allen et al. (1989) compared two rehabilitation facilities for the long-term mentally ill: a hospital unit and a purpose-built hostel in the community. They found the hospital unit to be more individually orientated in staff practices and attitudes. Staff were also more optimistic in the hospital setting.

Much of the research to date in the field of negative symptoms has been about diagnostic specificity, rather than treatment efficacy. In addition to the search for an organic basis, other areas which have drawn attention are: the nature of the link with positive symptoms, comparison with the effects of drug treatment and the relationship with depression. The distinction between positive and negative symptoms in schizophrenia is longstanding, and has been dated back to the work of Kraepelin at the beginning of this century (Wing, 1989). Although recent support has been shown for a further subdivision of positive symptoms into two categories (Liddle, 1987;

Arndt *et al.*, 1991) evidence would support the retention of negative symptoms as a separate syndrome. Sommers (1985) discusses three stages required to demonstrate the validity of a syndrome: that the signs and symptoms occur together, that they can be operationally defined and thereby reliably identified and rated, and that the syndrome has predictive power. Evidence would so far suggest that negative symptoms can be viewed as a separate syndrome.

Andreasen and Olsen (1982) found high internal consistency for negative symptoms. They also found that, relative to patients with positive symptoms, those with negative symptoms had poorer pre-morbid adjustment, lower overall functioning, more impaired cognitive functioning and evidence of structural brain changes. There are now a variety of scales for the assessment of negative symptoms (Krawiecka *et al.*, 1977; Andreasen, 1981). Negative symptoms have been found to be highly predictive of outcome, generally predicting poorer outcome (Andreasen *et al.*, 1985; Pogue-Geile and Harrow, 1985). Baron *et al.* (1992) evaluated the relationship of positive and negative symptoms to the familial transmission of schizophrenia. They found evidence of a reduced risk of developing schizophrenia in first degree relatives of probands with predominant negative symptoms, thus lending further support to the validity of a separate negative syndrome.

Crow (1980) tried to relate positive and negative symptoms to different underlying pathological processes: negative symptoms to structural brain abnormalities and positive to increased dopamine receptors. This model has been criticised as oversimplified. In particular, it is considered insufficient to explain some symptoms such as stereotypies (Frith, 1992) and mixtures of positive and negative symptoms as well as changes in phenomenology over time (Andreasen, 1989). There is some evidence, however, that negative symptoms are selectively associated with structural brain changes such as ventricular enlargement (Andreasen *et al.*, 1982; Marks and Luchins, 1990).

Of particular interest, especially in relation to treatment, is the observation by some researchers and clinicians of the phenomenon of secondary negative symptoms (Andreasen, 1989). Although not well researched, it does appear that some patients develop negative symptoms as a way of coping with distressing positive symptoms. For example, many patients withdraw socially in response to reality distortion such as the perceptual distortion of faces, or persecutory delusions (as illustrated by the case 'Jason' described above). This has been suggested as a possible explanation for why negative symptoms occurring in the acute phase of illness may differ from those occurring at other times in terms of correlation with other variables and prognostic value (Barnes, 1989).

The bradykinesia and other abnormal movements observed in people on long-term neuroleptic medication have raised concerns about the possibility of some negative symptoms being directly caused by medication.

There is no widespread support for this from research. Many people have negative symptoms before the emergence of positive symptoms and subsequent treatment. The view has been expressed that people who already have negative symptoms may be more vulnerable to drug side-effects. This might be because movement disorders induced by drugs and the movement disorders of negative symptoms have common underlying organic structures (Barnes and Liddle, 1985).

Depression commonly occurs in the context of schizophrenia. Birchwood et al. (1993) reviewed the literature on incidence and found figures varying from 20 per cent during the year following an acute episode to 65 per cent period prevalence (Johnson, 1988). This association has attracted particular attention because of the high incidence of suicide in this group (up to 10 per cent). Many theories have been proposed to explain the co-existence of depression and schizophrenia. It has been suggested that depression in this client group may be purely a consequence of drug therapy, a secondary reaction to the debilitating effects of the illness and its implications, or an integral part of the illness. An additional possibility is that negative symptoms are signs of depression rather than an independent phenomenon. The similarity in presentation between what are called negative symptoms in people with schizophrenia and depression is an obvious one. This may include reduced and/or slowed movements, poverty of speech, loss of pleasure, and social withdrawal. Research into the relationship between depression and negative symptoms would not support a common association between the two phenomena. Hirsch and colleagues (1989) found a prevalence rate of only 7 per cent in a population of chronic patients with a diagnosis of schizophrenia. Ragin et al. (1989) found poverty of speech to have a different time course in schizophrenia compared with depression: they found it to increase with time in schizophrenia and decrease or remain stable in depression. Also, there is evidence that some features commonly associated with depression are not commonly found in schizophrenics rated as having negative symptoms. These include depressed mood, somatic concern, guilt, tension, hopelessness, suicidal ideas, self-depreciation and early wakening (Kulhara et al. 1989; Norman and Malla, 1991).

From the research evidence, apparently negative symptoms are not merely depression by another name. However, given the similarity in presentation, it is possible for depression to be mistaken for negative symptoms in some individuals. Care needs to be taken in clinical work with people who have schizophrenia to assess for the presence of depression and to clarify the nature of any relationship with negative symptoms.

The current position in understanding negative symptoms is that although some people do develop negative symptoms in response to positive symptoms, some do become depressed, and others experience movement disorders akin to negative symptoms following drug treatment, none of these factors is sufficient to fully explain the presence of this crippling condition. The likelihood of organic impairment has, unfortunately, to some extent fostered therapeutic pessimism. This is regrettable because organic impairment is clearly only one of many factors that may be contributing to keeping someone in a debilitated state. Other factors, such as those mentioned above, may be more amenable to intervention. Also, psychological treatments have contributed much to the rehabilitation of people with brain damage.

In relation to assessment and treatment, there is much to be said for dispensing with diagnostic purity and instead working with symptoms. Such an approach is consistent with psychological treatments which are essentially empirical, where direction in treatment is based on detailed assessment of the individual and careful monitoring of progress.

UNDERSTANDING PEOPLE WITH NEGATIVE SYMPTOMS

Although the interview is well established as the primary method of cognitive–behavioural assessment, its use with negatively impaired patients is much less well established. The nature of negative symptoms can make it difficult and very time consuming to unearth important information. The benefits of perseverance cannot be overstated. Interventions based on a good understanding of the patient enable much more effective problem management than purely prescriptive approaches which are relatively more common with this client group.

It is crucial when working with someone who has negative symptoms to take the time to build a strong trusting relationship. Many people with negative symptoms may have had very unpleasant experiences of being compulsorily admitted to, and detained in, hospital. They may also have residual psychotic symptoms which may include an element of paranoia. They may have spent many years in a low-staffed long-stay ward where, unless they presented a threat to safety, it is likely that they received little attention for their negative symptoms. For all these reasons it is possible that the therapist may be perceived very suspiciously. It is important to allow time for the patient to express concerns or doubts about the therapy or therapist, and periodically to review how the patient feels about continuing in therapy. Giving the patient this degree of control over the therapy can have an important impact on the therapeutic relationship. The importance of collaboration is established from the outset.

Interview techniques need to be adapted for patients with negative symptoms. The pace of the interview needs to be much slower, although it is important to keep up the emotional tone to engage attention as much as possible. Patients with negative symptoms need plenty of time to respond. Questions need to be open rather than closed and stated clearly and simply:

twenty to thirty minutes is a reasonable maximum duration for the interview, but this needs to be flexible depending on the individual and circumstances. Frequent, short, fairly informal interviews are most effective with very impaired patients, perhaps partly because in making such an obvious commitment, the interviewer is showing interest and concern.

The function of the interview should be to gain a clear understanding of the patient's current difficulties as they perceive them. This might include how the problems have developed over time, how they interact with each other, and important contextual factors (e.g. living arrangements, resources which may be used for overcoming the problems, reactions of others, etc). Take care to assess the patient's thoughts and beliefs about their symptoms. This may reveal associated thoughts of a depressive nature. Alternatively, the negative symptoms may have an important function for the patient, such as a coping strategy for managing residual psychotic symptoms. It is crucial to agree goals for therapy with the patient. It is very common for therapists to make assumptions with negative symptoms about what would be a good outcome of therapy for the patient, usually based on their own values. MacCarthy et al. (1986) demonstrated that patients often have clear reasons for not performing tasks such as that they perceive them as too difficult or unimportant. It is important to explore such reasons in therapy. This may lead to therapy goals such as challenging the patient's belief that they could not manage, skills training, or considering further the pros and cons of performing the task. Obviously such further exploration would have to be a collaborative exercise to which the patient felt committed.

As with cognitive–behaviour therapy (CBT) in other conditions, assessment of the patient should lead to a preliminary formulation. This will enable a discussion about useful short-term goals for therapy planned to test hypotheses generated in the formulation. It is important that the formulation is shared with the patient and that they are given a copy to take home and consider further. With negatively impaired patients it is particularly important to back up any verbal discussion with written material, as attention and memory are often quite impaired. It is helpful to use a therapy notebook or folder in which patients can be encouraged to note down important learning points covered in therapy and any assignments agreed as homework. If the patient is agreeable, it can be particularly beneficial to tape record the sessions and give the patient the tape to take home to listen to before the next session. All these strategies both help the patient to process important information and add significance to the therapy.

THE IMPORTANCE OF CONTEXTUAL FACTORS

The importance of the milieu in which patients live is well established. Changing the milieu in a way which makes it more therapeutic has been one of the most effective interventions for people with negative symptoms (Wing and Brown, 1970). It is often quite illuminating to think what it would be like to be a patient and consider which aspects of the environment would make tasks easier or more difficult. The following factors might affect how likely any of us would be to persist in daily washing: basic washroom facilities, lack of privacy and personalisation, unavailability of soap and towels, insufficient money to afford pleasant toiletries, unclear expectations, poor models of self-care, uncomfortable or unappealing clothes to change into, and lack of compliments from peers. This is an extreme picture but it should highlight some factors that need to be considered when questioning why patients do not take better care of themselves. The availability of privacy, personal-isation, flexibility to accommodate individual preference, adequate and accessible tools for the job, clear expectations, adequate instructions, clear prompts, clear and immediate feedback are all crucial to consider in assessing reasons for absence of functioning.

Some of the above factors refer to the attitudes and behaviour of others. Much has been learned about the importance of the content and tone of communication between relatives and family members suffering from schizophrenia (see Chapter 10). Recently this knowledge has been applied to the interactions between mental health care staff and people suffering from schizophrenia living in supported accommodation (Moore et al., 1992). Moore and colleagues found that the clinical poverty syndrome and socially embarrassing or difficult behaviour were the two categories of residents' functioning most often criticised by staff working in these settings. Looking after people with severely disabling negative symptoms in the long term certainly presents a major challenge for staff. Besides this, other pressures, both internal (beliefs about inadequacy in helping people change etc) and external (clinical audit procedures, visits from managers or inspection teams) may have a deleterious effect in increasing stress in staff, and reducing tolerance. Clearly frustration and intolerance in staff can only have an unhelpful effect on staff–resident relationships and there-fore the likelihood that the resident will change. When criticised, most people comply less. Care programmes for severely impaired people need to be sensitive to the needs of direct care staff and establish a milieu conducive to discussing frustrations openly and using this to inform care planning. Ranz et al. (1991) describe an interesting residential programme based on the psychoeducational work with families which attempts to modify the negative aspects of both staff–resident and resident–resident interactions.

Another contextual factor to consider is the roles of others in the residential or day care setting. Family members and professionals often take over the roles of people with negative symptoms for many very sound reasons. However, this can have the unfortunate consequence of making it easier for the person with negative impairments to remain inactive. A good example is the employment of housekeepers in supported long-stay settings. It is common to hear patients say "I don't see why I should tidy up, they're paid to do it".

There is no simple checklist of factors to consider in understanding people with negative symptoms. What is needed is time, and careful, thoughtful analyses of what might be important for each individual in their particular context. Only once this has been achieved should intervention be attempted.

INCREASING ACTIVITY LEVELS

Reduced activity, lethargy, poor motivation and social withdrawal are probably the most common negative symptoms, and certainly some of the most troublesome for carers to cope with. They also have implications for other problems. For example, if people are not able to get out of bed, leave the house, join in social activities, then they are less likely to feel that they are achieving, less able to develop and maintain friendships, and much less likely to experience any pleasure. Hopelessness and worthlessness are common problems in schizophrenia (Drake and Cotton, 1986) both of which are often made worse by inactivity. For these reasons, it is important to target inactivity early on in treatment, where this exists.

Depression may not necessarily accompany inactivity, or may not be readily apparent. Cognitive–behavioural techniques for activating depressed patients are, however, very helpful for people with negative symptoms also. These techniques include: activity scheduling, rating mastery and pleasure, and graded task assignment.

Activity scheduling is one of the simplest and most useful techniques for helping patients with negative symptoms. It can be used in several ways. Initially, patients can be encouraged to note down in a diary what they do during each day. This is usually done hourly, but for very impaired patients it may be sufficient to get them to make a list each day of things they did, preferably as they did them. Table 9.2 is an example of an activity schedule kept by a patient with negative impairments. Such recording is a useful way of both engaging the patient in a constructive activity, and obtaining a baseline which can be used to plan increasing activities or to monitor progress. Less-impaired patients can often manage this task on their own each day after careful verbal instruction, supported by written or tape recorded instructions. More impaired patients will need help to complete this task. This may require a carer sitting down with them at intervals during each day, or at the end of the day, to record as accurately as possible what they did during that day. It is vitally important for success that the patient sees this task as important. As with depressed patients, a common problem that can interfere with activity scheduling is hopelessness. Tasks the patient attempts may be seen as trivial, or activities accomplished dismissed as achieving nothing compared to past performance or future

159

Table 9.2 Weekly activity schedule

	M	T	W	T	F	S	S
9–10	asleep	asleep	asleep	asleep	asleep	asleep	asleep
10–11	watched telly	asleep	watched telly	asleep	asleep	asleep	asleep
11–12	cooked meal	watched telly	watched telly	asleep	asleep	asleep	asleep
12–1	went to day centre	at day centre	at day centre	watched telly	watched telly	watched telly	watched telly
1–2	working at day centre	"	"	talked to friends	went to club	made a phone call	went to shops
2–3	"	"	hospital appointment	watched telly	at club	watched telly	watched telly
3–4	"	"	"	cashed cheque in town	"	dozed	"
4–5	talked to friend	watched telly	watched telly	watched telly	watched telly	"	"
5–6	watched telly	drank tea	dozed	dozed	"	"	had shower
6–7	"	cooked meal	"	"	dozed	watched telly	cleaned floor
7–8	went shopping	"	cooked meal	cooked meal	talked to friend	"	watched telly
8–12	cooked meal	"	went to bed	watched telly	watched telly	got meal	went to bed

aspirations. Patients need to be encouraged to see the task as a means to an end, and initially to evaluate progress relative to their starting point not ultimate goal.

Once a baseline has been established, the activity schedule can be used to add structure to a patient's day. Activities can be planned in advance and the outcome of an increase in activities recorded. Any planned activities should be agreed collaboratively with the patient so that they are seen as worthwhile. It is pointless to encourage patients to attend a day centre or ward-based activity programme that they do not see as pleasurable or helpful. This can often be a reason for poor attendance at ward activity sessions set up without consultation with prospective attenders.

Activity schedules are also a good way of helping patients to identify those activities that give them the greatest sense of achievement and pleasure. Patients are asked to rate, usually on a scale of 0–10, the degree of mastery and pleasure they obtain from each activity they engage in. For more impaired patients, or at the beginning of therapy, simply rating whether activities elicited any sense of mastery or pleasure can be sufficient. Patients can then be encouraged to focus selectively on those activities that rate highly on each of these dimensions.

It is important to work very gradually in scheduling new activities, perhaps planning new activities for only once or twice in the week. Many patients with negative symptoms may have cognitive impairments or have had years of inactivity; it takes time to educate them into therapy. The difficulty of tasks should also be increased gradually. For example, if a patient's ultimate goal is to talk more with the other residents in a group home, then setting an initial target of sitting in the television room for the duration of one programme each night when other residents are there may be a suitable and achievable initial target in a graded task hierarchy.

Activity scheduling can be helpful in achieving the following main aims:

1. demonstrating to the patient that change is possible, even if slow; and
2. helping the patient to achieve things that they may perceive as very difficult or impossible.

Operant learning theory has made an important contribution to the management of negative impairments. It has emphasised the importance of contingency management, through the use of effective cues for behaviour and appropriate reinforcement (Matson, 1980). Interventions based on increasing the rewards inherent in performing activities as a way of increasing motivation are well documented. The most well-known example of this is the ward-based Token Economy regime, in which performance of prespecified target behaviours is immediately followed by reinforcement of a social and tangible nature (Kazdin, 1982). The effectiveness of reinforcement in increasing motivation to become more active is important to bear in mind in working with individual patients also. Activities which

161

bring immediate, as opposed to delayed, rewards are particularly important to include in scheduling activities. Such activities may be identified
through mastery and pleasure ratings, reviewing activities the patient used
to find pleasurable, or the therapist may have to be quite active in making
suggestions. Other less obvious rewards can also be used, such as the
therapist contacting the patient immediately after a planned activity to
review and praise progress.

To maximise the likelihood of success, the therapist should discuss in
detail with the patient the steps necessary to carry out a particular activity.
For example, if the patient plans to visit the swimming pool they will need
to know how to get there, the times that the pool will be open, what to do
with their clothes once they have changed, etc. On careful consideration, it
becomes clear that many activities are very complex and require careful
and detailed planning. It may be sufficient for some patients to begin by
checking the swimming pool and bus timetable and leave actually going
there until a later stage in therapy. Patients should be encouraged to think
through the stages involved in each activity and anticipate as many things
that could go wrong as possible. The therapist can then work with the patient
to generate ways that they might prevent these happening, or cope if they
did. In breaking tasks down, it can be necessary to break down the actions
involved in performing the task. For example, a patient may be encouraged
to get out of bed by listing the sequence of actions needed such as:

1. open eyes,
2. throw back the covers,
3. swing legs to the side of the bed,
4. pull body into a sitting position on the side of the bed, and
5. stand up.

Some patients find it helpful to have such a preprepared list, or cue card,
with them when they need to perform the activity in question, for example,
on the bedside table to help them get up in the morning. It may even be
necessary to go a stage further and encourage patients to verbally direct
their limbs to move, at times of excessive retardation. Cue cards can also be
used to help patients challenge self-defeating thoughts, such as "It's too
difficult", "I won't be able to do it", "There's no point", "I won't enjoy it
anyway". The therapist can help the patient generate helpful answers to
these negative thoughts that will enable them to continue with the planned
activity. For example, a patient who is undermined by the thought "I won't
be able to do it" could be encouraged to respond to such a thought by saying
to themselves "I don't know that I won't be able to do it until I give it a try.
I'll just take it nice and easy. Even if I do get stuck, at least I tried and I'll be
able to tell my therapist exactly where I got stuck so that we can work out
how to sort the problem out for next time." Bentall *et al.* (1987) evaluated
the effectiveness of self-instructional training as a means of helping patients

with negative impairments to perform activities. Patients were initially trained to direct themselves by speaking aloud. As they became more proficient, they then learned to direct themselves silently. Unfortunately, Bentall *et al.* found that patients were unable to generalise from the experimental to real-life tasks. It is an open question whether patients with schizophrenia can be taught interventions that have a continuing therapeutic effect long after the therapist input has ended. In practice, it is often necessary to encourage patients to use specific coping strategies in the long term. Lengthy follow-up may be necessary or the use of relatives as cotherapists to facilitate continued use.

SKILLS TRAINING

For many people with negative symptoms, some training in specific skills may be required. It may be that people have never developed skills, perhaps due to lack of opportunity (e.g. conversational skills, work skills, cooking skills). Alternatively, it may be that a refresher course is required. Skills in relating to others might be considered the most crucial to address in therapy. In people with negative symptoms the extent of impairment in social functioning can vary enormously, from inability to converse on more than a very limited number of topics, to complete inability to speak, or mutism.

The most effective interventions to date for mutism or very limited speech skills have been operant procedures (Wilson and Walters, 1966; Baker, 1971). Individuals are selectively reinforced for making gradually increasing approximations to normal words. Although limited in the range of verbalisations able to be produced, generalisability, and normality of emotional expression, such procedures have made a valuable contribution to the rehabilitation of very impaired patients by enabling some degree of communication.

There are many texts on how to conduct skills training and research into its efficacy. Much of the present research has focused on teaching component skills of conversational ability, such as appropriate eye contact, listening skills, speech skills, assertiveness, etc. Such programmes, although effective in the short term and within the confines of what is required within the treatment setting, have been generally less successful in equipping people with skills which will last in the longer term and generalise to other settings. Attention has been drawn to the need to provide people with valued roles and social settings appropriate to their needs prior to skills training (Shepherd, 1988). This is important for two main reasons:

1. it provides meaning and therefore motivation to perform the skill, and
2. it enables crucial practise of the newly acquired skill.

It is also important that training covers skills which are relevant for

163

individuals rather than those which the therapist has chosen as generally relevant. For example, learning to use the telephone or reading a bus timetable may be more directly useful than becoming confident in taking faulty goods back to a department store.

There have been some interesting attempts to teach patients with negative symptoms specific skills such as problem solving. Hansen and colleagues (1985) were able to train seven subjects with diagnoses of schizophrenia or manic depression how to problem solve. Competence in each stage of problem solving improved following training, skills acquired generalised to unfamiliar situations, and effectiveness in selecting viable solutions to problems was maintained at one and four months follow-up. Effectiveness in solving problems in vivo was not assessed, however. Brenner (1989) has developed a treatment programme for people with schizophrenia which addresses both cognitive and behavioural skills deficits. Patients are taught strategies for improving attentional and perceptual difficulties, followed by communication skills, social skills and interpersonal problem solving in a stepwise progression. Using this approach, improvements have been found on measures of cognitive functioning, social adjustment and psychopathology (Brenner *et al.*, 1990).

CONCLUSIONS

Traditional approaches to the management of negative symptoms include environmental change, operant procedures and social skills training. These have been well evaluated and found to be effective, although effects can be short lived and limited to the criterion situation. They still have a very important role to play. However, there have been a number of changes in the care of people with negative symptoms over the last 30 years or so which suggest the need for a fresh look at approaches to management. The settings in which people live, work and socialise have become more varied (Hafner, 1985). As clinicians, we are no longer faced with large groups of relatively homogeneous patients all facing the same prospects and therefore with similar requirements. More importantly, our ability to relate to patients and therefore understand them has improved. This has brought with it the realisation that even very impaired patients can be engaged in a collaborative therapeutic process, do have goals and priorities and do attribute meaning to their experiences. We need to use this valuable information and insight to further our ability to help people debilitated by negative symptoms, and their carers, to manage such symptoms better. Much of the work presented here is exploratory and based on clinical experience. The author hopes it will have encouraged greater interest in the study, and optimism about the treatment, of negative symptoms. More research into the efficacy of different clinical approaches with this client group is much needed. Negative symptoms are probably the most persistent, debilitating and distressing aspect of schizophrenia. They are certainly the most burdensome for carers.

REFERENCES

Allen, C. I., Gillespie, C. R. and Hall, J. N. (1989) 'A comparison of practices, attitudes and interactions in two established units for people with a psychiatric disability', *Psychological Medicine* 19: 459–67.

Alpert, M. (ed.) (1985) *Controversies in Schizophrenia*, New York: Guildford Press.

Andreasen, N. C. (1981) *Scale for the Assessment of Negative Symptoms (SANS)*, Iowa City: University of Iowa.

—— (1989) 'Neural mechanisms of negative symptoms', *British Journal of Psychiatry* 155 (suppl. 7): 93–8.

—— (ed.) (1990) *Modern Problems of Pharmacopsychiatry: Positive and Negative Symptoms and Syndromes* (Vol. 24), Basel: S. Karger, A. G.

Andreasen, N. C. and Olsen, S. A. (1982) 'Negative versus positive schizophrenia: Definition and validation', *Archives of General Psychiatry* 39: 789–94.

Andreasen, N. C., Hoffman, R. E. and Grove, W. M. (1985) 'Mapping abnormalities in language and cognition', in M. Alpert (ed.) *Controversies in Schizophrenia*, New York: Guildford Press.

Andreasen, N. C., Olsen, S. A., Dennert, J. W. and Smith, M. R. (1982) 'Ventricular enlargement in schizophrenia: Relationship to positive and negative symptoms', *American Journal of Psychiatry* 139: 297–302.

Arndt, S., Alliger, R. J. and Andreasen, N. C. (1991) 'The distinction of positive and negative symptoms: The failure of a two-dimensional model', *British Journal of Psychiatry* 158: 317–22.

Baker, R. (1971) 'The use of operant conditioning to reinstate speech in mute schizophrenics', *Behaviour, Research and Therapy* 9: 329–36.

Barnes, T. R. E. (1989) 'Introduction', *British Journal of Psychiatry* 155 (suppl. 7): 8–9.

Barnes, T. R. E. and Liddle, P. F. (1985) 'Tardive dyskinesia: Implications for schizophrenia?', in A. A. Schiff, M. Roth and H. L. Freeman (eds) *Schizophrenia: New Pharmacological and Clinical Developments*, Royal Society of Medicine International Congress and Symposium Series No. 94: 81–7.

Baron, M., Gruen, R. S. and Romo-Gruen, J. M. (1992) 'Positive and negative symptoms: Relation to familial transmission of schizophrenia', *British Journal of Psychiatry* 161: 610–14.

Bebbington, P. and McGuffin, P. (eds) (1988) *Schizophrenia: The Major Issues*, Oxford: Heinemann.

Bentall, R. P., Higson, P. J. and Lowe, C. F. (1987) 'Teaching self-instructions to chronic schizophrenic patients: Efficacy and generalisation', *Behavioural Psychotherapy* 15: 58–76.

Birchwood, M., Mason, R., MacMillan, F. and Healy, J. (1993) 'Depression, demoralisation and control over psychotic illness: A comparison of depressed and non-depressed patients with a chronic psychosis', *Psychological Medicine* 23: 387–95.

Brenner, H. D. (1989) 'The treatment of basic psychological dysfunctions from a systemic point of view', *British Journal of Psychiatry* 155 (suppl. 5): 74–83.

Brenner, H. D., Hodel, B. and Roder, V. (1990) 'Integrated cognitive and behavioural interventions in the treatment of schizophrenia', *Psychosocial Rehabilitation Journal* 13 (3): 41–3.

Creer, C. and Wing, J. (1974) *Schizophrenia at Home*, Surbiton: National Schizophrenia Fellowship.

Crow, T. J. (1980) 'Molecular pathology of schizophrenia: More than one disease process?', *British Medical Journal* 280: 66–8.

Crow, T. J., Cross, A. J., Johnson, A. J., Johnstone, E. C., Joseph, M. H., Owen, F., Owens, D. G. C. and Poulter, M. (1984) 'Catecholamines and schizophrenia: an assessment of the evidence', in E. Usdin, A. Carlsson, A. Dahlstrom and J. Engel (eds) *Catecholamines. Part C: Neuropharmacology and Central Nervous System–Therapeutic Aspects*, New York: Liss.

Drake, R. E. and Cotton, P. G. (1986) 'Depression, hopelessness and suicide in chronic schizophrenia', *British Journal of Psychiatry* 148: 554–9.

Frith, C. D. (1992) *The Cognitive Neuropsychology of Schizophrenia*, Hove: Lawrence Erlbaum Associates.

Gattaz, W. F., Kohlmeyer, K. and Gasser, T. (1991) 'Computer tomographic studies in schizophrenia', in H. Hafner and W. F. Gattaz (eds) *Search for the Causes of Schizophrenia (vol. II)*, Berlin: Springer.

Hafner, H. (1985) 'Changing patterns of mental health care', *Acta Psychiatrica Scandinavica*, 71 (suppl. 319): 151–64.

Hafner, H. and Gattaz, W. F. (eds) (1991) *Search for the Causes of Schizophrenia (Vol. II)*, Berlin: Springer.

Hansen, D. J., Lawrence, J. S. and Christoff, K. A. (1985) 'Effects of interpersonal problem solving training with chronic aftercare patients on problem solving component skills and effectiveness of solutions', *Journal of Consulting and Clinical Psychology* 53, 167–74.

Hirsch, S. R., Jolley, A. G., Barnes, T. R. E., Liddle, P. F., Curson, D. A., Patel, A., York, A., Bercu, S. and Patel, M. (1989) 'Dysphoric and depressive symptoms in chronic schizophrenia', *Schizophrenia Research* 2, 259–64.

Johnson, D. A. W. (1988) 'The significance of depression in the prediction of relapse in chronic schizophrenia', *British Journal of Psychiatry* 152: 320–3.

Kazdin, A. E. (1982) 'The token economy: A decade later', *Journal of Applied Behaviour Analysis* 15: 431–55.

Krawiecka, M., Goldberg, D. and Vaughan, M. (1977) 'A standardized psychiatric assessment scale for rating chronic psychotic patients', *Acta Psychiatrica Scandinavica* 55: 299–308.

Kulhara, P., Avasthi, A., Chadda, R., Chandiamani, K., Mattoo, S. K., Kota, S. K. and Joseph, S. (1989) 'Negative and depressive symptoms in schizophrenia', *British Journal of Psychiatry* 154: 207–11.

Liddle, P. F. (1987) 'The symptoms of chronic schizophrenia: A re-examination of the positive–negative dichotomy', *British Journal of Psychiatry* 151: 145–51.

MacCarthy, B., Benson, J. and Brewin, C. R. (1986) 'Task motivation and problem appraisal in long term psychiatric patients', *Psychological Medicine* 16: 431–8.

Marks, R. C. and Luchins, D. J. (1990) 'Relationship between brain imaging findings in schizophrenia and psychopathology: A review of the literature relating to positive and negative symptoms', in N.C. Andreasen (ed.) *Modern Problems of Pharmacopsychiatry: Positive and Negative Symptoms and Syndromes (vol. 24)*, Basel: S. Karger, A. G.

Matson, J. L. (1980) 'Behaviour modification procedures for training chronically institutionalized schizophrenics', *Progress in Behaviour Modification* 9: 167–204.

Moore, E., Kuipers, L. and Ball, R. (1992) 'Content analysis of expressed emotion interviews: Staff–patient relationships in the care of the long term adult mentally ill', *Social Psychiatry and Psychiatric Epidemiology* 27: 28–34.

Norman, R. M. G. and Malla, A. K. (1991) 'Dysphoric mood and symptomatology in schizophrenia', *Psychological Medicine* 21: 897–903.

Pogue-Geile, M. F. and Harrow, M. (1985) 'Negative symptoms in schizophrenia:

166

their longitudinal course and prognostic importance', *Schizophrenia Bulletin* 11: 427–39.

Ragin, A. G., Pogue-Geile, M. and Oltmanns, T. F. (1989) 'Poverty of speech in schizophrenia and depression during in-patient and post-hospital periods', *British Journal of Psychiatry* 154, 52–7.

Ranz, J. M., Horen, B. T., McFarlane, W. R. and Zito, J. M. (1991) 'Creating a supportive environment using staff psychoeducation in a supervised residence', *Hospital and Community Psychiatry* 42: 1154–9.

Roberts, G. W. and Bruton, C. J. (1990) 'Notes from the graveyard: Schizophrenia and neuropathology', *Neuropathology and Applied Neurobiology* 16: 3-16.

Schiff, A. A., Roth, M. and Freeman, H. L. (eds) (1985) *Schizophrenia: New Pharmacological and Clinical Developments*, Royal Society of Medicine International Congress and Symposium Series No. 94, 81–7.

Shepherd, G. (1988) 'The contribution of psychological interventions to the treatment and management of schizophrenia', in P. Bebbington and P. McGuffin, (eds), *Schizophrenia: The Major Issues*, Oxford: Heinemann.

Sommers, A. S. (1985) '"Negative symptoms": Conceptual and methodological problems', *Schizophrenia Bulletin* 11: 364–79.

Usdin, E., Carlsson, A., Dahlstrom, A. and Engel, J. (eds) (1984) *Catecholamines. Part C: Neuropharmacology and Central Nervous System – Therapeutic Aspects*, New York: Liss.

Wilson, F. S. and Walters, R. H. (1966) 'Modification of speech output of near mute schizophrenics through social learning procedures', *Behaviour Research and Therapy* 4, 59–67.

Wing, J. K. (1989) 'The concept of negative symptoms', *British Journal of Psychiatry* 155 (suppl. 7): 10–14.

Wing, J. K. and Brown, G. W. (1970) *Institutionalism and Schizophrenia*, Cambridge: Cambridge University Press.

Part III

INTEGRATING WITH OTHER THERAPEUTIC STRATEGIES

10

EARLY INTERVENTION IN PSYCHOTIC RELAPSE: COGNITIVE APPROACHES TO DETECTION AND MANAGEMENT

Max Birchwood

The control of relapse is one among many of the needs of people with a psychosis. It is important, however, as each relapse brings with it an increased probability of future relapse and residual symptoms (McGlashan, 1988) as well as accelerating social disablement (Hogarty *et al.*, 1991). Even an ideal combination of pharmacological and psychosocial intervention does not eliminate the potential for relapse (ibid.).

These facts are not lost on those who themselves experience recurring psychotic symptoms. A survey by Mueser and colleagues (1992) found that patients expressed a strong interest in learning about 'early warning signs of the illness and relapse' and this was ranked second in importance out of an agenda of over forty topics. Their thirst for knowledge and understanding on this matter would seem to be driven by a perceived need for control rather than mere curiosity. In a study of 'secondary' depression in schizophrenia (Birchwood *et al.*, 1992) we found that 'perceived control over illness' was the variable most closely linked to depression, more so than illness variables, locus of control or self-evaluative beliefs derived from culture-bound beliefs about mental illness (see Table 10.1). The propensity of individuals to seek control of psychotic disorder is now well understood (Breier and Strauss, 1983; Kumar *et al.*, 1989) and the question is raised as to the possibility of empowering individuals with real control over an event they fear most: relapse.

DSM-III-R (APA, 1987) recognises that relapse, when defined as the re-emergence or exacerbation of positive symptoms, tends to be preceded by subtle changes in mental functioning up to four weeks prior to the event. Not only is this perceived as a loss of well-being by the individual but it appears to trigger a set of restorative manoeuvres, as McCandless-Glincher *et al.* (1986) show in their study.

171

Table 10.1 Items from the scale 'perceived control of psychotic illness'

If I am going to relapse there's nothing I can do about it.
I cannot cope with my current symptoms.
My illness frightens me.
I am powerless to influence or control my illness.

McCandless-Glincher and colleagues (1986) studied 62 individuals attending for maintenance therapy, and inquired about their recognition of, and response to, reduced well-being. The patients were drawn from those routinely attending two medical centres; their age range (20–75 years), with a mean illness duration of 28 years, suggests that such a group would be well represented in ordinary clinical practice. Sixty-one said they could recognise reduced well-being; of these only thirteen relied entirely upon others to identify symptoms for them. Nine were assisted by others and thirty-six identified the problem themselves. The majority (fifty out of sixty-one) of patients initiated some change in their behaviour when they recognised reduced well-being, including engaging in diversionary activities, seeking professional help and resuming or increasing their neuroleptic medication. Only three of this group had ever been encouraged to self-monitor by mental health professionals, and a further seven had received encouragement from relatives. Thus, these schizophrenic patients had initiated symptom monitoring and a range of responses almost entirely on their own initiative. The study by Kumar *et al.* (1989) comes to rather similar conclusions.

In essence, there may be a relatively untapped pool of information which is not accessed adequately enough to initiate early intervention, except perhaps by individuals themselves. If individuals can recognise and act on symptoms suggestive of reduced well-being, then it is possible that patterns of early ('prodromal') symptoms heralding relapse may be apparent and identifiable, and may offer further avenues for relapse management in partnership with the individual with the psychosis. In this chapter, the scientific data on the predictive validity of early symptoms is reviewed and a process of collaborative early intervention is described with case examples. The main thrust of this chapter, however, is to explore theoretically, and with case examples, the basis for a cognitive approach to early intervention based on the appraisal of early symptoms and its direct and indirect impact on relapse and delusion formation.

DOES A PRODROME HERALD PSYCHOTIC RELAPSE?

Clinical, retrospective and prospective studies have addressed and continue to address this question. In this section we shall concentrate on the last two and consider the implications of the clinical studies in trying to interpret the empirical investigations.

Psychiatric services are, by and large, organised to respond to crises such as relapse; this constrains our ability to develop clinical experience of prodromal changes. Thus, the first systematic studies of the prodrome adopted the simple expedient of asking the patient and his relative or carer.

The interview study by Herz and Melville (1980) in the USA attempted systematically to collect data retrospectively from patients and relatives in this manner. It is widely regarded as definitive since they interviewed 145 schizophrenic sufferers (forty-six following a recent episode) as well as eighty of their family members. The main question, 'could you tell that there were any changes in your thoughts, feelings or behaviours that might have led you to believe you were becoming sick and might have to go into hospital?', was answered affirmatively by 70 per cent of patients and 93 per cent of families. These, and the results of a similar British study (Birchwood et al., 1989), are shown in Table 10.2.

Generally the symptoms most frequently mentioned by patients and family members were dysphoric in nature: eating less, concentration problems, troubled sleep, depressed mood and withdrawal. The most common 'early psychotic' symptoms were 'hearing voices', 'talking in a nonsensical way', 'increased religious thinking' and 'thinking someone else was controlling them'.

There is considerable agreement about the nature of these 'early signs' although somewhat less in their relative salience. Both studies concur in finding 'dysphoric' symptoms the most commonly prevalent. In the Herz and Melville study, although more families than patients reported the presence of early signs, there was considerable concordance between patients and families in the content and relative significance of early symptoms. There was substantial agreement between patients that non-psychotic symptoms such as anxiety, tension and insomnia were part of the prodrome, but less agreement as to the characteristics of the earliest changes. Fifty per cent of the patients felt that the characteristic symptoms of the prodrome were repeated at each relapse. A number of these patients also reported that many of the non-psychotic symptoms persisted between episodes of illness – an important issue to which we shall return below.

Both studies carefully questioned respondents about the timing of the onset of the prodrome. Most of the patients (52 per cent) and their families (68 per cent) in the Herz and Melville study felt that more than a week elapsed between the onset of the prodrome and a full relapse. Similarly, Birchwood et al. (1989) found that 59 per cent observed the onset of the prodrome one month or more prior to relapse, and 75 per cent two weeks or more; 19 per cent were unable to specify a time scale.

Table 10.2 Percentages of relatives reporting early signs

Category	Birchwood et al. (1989) (n = 42)		Herz and Melville (1980) (n = 80)	
	%	Rank*	%	Rank*
Anxiety/agitation				
Irritable/quick tempered	62	2 (eq)	–	–
Sleep problems	67	1	69	7
Tense, afraid, anxious	62	2 (eq)	83	1
Depression/withdrawal				
Quiet, withdrawn	60	4	50	18
Depressed, low	57	5	76	3
Poor appetite	48	9	53	17
Disinhibition				
Aggression	50	7 (eq)	79	2
Restless	55	6	40	20
Stubborn	36	10 (eq)	–	–
Incipient psychosis				
Behaves as if hallucinated	50	7 (eq)	60	10
Being laughed or talked about	36	10 (eq)	14	53.8
'Odd behaviour'	36	10 (eq)	–	–

* There were many other symptoms assessed. Percentage reporting only shown for parallel data.

The true predictive significance of prodromal signs can be clearly established only with prospective investigations. Such studies need to examine three issues:

1. Whether prodromes of psychotic relapse exist;
2. their timing in relation to full relapse, and
3. how often the 'prodromes' fail as well as succeed to predict relapse (i.e. 'sensitivity' and 'specificity').

The clinical implications of this research will largely depend on the degree of specificity which early signs information affords. In particular a high false positive rate will tend to undermine the use of an early intervention strategy, in particular that which uses a raised dose of neuroleptic medication, since in such cases, patients will have been needlessly exposed to additional medication.

In the course of a study comparing low and standard dose maintenance medication, Marder et al. (1984) assessed forty-one patients on a range of psychiatric symptoms at baseline, two weeks later, monthly for three months and then every three months. Relapse was defined as the failure of an increase in medication to manage symptoms following a minor exacerbation of psychosis or paranoia. Thus, under this definition, it is not known how many genuine prodromes were *aborted* with medication and whether those that responded to medication were similar to those that did not. Patients were assessed using a standard psychiatric interview scale (Brief Psychiatric Rating Scale, BPRS; Overall and Gorham, 1962) and a self-report measure of psychiatric symptoms (SCL90; Derogatis *et al.*, 1973). Changes in scores 'just prior to relapse' were compared with the average ('spontaneous') change for a given scale during the course of the follow-up period. Marder *et al.* found increases in BPRS depression, thought disturbance and paranoia and SCL90 scores for interpersonal sensitivity, anxiety, depression and paranoid ideation prior to relapse. They note that the changes they observed were very small (equalling two points on a 21 point range) and probably not recognisable by most clinicians. A discriminant function analysis found the most discriminating ratings were paranoia and depression (BPRS) and psychoticism (SCL90). They suggest: 'such a formula if used in a clinic could probably predict most relapses although there would be a considerable number of ... false positives' (Marder *et al.*, 1984, p. 46). While this study strongly supports the presence of the relapse prodrome, it was unable to control for timing. The last assessment before relapse varied from between one and twelve weeks, weakening the observed effects. One would anticipate the prodrome to be at its maximum in the week or two prior to relapse; assessments carried out prior to this would measure an earlier and weaker stage of the prodrome, or miss it entirely.

A subsequent report from this laboratory (Marder *et al.*, 1991) studied 50 schizophrenic patients monitored weekly for non-psychotic prodromal episodes. This study compared different methods of monitoring for prodromes using experimenter administered scales (Brief Psychiatric Rating Scale, anxiety-depression cluster and their Individualised Prodromal Scale), systematically varying the sensitivity of their instruments and observing the impact on their predictive efficacy. Thus, Figure 10.1 plots the hit rate against the rate of false positives under varying degrees of change in BPRS anxiety and depression from one to five points. This shows that using a change score of three, 50 per cent of relapses are accurately predicted with a 20 per cent false positive rate; this was achieved only when patients with a relatively stable mental state were included.

Subotnik and Nuechterlein (1988) considerably improved upon the Marder *et al.* studies by administering the BPRS fortnightly to fifty young, recent onset schizophrenic patients diagnosed by RDC criteria. Twenty-three patients relapsed and their BPRS scores two, four and six weeks prior to the relapse were compared with their scores in another six week period not associated with relapse, and with scores of a non-relapse group (n=27) over a similar period. This research found that BPRS anxiety-depression (which includes depression, guilt and somatic concern) and thought disturbance (hallucinations and delusions) were raised prior to relapse, with the

175

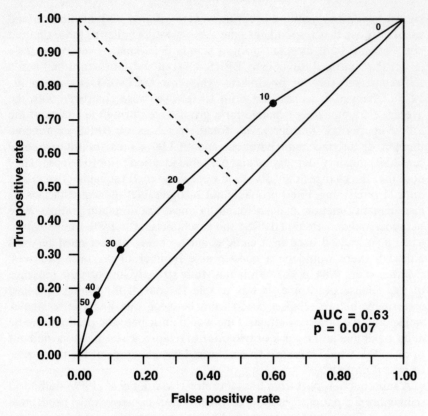

Figure 10.1 The relationship between sensitivity and error rates using various
BPRS thresholds to define prodromes (from Marder *et al.*, 1991)

latter more prominent as relapse approached (two to four weeks prior to
relapse). The contrast with the *non*-relapsed patients revealed a rise in
low-level 'psychotic' symptoms as part of the prodrome, but not of the non-
psychotic items (depression, somatic concern, guilt, etc). This suggests that
the non-psychotic symptoms are sensitive to relapse but not specific to it. If,
however, they were followed by low-level psychotic symptoms, this study
suggests that relapse is more probable. Subotnik and Nuechterlein note:

> mean elevations in prodromal symptoms were small ... 0.5–1.00 on a
> 7 point scale ... but in three patients no prodromal symptoms
> were present ... in several others they did not begin to show any
> symptomatic change until 2–4 weeks prior to relapse ... thus lowering
> the magnitude of the means.
>
> (Subotnik and Nuechterlein 1988, p. 411)

These results support clinical observations that the nature and timing of prodromal signs are like relapse itself – not universal, but include considerable

between-subject variability. Nevertheless, Subotnik and Nuechterlein reported that a discriminant function analysis using two BPRS 'psychotic' scales correctly classified 59 per cent of relapses and 74 per cent of non-relapse periods, suggesting a false positive rate of 26 per cent.

Hirsch and Jolley (1989), in the course of an early intervention study, measured putative prodromes ('neurotic or dysphoric episodes') in a group of fifty-four patients with DSM-III-R schizophrenia using the SCL90 and Herz's Early Signs Questionnaire (ESQ; Herz *et al.*, 1982). Patients and their key workers received a one hour teaching session about schizophrenia, particularly concerning the significance of the 'dysphoric' syndrome as a prodrome for relapse. It was hoped that this would enable them to recognise 'dysphoric' episodes. All subjects were symptom free at the onset of the trial. At each dysphoric episode, the SCL90 and the ESQ were administered and then weekly for two further weeks; otherwise each was rated monthly. Relapse was defined as the re-emergence of florid symptoms, including delusions and hallucinations. Seventy-three per cent of the relapses were preceded by a prodromal period of dysphoric and neurotic symptoms within a month of relapse. These prodromes were defined clinically, but confirmed by SCL90 scores, which were similar to those reported by the other two prospective studies, and included depression, anxiety, interpersonal sensitivity and paranoid thinking. Interpretation of this study is complicated by the design, in which half the subjects received active, and half placebo, maintenance medication and all patients showing signs of dysphoric (prodromal) episodes were given additional active medication (Haloperidol, 10mg per day). Dysphoric episodes were much more common in the placebo (76 per cent) than in the active group (27 per cent) but the prompt pharmacological intervention does not allow us to ascertain whether these dysphoric episodes were part of a reactivation of psychosis (i.e. true prodromes) aborted by medication and to what extent these included 'false positives' related, perhaps, to the use of placebo.

Malla and Norman (1994) report a prospective study of fifty-five DSM-III-R schizophrenic patients in which monthly recordings of positive symptoms, thought disorder and putative prodromal 'dysphoric' symptoms were taken, both using standard self-report scales (including the Beck Depression Inventory and the Scale for the Assessment of Positive Symptoms). They found that minor undulations in psychotic symptoms were not linked to dysphoric symptoms recorded one month previously. However, major exacerbations of positive symptoms were nearly always preceded by elevations (less than one standard deviation) of prodromal symptoms above baseline (specificity: 90 per cent); 'prodromes' anticipated only 50 per cent of relapses, but this may have increased with *fortnightly* monitoring as adopted by Subotnik and Nuechterlein (1988) and Birchwood *et al.* (1989). Indeed, Gaebel *et al.* (1993), in an analysis based on an early intervention design (see below), found greater predictive efficacy of prodromal symptoms two weeks prior to a relapse.

177

A further prospective study (Birchwood *et al.*, 1989) used a scale designed to tap the specific characteristics of the prodrome, rather than that of general psychopathology. Construction of the scale was informed by the retrospective study reported in the same paper. Two versions of the scale were used for completion by both the patient *and* a chosen observer (e.g. relative, carer, hostel worker). It was reasoned that the behavioural observations by the observers might provide additional information if the individual under-reported or lost insight. *Changes* in baseline levels were readily apparent, which is particularly important if the individual experiences persisting symptoms.

The authors reported an investigation of nineteen young schizophrenic patients diagnosed according to the broad CATEGO 'S' class (Wing *et al.*, 1974). All except one were on maintenance medication, monitored in the context of a routine clinical service and were not involved in a drug trial. Eight of the nineteen relapsed in the course of nine months and, of these, 50 per cent showed elevations on the scales between two and four weeks prior to relapse. A *post hoc* defined threshold on their scale (less than or more than thirty) led to a sensitivity of 63 per cent, specificity of 82 per cent and an 11 per cent rate of false positives.

Figure 10.2 shows some of the results of individual prodromes. Figure 10.2a is that of a young male who relapsed sixteen weeks following discharge. In this case, the first change was that of dysphoria/withdrawal which was apparent five weeks prior to relapse. One to two weeks later he became steadily more agitated and within two weeks of relapse, low-level ('incipient') psychotic symptoms appeared. Disinhibition was unaffected. In contrast, the individual shown in Figure 10.2b reported dysphoria/withdrawal and incipient psychotic symptoms simultaneously together with signs of disinhibition; anxiety/agitation did not peak until somewhat later. It is interesting to note that the observer's behavioural observations showed striking concordance to self-report in respect of dysphoria but lagged behind by up to two weeks in respect of the behavioural concomitants of incipient psychosis. These two examples also reveal an apparent *improvement* in well-being just prior to the onset of the prodromes. The third case (Figure 10.2c) is a young male, where the rise in anxiety/agitation, dysphoria and incipient psychosis were noted by the observer, but the individual reported a slight rise in symptoms followed immediately by a sharp fall, presumably due to loss of insight. Case four (Figure 10.2d) demonstrates a definite rise in the scales which returned to baseline four weeks later and was not followed by a relapse. While the increase in scores did not lead to relapse, this individual had learnt that he had secured employment which seemed to be associated with a feeling of well-being noted by the individual and his mother; as the start of his job approached, his symptoms increased then returned to baseline a few weeks after the start of his job. What was witnessed here was probably the impact of a stressful life event which on this occasion did not culminate in relapse.

CONTINUING QUESTIONS
Sensitivity and specificity

The results of the five prospective studies are consistent with the clinical and retrospective studies, particularly supporting Herz and Melville's (1980) seminal investigation. The studies all found that psychotic relapse is nearly always preceded by non-psychotic, 'dysphoric' symptoms including anxiety, dysphoria, interpersonal sensitivity/withdrawal and low-level psychotic thinking, including ideas of reference and paranoid thoughts. In two of these studies (Marder *et al.*, 1984; Hirsch and Jolley, 1989), the observations were confounded by a targeted medication strategy, so it was not clear how many of their putative prodromes were actually false positives. It is also possible that the use of an early intervention strategy exaggerated the magnitude of the recorded prodromes. Under normal conditions, the baseline levels of psychopathology would be increased in the non-relapsed patients by transient fluctuations in dysphoric symptoms which were not part of a relapse (i.e. the false positives) which might respond to medication, thus reducing the contrast between relapsed and non-relapsed groups.

The possibility of between-subject variability in the nature and timing of prodromes will, however, act to reduce their apparent amplitude in group studies. Subotnik and Nuechterlein (1988) reported that some patients showed no prodromal symptoms. Among the patients who did show prodromal signs, some were elevated six weeks prior to relapse while in others this occurred a full month later, thus lowering the mean value for the whole group within the time frames (six, four or two weeks prior to relapse). The study by Birchwood *et al.* (1989) raises further potential complications, as not only does it reveal differences in the amplitude and timing of symptoms, but also that the pattern of prodromal symptoms showed subject variability—some may 'peak' on anxiety symptoms, others on disinhibition, and so forth.

Prodromes: discrete or continuous?

The prospective studies rather assume that prodromal and psychotic symptoms are discrete, dichotomous variables that may be scored as present or absent. Each study uses slightly different definitions of prodrome and relapse that may well contribute to differences in figures for sensitivity and specificity (Malla and Norman, 1994). The notion of 'prodrome' is, of course, taken from general medicine where non-specific symptoms (e.g. malaise) precede the illness proper (e.g. AIDS). In fact, most of the prospective studies do not maintain such a clear distinction: Tarrier *et al.* (1991) included hallucinations in the prodrome, as did Herz and Melville

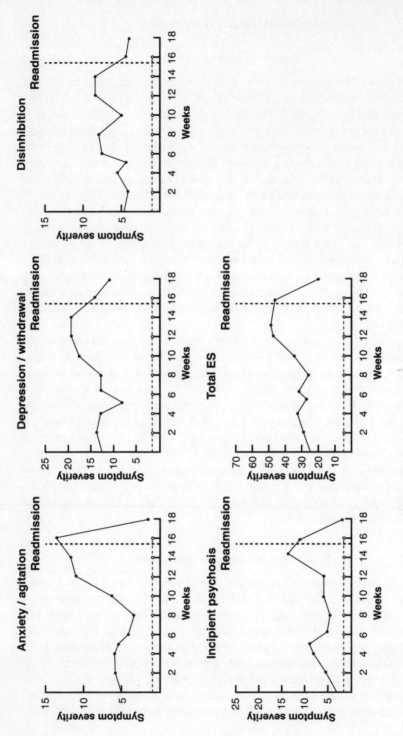

Figure 10.2 Four prodromes detected using the ESS scales

Note: Self = ————————
      Observer = — — — — — — —

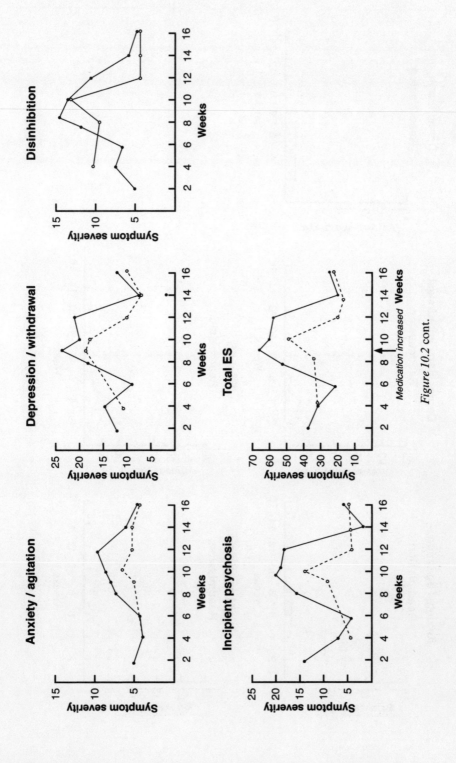

Figure 10.2 cont.

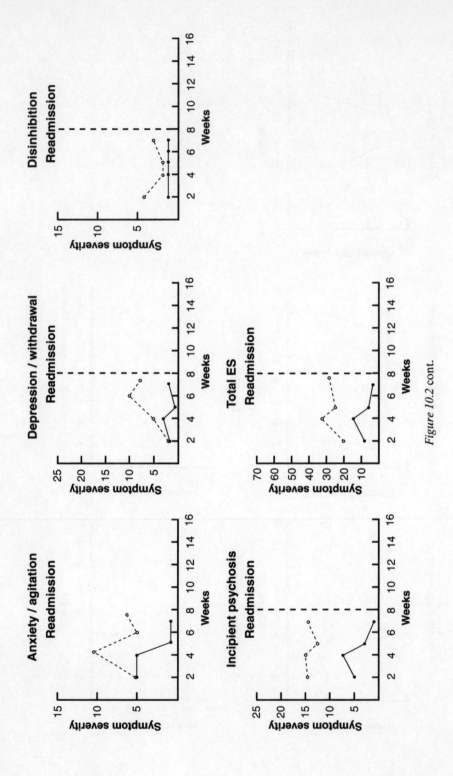

Figure 10.2 cont.

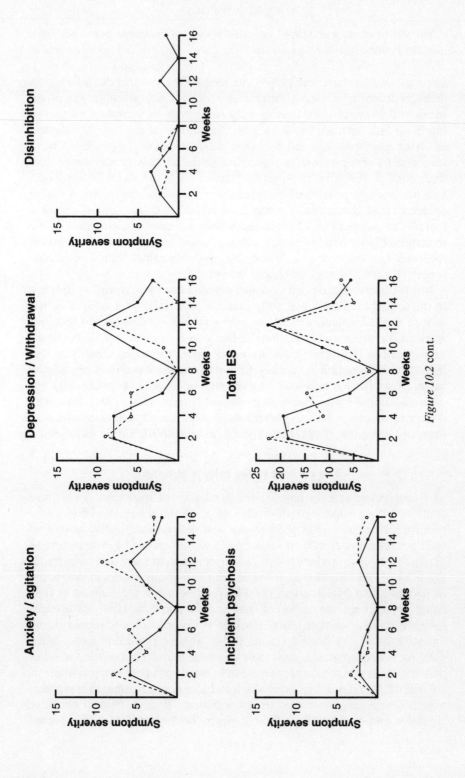

Figure 10.2 cont.

(1980); Birchwood *et al.* (1989) included a scale of 'incipient psychosis' with items indicating low-level psychotic signs ('something odd is going on which cannot be explained'; 'feeling people are taking unusual notice of me'). Subotnik and Nuechterlein (1988) included BPRS 'thought disturbance' in their prodrome which is, of course, not strictly a non-psychotic symptom. Malla and Norman (1994), using only *non*-psychotic symptom measures, found no link between prodromes and psychosis, where both are viewed as continuous, but they did find that major increases in psychosis were preceded by non-psychotic signs, although the sensitivity was lower than that found in the other prospective studies. Even the status of dysphoria as a non-specific prodromal symptom is contentious since there is sound evidence that dysphoria accompanies acute psychosis and depression features as a dimension of psychopathology in some of the studies of the structure of psychotic symptoms. Also, in some formulations, dysphoria is regarded as a reaction to a developing psychosis rather than a prodrome proper (Birchwood *et al.*, 1992; and below).

It is probably of little consequence whether the 'prodromal' symptoms, in the formal medical sense, truly precede psychosis: what is clear is that relapse in most instances builds up over a period of between two and four weeks. Like psychosis itself, there is likely to be a considerable between-subject variability in timing and nature of early symptoms. Identifying this individual information is the key to early intervention and is considered below. Also, there is now a well-established relationship between duration of psychosis and susceptibility to treatment (Loebel *et al.*, 1992); thus even if early intervention fails to prevent the breakthrough of severe hallucinations and delusions, it can, theoretically, at least shorten their duration.

The concept of the relapse signature

The prospective studies have raised a number of questions. They have confirmed the existence of prodromes of psychotic relapse and find a true positive rate in the region of 50–60 per cent with a false positive rate of up to 25 per cent; however, their limitations have not enabled a clear picture to emerge of the true predictive significance of apparent early warning signs. If the work of Birchwood *et al.* is borne out, then group studies in the mould of Subotnik and Nuechterlein (1988) would be inherently limited as they could not capture the apparent quantitative and qualitative differences between patients in their early signs or symptoms. This is supported by Subotnik and Nuechterlein's finding that greater prediction came when patients were compared against their own baseline, rather than that of other patients. It may be more appropriate to think of each patient's prodrome as a personalised *relapse signature* which includes core or common symptoms together with features unique to each patient. If an individual's relapse signature can be identified, then it might be expected that the overall predictive power of 'prodromal' symptoms will be increased. Identifying the unique characteristics of a relapse signature can be achieved only once a relapse has taken place; with each successive relapse further information becomes available to build a more accurate image of the signature. This kind of learning process has been acknowledged by patients (Breier and Strauss, 1983) and could be adapted and developed by professionals and carers as well. We are currently collecting data relevant to the validity of this concept by comparing signatures of those clients who have relapsed more than once. Two such cases are presented later in this chapter.

The relevance of individual and illness factors

An issue not directly examined in the prospective studies concerns the existence of a prodrome of relapse where the individual continues to experience significant residual symptoms. Where the patient experiences continued negative symptoms such as anergia and withdrawal, a prodrome presumably may involve an apparent *exacerbation* of these symptoms, as shown in some of the cases in Figure 10.2. Where individuals continue to suffer from symptoms such as delusions and hallucinations, a 'relapse' will involve an exacerbation of these symptoms; whether these relapses will also be preceded by prodromes of a similar character is unknown. Patients in the Hirsch and Jolley and Subotnik and Nuechterlein studies were generally symptom free; there was somewhat more variability in residual symptoms than in the Birchwood *et al.* and Marder *et al.* studies. Residual symptoms will tend also to be associated with unstable mental state: Marder *et al.* (1991) found better prediction when 'unstable' patients were excluded. In view of the large numbers of patients with even moderate residual symptoms, this issue deserves serious and careful examination.

Patients participating in the prospective studies generally were young (18–35 years), with a relatively brief psychiatric history. Such individuals may be more prone to relapse and tend to be recruited at acute admission or because they were thought to be appropriate for low-dose or intermittent drug strategies (cf., Hirsch and Jolley, 1989). The application of this methodology to older, more stable individuals is another important area for further investigation.

THE SEARCH FOR MEANING AND ITS IMPLICATIONS

The prodrome studies suggest at least two stages in the process of relapse: dysphoria (including anxiety, restlessness, blunting of drives) followed by early psychotic symptoms (including suspiciousness, ideas of reference, misinterpretations). Should we interpret this as 'neurotic' symptoms, preceding psychotic ones in the sense of Fould's (1976) notion of a hierarchy of psychiatric symptoms, according to which, schizophrenia at the top of the hierarchy will concurrently incorporate dysphoria, anxiety and other neurotic symptoms?

In this welter of data on signs and symptoms, it would be sensible to enquire what the individual is making of all these changes to his mental life; we know, after all, that loss of insight is one of the *last* changes to occur (Heinrichs *et al.*, 1985).

The Hirsch and Jolley (1989) study using the ESQ found that 'loss of control', 'fear of being alone', 'puzzlement about objective experience' and 'fear of going crazy' were strong features of the prodrome, the latter in fact was the most common of all symptoms (70 per cent of relapsing patients). The clinical studies of relapsing patients suggest that a set of early symptoms has been overlooked. Some patients report a feeling of over-stimulation involving a difficulty in preventing external or internal events invading consciousness (Chapman, 1966). Visual, proprioceptive and time distortions are common resulting in visual illusions and feelings of derealisation and depersonalisation:

> irrelevant thoughts and feelings appear from nowhere and cannot be separated from more meaningful ones ... the patient becomes a passive recipient ... past memories and present occurrences, varying in length, relevance and emotional tone that run through his mind, leaving him fearful and perplexed.
>
> (Donlon and Blacker, 1975, p. 324)

It is perhaps not surprising that confusion and inability to think clearly is prodromal in 50 per cent of patients (Kumar *et al.*, 1989).

Perhaps what is happening here is a juxtaposition of symptoms intrinsic to the relapse, with a psychological response that centres on a search for meaning and control. Those with little experience of relapse, and without appropriate constructions and vocabulary to describe their experiences, may be puzzled by these perceptual changes and feel a sense of perplexity and fear; those with greater experience may catastrophise these experiences as 'dangerous' and will respond with a sense of foreboding that something is about to happen over which they may have little control (i.e. relapse).

The search for meaning: The case of PT

We have been attempting to examine the attributional processes of individuals during their prodromal phase. This is not a straightforward task as the prodromes are brief and relatively infrequent. We have accumulated a number of single cases whom we have interviewed and captured on video tape in an attempt to unpack the distinction between these primary prodromal changes and secondary attributions. In the case study that follows, the changes in perception and thought were documented, together with the patient's attributions (ideas of causality) that are attached to them. In a case later in this chapter we describe how this might form the basis of a cognitive approach to intervention.

PT was a 29-year-old male chemistry graduate with a one year history of diagnosed schizophrenia. He sought the assistance of his case manager following a "definite change in my thinking". He had not slept for three nights and appeared unkempt and drawn. His affect was one of puzzlement and concern. He was interviewed using the prodrome interview, and his explanation for his symptoms was sought. This is shown in Table 10.3.

The results reveal a predomination of changes in perception. He entertained three explanations for his changed mental life. First, PT conjectured that his medication was responsible for his abrupt change in thinking and perception. He disclosed that he had tested this by discontinuing with his medication but later discounted this possibility as it seemed to bring no improvement to his mental life. Second, he considered that it was something to do with the return of his 'illness'. This aroused considerable anxiety and fear and he did not like to dwell on this prospect and preferred to think of it as his 'old' (pre-morbid) personality returning.

A third possibility was entertained. He considered that his diminished capacity for clear thinking led him to believe that he would not be understood by others; he subsequently changed this view to "they don't *want* to understand, they're not interested in me". As evidence for this he asserted that "their body language is saying something about me" – his intense sensations of heightened perception and derealisation possibly driving his hypervigilance.

What is clear about his account is that in the early stage of relapse, PT was actively speculating about the meaning of his changed mental life, and this was preoccupying his thoughts. Each idea was tentative and he was prepared to discount it, although some were directly tested, and in the case of the hypothesis about medication, with possible negative consequences. He showed a strong tendency to externalise which began to embrace even his family and friends whom he showed signs of avoiding. The attribution concerning relapse filled him with fear and foreboding, and he was less inclined to consider this seriously.

EARLY RELAPSE: A COGNITIVE ANALYSIS

Maher's model of delusions (1988) dovetails neatly with the early signs phenomenon: ambiguous and novel perceptual-cognitive changes are provided with a construction which is likely to be abnormal in view of the initial experience, but which nevertheless offers the individual some relief, thus reinforcing the tenacity with which it is held. Delusions, then, are regarded as an adaptive response preserving order, integrity and meaning (Roberts, 1991; Strauss, 1991). And yet, if such a conscious or

Table 10.3 Explanations for symptoms (PT)

Prodrome	Attributions	Outcomes
Thinking	*1. External: people*	
Loss of mental agility	'They're not going to understand me . . .'	Suspiciousness
Racing thoughts	'They're not understanding the point I'm making . . .'	Social withdrawal
Confused and disjointed	'Their body language is saying something about me . . .'	Affect: fear
	'People are not interested in me . . . they don't want to know me'	
Perception	*2. External: medication*	
Derealisation	'I thought it was my medication affecting me this way'	Stops medication
Heightened perception;	*3. Internal: illness*	
Loss of ability to filter	'I'm relapsing . . . why why the illness? . . . it seems to be setting in'	Affect: dysphasia
	4. Internal	
	'I thought it was my old obsessions coming back'	Affect: dysphasia? Guilt

semi-conscious attributional process does occur, why in the context of relative insight and prior experience of relapse, does the individual choose such an apparently disempowering (externalising) attribution? Attribution theory itself might offer some help here.

Weiner's attribution theory (1985, 1986) argues that perceived causes of an event differ on the dimensions of internality, stability and controllability. To label early symptoms as relapse is to make an attribution that is internal, stable and global and, for most individuals, uncontrollable. As Brewin (1988) suggests, to attribute negative outcomes to stable factors (e.g. schizophrenic vulnerability) leads to lowered expectations of success and a tendency to give up trying. Internality and controllability dimensions are thought to be particularly involved in the genesis of esteem-related emotions. The relapse attribution then is likely to arouse guilt and lowered self-esteem; externalising (e.g. paranoid) attributions may be self-esteem preserving as well as inherently more controllable (e.g. through the use of avoidance).

It may be hypothesised that this attributional process and the negative affect it generates is instrumental in accelerating, or conversely retarding or arresting, the process as some individuals feel they can do (Breier and Strauss, 1983). Dysphoria, then, might be regarded as arising out of fear of forthcoming relapse or a failure to explain and control what might be highly disturbing and dangerous symptoms. The stress and anticipation of this could accelerate the process of relapse. The external attribution of causality that was apparent in PT may sow the seeds of delusional beliefs, as Maher (1988) suggests in his general model of delusions, as constructions arising out of aberrant experiences (see Figure 10.3). Symptom exacerbation is hypothesised to occur (or indeed be prevented) through two routes. The tension, uncertainty and danger inherent in some attributions could accelerate the relapse process in line with the stress-vulnerability model.

This has many parallels with the cognitive model of panic in which a catastrophic misinterpretation of bodily sensation triggers panic through the 'wired in' danger signalling system of the 'flight or fight' response. The 'wired in' equivalent in psychosis is the supposed relationship between stress and its impact on the threshold for expression of the vulnerability as symptoms (Clements and Turpin, 1992). The second, and more direct route is through an externalising attribution process which, while preserving self-esteem and control, drives delusion formation.

This 'two process' theory requires a manifold replication of the observations surrounding PT: the coexistence of internal and external attributions slowly giving way to one which is solely external, and a concomitant change in affect from dysphoria to suspicion and anger. The strength of the theory lies in the twin opportunities for cognitive early interventions that are discussed later.

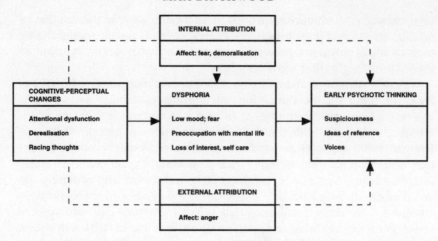

Figure 10.3 Psychological aspects of early relapse: an attributional model

COLLABORATIVE EARLY INTERVENTION

Engagement and education

Early intervention rests on a close cooperation between patient, carer/relative and professionals. In common with many interventions, an ethos of trust and 'informed partnership' between these groups must be developed (Smith and Birchwood, 1990). Education about prodromes and early intervention opportunities need to be provided, which might be given in the context of general educational intervention about psychosis (Birchwood *et al.*, 1992; Smith and Birchwood, 1990). Education must emphasise that some responsibility is being placed on the individual and relative to recognise a potential relapse and to initiate treatment. Engagement and compliance will be enhanced where the client has a stable, trusting relationship with individuals in the mental health services. As the experience of Jolley *et al.* (1990) illustrates, this requires psychoeducation to be a continuous feature of this relationship. The continuity of care inherent in the case management approach provides an appropriate support structure (Shepherd, 1990).

Suitable clients

Individuals with a history of repeated relapse or who are at high risk of relapse, for reasons of non-adherence with a maintenance medication regime, recovery from a recent relapse, living alone or in a high Expressed Emotion family environment, may be appropriate to participate in early intervention, as will those who fear relapse and are demoralised by their apparent inability to control it. For those with severe drug-refractory positive symptoms, discriminating a prodrome against such a background is likely to prove extremely difficult (indeed its very existence is questionable) and early intervention becomes less meaningful in this context. The absence of insight may preclude an individual's acceptance of an early intervention strategy; indeed the ultimate test will be the individual's acceptance of the approach, which in our experience has much to do with his or her dislike of the dislocation which relapse/readmission can cause, as well as fear of the experience itself. The availability of a close relative or carer, to maximise information about prodromal signs and provide support, can be helpful but must be selected in collaboration with the individual.

Identifying the time window and relapse signature for early intervention

The previous review of the literature suggests four problems which need to be overcome if our knowledge about prodromes is to have clinical application. First, the identification of 'early signs' by a clinician would require intensive, regular monitoring of mental state at least fortnightly which is rarely possible in clinical practice. Second, some patients choose to conceal their symptoms as relapse approaches and insight declines (Heinrichs *et al.*, 1985). Third, many patients experience persisting symptoms, cognitive deficits or drug side-effects which may obscure the visibility of the prodromes. Indeed, the nature of a prodrome in patients with residual symptoms (in contrast to those who are symptom free) has not been studied, and is important, since in clinical practice the presence of residual symptoms is extremely common. Fourth, the possibility is raised that the characteristics of prodromes might vary from individual to individual and this information may be lost in scales of general psychopathology and the group designs of research studies.

With regard to the latter, precise information about the nature and duration of an individual's prodrome or 'relapse signature' may be obtained through careful interviewing of the patient (and, if possible, relatives and other close associates) about the changes in thinking and behaviour leading up to a recent episode. Where this is fed back, it may enable a more accurate discrimination of a future prodrome.

Such an interview (used by the author) is shown in Table 10.4. This involves five stages. The first establishes the date of onset of the episode and the time between this and any admission. The second establishes the date when a change in behaviour was *first* noticed; and in the third and fourth stages the sequence of subsequent changes is established using specific prompts if necessary. Finally, the prodrome is summarised. Figure 10.4 represents the outcome of one such interview which was drawn by the client herself. A cognitive intervention developed for this individual is described in the next section.

Table 10.4 Early Signs interview: relatives' version

Stage One : Establish date of onset/admission to hospital and behaviour at height of episode.
'On what date was X admitted to hospital?'
　　Prompt: date, day, time; contemporary events to aid recall.
'When did you decide he needed help?'
　　Prompt: date.
'What was X's behaviour like at that time?'
　　Prompt: What kind of things was he saying?
　　　　　　What kind of things was he doing?

Stage Two : Establish date when change in X was first noticed
'So X was admitted to hospital weeks after you decided (s)he needed help
. . .'
'Think back carefully to the days or weeks before then'
'When did you first notice a change in X's unusual behaviour or anything
out of the ordinary?'
　　Prompt: Nature, time of change.
'Were there any changes before then, even ones which might not seem
important?'

Stage Three : Establish sequence of changes up to relapse
'Id like to establish the changes that took place after that up to (date) when
you decided X needed help . . .'
'What happened next (after last change)?'
　　Prompt: Was this a marked change?
　　　　　　When did this happen?
　　　　　　Can you give me some examples?
　　　　　　Repeat question until point of relapse is reached.

Stage Four : Prompting for ideas not already elicited
'During this build up to his relapse/admission to hospital . . .'
'Was he unusually anxious or on edge?'
　　Prompt: When did you notice this?
　　　　　　Prompt items from relevant Early Signs checklist.
'Did he seem low in his/her spirits?'
　　Prompt: As above.
'Did he seem disinhibited (excitable, restless, aggressive, drinking, etc).'
　　Prompt: As above.
'Did he seem suspicious or say/do strange things?'
　　Prompt: As above.

Stage Five : Summary
'Let me see if I'm clear on what happened before X's admission'
'X was admitted on (date), (number) weeks after you decided he needed
help; he was (describe presentation)'.
'You first noticed something was wrong on (date) when he (describe
behaviour) . . . then s(he) began to . . .'.
(Complete description of prodrome)
'Have I missed anything out?'

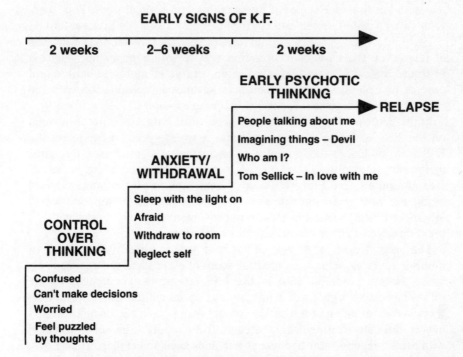

EARLY SIGNS OF K.F.

| 2 weeks | 2–6 weeks | 2 weeks |

EARLY PSYCHOTIC
THINKING

RELAPSE

People talking about me

Imagining things – Devil

ANXIETY/
WITHDRAWAL

Who am I?

Tom Sellick – In love with me

Sleep with the light on

CONTROL
OVER
THINKING

Afraid

Withdraw to room

Neglect self

Confused
Can't make decisions
Worried
Feel puzzled
by thoughts

Figure 10.4 A hypothesis about the relapse signature (K.F.)

Monitoring and intervention

In our work, individuals engage in a process of monitoring using the ESS scales described earlier.

This has four objectives:

1. To develop a baseline measure against which changes can be discerned and compared.
2. To reinforce the discrimination of the changed perceptual, cognitive and affective processes through use of appropriate labels.
3. To educate individuals, their carers and professionals about the precise nature of the 'relapse signature'.
4. To promote client's engagement in services, and to share responsibility for prodrome detection between individual and professionals.

Thus, monitoring is conceived not as a lifetime activity but as a relatively short-term manoeuvre to learn about prodromes, to engage patient and professional in meaningful activity to enhance control and to demonstrate that control can be achieved.

In the next stage, decision rules are discerned to define the onset of a prodrome operationally; these include a quantitative change on the ESS

193

scales and/or the appearance of individualised prodromal signs. This, then, is an entirely client driven and controlled system, as is the intervention.

Early intervention seeks to intervene as early as possible in the process of relapse on the basis of information that relapse is probable. Where a pharmacological intervention is indicated, a targeted and time-limited oral dose of neuroleptics may be chosen in advance in consultation with the client. Figure 10.5 gives three individual case examples.

In the first case (Figure 10.5a), SH achieved a baseline score of thirteen on the ESS scale; his decision rule was a twenty point increase on the ESS scale including the presence of idiosyncratic signs: racing thoughts, inefficient and confused thinking, poor concentration and a 'giggly' affect. He self-administered a targeted dose of 20mg Stelazine which was increased by 50 per cent if an improvement was not observed within one week. His record clearly shows a steady improvement over six weeks with no breakthrough of either hallucinations or delusions.

The second case, a 28-year-old female with a three year history of multiple relapses, achieved a baseline score of eleven and the decision rule was a twenty point increase in the ESS scores, in the context of the following relapse signature: irritability and social withdrawal, entertaining thoughts about being in telepathic contact with people she once knew and having difficulty distinguishing dreams from reality. She self-medicated with Stelazine, and after five weeks her signs subsided (Figure 10.5b).

In the third case, targeting began when TS experienced a relapse signature, including: poor concentration, inefficient thinking, social withdrawal and a loss of appetite for up to a week accompanied by a change of ESS scores of twenty points. Again, the impact of self-medication was readily apparent and shown in Figure 10.5c.

A sense of ownership over these data should be fostered with patients and their families so that responsibility for initiating early intervention is a shared one; for example in the author's work, regular updated copies of the graphs are available to participants, many of whom are taught to interact with the computer-based system. Educating patients and relatives about early signs of relapse, collaboration in monitoring, feeding back to them information from the early signs interview and any detected prodromes should significantly raise the likelihood of future early detection and therefore intervention.

Support and counselling

Once a prodrome has been declared, the individual and family need intensive support. The psychological reaction to a loss of well-being, and the possibility that this may herald a relapse, places a significant strain on both parties, which, if unchecked, could accelerate the decompensation process. The availability of support, quick access to the team, the use of

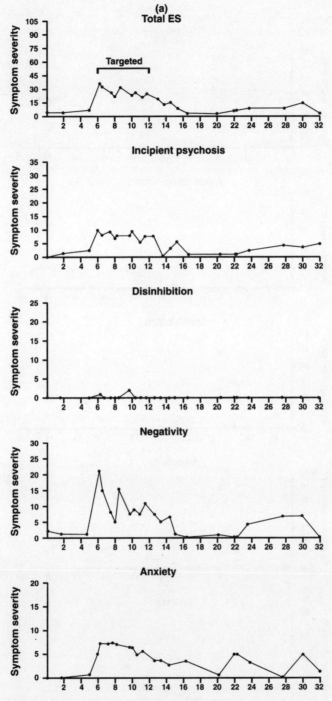

Figure 10.5 The impact of early pharmacological intervention: 3 case examples

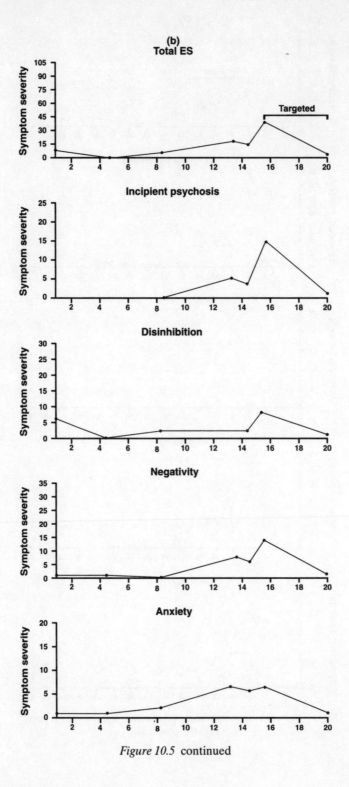

Figure 10.5 continued

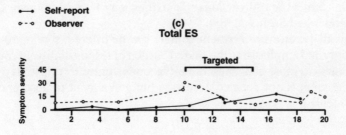

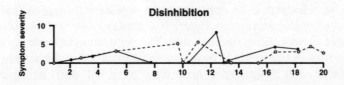

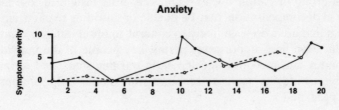

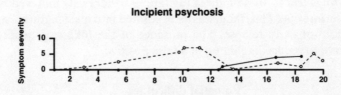

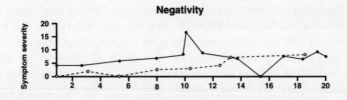

Figure 10.5 continued

MAX BIRCHWOOD

stress management and diversionary activities may help to mitigate these effects (Breier and Strauss, 1983).

Weekly, daily, or even inpatient contact can be offered, serving to alleviate anxiety and emphasising the shared burden of responsibility. In routine clinical practice, most clinicians value the opportunity to utilise day care where admission is not deemed necessary but an element of decompensation is evident.

Clarifying the relapse signature

Impending or actual crises present an important opportunity to 'sharpen the image' of the signature for client, carer and professional; in this respect the crisis can be reframed as an opportunity to acquire information that can facilitate control and prevention. Figure 10.6 illustrates a client who showed early relapse on more than one occasion. The prodromes of these episodes are juxtaposed in the figure. Considerable consistency in the nature and timing of the early symptoms is apparent, consistent with the signature concept. In the case of TF, the record clarifies that the time window is at least two weeks; the onset of 'psychotic thinking' coincides with increases in agitation and withdrawal. Two weeks prior to this, TF showed clear evidence of an *improvement* in these indices (agitation/withdrawal) followed by an abrupt deterioration. This, then, was incorporated into his signature, 'raising the question' of early relapse. The presence of the following qualitative aspects serve to reduce likelihood of a false positive.

Potential difficulties

Notwithstanding its potential therapeutic value, the notion of self-monitoring does raise a number of concerns about sensitising patients and carers to disability, promoting the observations as critical responses, burdening individuals at frequent intervals, or increasing the risk of self-harm in an individual who becomes demoralised by an impending relapse. There is, as yet, no evidence that self-monitoring is likely to increase the risk of self-harm; indeed, florid and uncontrolled relapse may be more dangerous and more damaging. Engaging patients and carers more actively in the management of the illness may also promote a sense of purposeful activity and have therapeutic benefits per se. However, it is probable that a substantial group of patients, who retain very little insight or lose insight very early in decompensation, may be unable or unwilling to entertain self-monitoring, and are also least likely to consent to observation by another. Family education and support may permit key people in the individual's life to monitor and recognise specific early warning signs, and to initiate preventative strategies such as seeking professional help promptly if relapse is predicted.

198

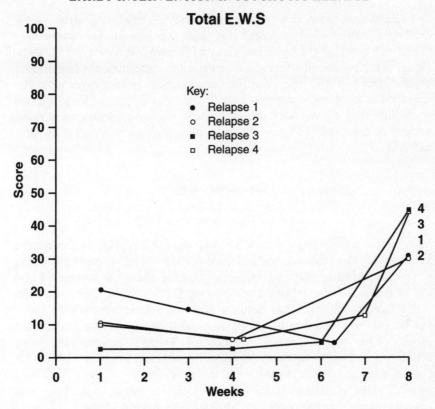

Figure 10.6 Clarifying the relapse signature (T.F.)

COGNITIVE EARLY INTERVENTION

The pursuance of control and the 'search for meaning' framework described earlier offers options for a cognitive approach to the enhancement of self-care. Three components might be considered. The first step involves identifying the attributions that individuals make about their symptoms, which may include catastrophisation (e.g. "I am relapsing and I can't control it"), the employment of an externalising attribution linked to the appraisal of changed mental life (e.g. "something is happening to me") or social attribution (e.g. "people are saying they're not interested in me").

Second, a modified form of cognitive therapy (CT) may be employed to facilitate reattribution that emphasises control: *decatastrophisation* is a CT technique frequently employed in the management of panic attacks and involves the examination of supposed catastrophic consequences

199

and emphasises those aspects that are within the clients' control; *verbal challenge*, *hypothetical contradiction* and the *search for alternatives* (Chadwick and Lowe, 1990; Chadwick and Birchwood, 1994) are CT techniques that have found a therapeutic role in the management of delusional beliefs. Third is the use of stress management manoeuvres and the rehearsal of a coping repertoire, including the challenging of these various cognitions that disempower the individual. We have conducted a small number of case studies to develop these ideas, and below we offer a recent example.

Case Study: KF

Assessment

Six weeks into a training course at a local college, KF reported a diminution in her ability to sustain concentration on her studies and further disturbing symptoms including restlessness, anxiety, racing thoughts, low mood and loss of sleep. She also reported entertaining themes about the relationship with a famous actor and had begun to feel that people were talking about her on the bus, referring to her past sexual behaviour and fantasies and aspects of her family's feelings towards her. These referential ideas were often triggered while watching the television or travelling on her own. This constellation of symptoms conformed to her prodrome, and was confirmed by an elevated score on the ESS scales from eight to twenty-eight. Interview enlisted three recurring cognitions associated with her distress:

1. "I'm relapsing, it's my fault and I'm going right back to the beginning (of my recovery)."
2. "I'm immature for having these sexual fantasies."
3. "Everyone knows about my past."

Intervention

Within a collaborative atmosphere, the three cognitions were discriminated and addressed. The first two cognitions were generalised ones and appeared to be linked to periods of restlessness and agitation.

Regarding the first cognition, it was suggested that the tendency to relapse was a feature of the illness for which she bore no responsibility: she was invited to consider the case of her friends at the hostel where she lived who had shown signs of relapse following a stressful period and whether she would consider *them* responsible. She reasoned that to avoid training courses and the like was a sign of being defeated by her illness; at least she had tried. The factors within her control were reviewed. In order to decatastrophise her thinking about relapse, a short-term stress control

200

measure was agreed involving a reduction in her attendance at college from four days a week to two, and similarly a reduction in the time she spent watching the television, as this was a trigger for her ideas of reference. To reinforce the stress attribution, KF was taught some anxiety management techniques including breathing control and muscular relaxation.

The cognition that she was immature was countered by asking her to consider whether this held true in the light of evidence of her past relapses. Even though her last relapse was a full one, she nevertheless managed to get to the point of returning to college: the fact that on this occasion she had caught her relapse early was offered as evidence for her learning greater control which would improve, and not adversely affect her recovery and well-being. Through a process of 'live' rehearsal she was encouraged to challenge these cognitions concurrently with the stress management techniques.

KF felt guilty that "someone of my age should not be having these [sexual] thoughts". A distinction was made between her sexual fantasies and the re-emergence of the delusional theme about the famous actor. With regard to the former, therapy focused on normalising such fantasies and these were tested by encouraging her to discuss these in confidence with a trusted friend and her key worker. The thought about the famous actor was caricatured as a 'fossilised' thought that had been laid down during the time of her life when her illness began (her teens) which re-emerged on these occasions, and thus it was suggested had no meaning. As evidence of this she declared that this actor was no longer attractive to her and was simply a teenage idol. This re-framing approach served to disengage her from the thought and enabled her to dismiss it.

The third, referential, cognition was examined by use of a verbal challenge (see Chadwick and Birchwood, Chapter 4 in this book) centring on the motive and means by which others would try to achieve this. The fact that the referential ideas centred only on her guilty thoughts about her past was considered. KF acknowledged that guilty thoughts do lead to 'paranoid vigilance' and day-to-day examples were identified to support this. This was tested by rehearsing some distraction techniques – it was predicted that the more she was able to distract her thoughts, the less she would experience referential thinking. This was made achievable through use of brief programmed bus journeys which were the main setting conditions for her ideas of reference.

Outcome

KF was seen three times a week for two weeks. Her EWS score reverted to baseline as did her insight score. No pharmacological intervention was used and KF slowly increased her days at college.

THE EFFICACY OF EARLY INTERVENTION

In the opening section of this chapter it was argued that perceived loss of control over 'illness' (relapse, residual symptoms), the life goals they affect as well as relapse itself can lead to deleterious outcomes for people with a psychosis (depression/demoralisation, suicide, raised relapse risk). In addition to any further opportunities that early pharmacological and/or cognitive intervention may offer the control of relapse, the collaborative ethos of early intervention which places the individual in the 'driving seat' may promote control and self-efficacy. The important evaluative questions then become:

1. Can pharmacological interventions initiated at the onset of apparent early symptoms slow down or arrest the relapse process?
2. Is cognitive early intervention effective and can it achieve a similar or better outcome than pharmacological early intervention and is their combination better than either alone?
3. Does the process of early intervention (education, collaborative monitoring, etc.) improve clients' understanding and discrimination of prodromes and control of relapse and promote a 'collaborative' style of engagement with services?

Pharmacological early intervention

All the reviewed drug studies have involved withdrawing patients from maintenance regimes, monitoring clinical state and providing brief pharma-cotherapy at the onset of a prodrome. This paradigm has been chosen with the goal of minimising drug exposure and therefore side-effects, without prejudicing prophylaxis, rather than as a means of further controlling relapse. This issue will be returned to at the conclusion of this section.

Three well-controlled studies have been reported (Table 10.5) using this paradigm. Jolley *et al.* (1989, 1990) studied 54 stabilised, symptomatic and, thus, highly selected patients who were randomly assigned to active or placebo maintenance therapy conditions, with both receiving early drug intervention at the onset of a prodrome which involved the administration of 5–10 mg daily of Haloperidol. Patients received a brief educational session on entry to the study about prodromes and early intervention, as reliance was placed on patients to recognise their early signs of relapse and to contact the clinical team. Outcome at one year revealed that significantly more patients experienced prodromal symptoms in the intermittent group (76 per cent) than in the control group (27 per cent), which was accompanied by an increased rate of relapse in the intermittent group (30 per cent versus 7 per cent), although there was good evidence that 'severe' relapse was not affected and was indeed low in both groups. Nevertheless, the large difference between the number of prodromes and number of relapses

Table 10.5 Pharmacological early intervention studies

	Maintenance and targeted		Targeted only	
	Jolley	Carpenter	Jolley	Carpenter
Relapse – 1 year	7%		30%	
– 2 year	12%	36%	50%	53%
Readmissions – 1 year	7%		13%	
Prodromes	27%	1.6/year	76%	3.18/year
Side-effects	55	?	24	?
Drug-free period	0%	0%	?	48%
Non-adherence		19%		51%

does suggest that prompt action can abort relapse in many instances. During the first year of the study, 73 per cent of relapses were preceded by identified prodromal symptoms; during the second year this fell to 25 per cent, as reliance was placed on patients and families to identify and seek assistance for prodromal symptoms. This suggests 'that the single teaching session at the start of the study does not provide patients and families with an adequate grasp of the intermittent paradigm ... ongoing psycho-educational intervention should be an essential component of further studies' (Jolley et al., 1990, p. 841).

Carpenter et al. (1990) report the outcome of a study of similar design to Jolley and colleagues with largely similar outcomes. However, in their study, not only was the intermittent regime less effective, it was less popular too: 50 per cent refused to continue with the regime (versus 20 per cent in continuous treatment), presumably due to the higher rate of prodromes and hospitalisation and perhaps also due to the fact that patients found the responsibility placed on them to recognise relapse an excessive one.

Gaebel et al. (1993) report a multi-centre open German trial comparing maintenance and targeted medication, targeted medication alone ('early intervention') and no pharmacotherapy. Six 'prodromal' symptoms were measured by the participating psychiatrists using a four point scale of severity on a 'regular' basis; impending relapse was defined on the basis of a 'significant increase' in these symptoms, but was essentially determined by the psychiatrist. The study found that relapse under targeted pharma-cotherapy alone (49 per cent) was less than no pharmacotherapy (63 per cent) but was greater than maintenance and targeted pharmacotherapy combined (23 per cent). This study suffered from a massive drop-out of over 56 per cent, on a par with the Carpenter study, and no data are presented regarding selectivity of drop-outs by experimental condition. Unlike the other studies, the results do suggest that targeted medication alone is effective in controlling relapse compared to no treatment, but again the value and relative popularity of maintenance medication is clearly underlined.

The methodology used to identify relapse prodromes has relied heavily upon patients' skill and their initiative to alert services. Jolley *et al.* (1990) have suggested that a brief educational session is insufficient for patients to sustain a grasp of the prodrome concept and early intervention; and the high drop-out rate noted by Carpenter *et al.* (1990) underlies its unpopularity. This experience suggests that this responsibility is viewed best as one that is very clearly shared between patient, carer and services.

Experimental designs ask specific questions and hitherto the early intervention studies have asked only limited questions, namely, whether a targeted regime alone yields comparable prophylaxis to one which combines maintenance and targeting yet minimises side-effects. The answer to this is clearly negative, although the Gaebel study does suggest that targeted treatment is not without benefit. For present purposes, therefore, our question then becomes, can a 'standard' dose maintenance medication combined with a targeting paradigm control relapse to an adequate degree?

The study of Jolley *et al.* found an unusually low rate of relapse over two years in the group receiving continuous and targeted regimes (12 per cent) suggesting a possible additive effect. Marder *et al.* (1984, 1987) studied patients assigned to a low (5 mg) or standard (20 mg) dose maintenance regime of Fluphenazine Decanoate over two weeks and at the first sign of exacerbation the dose was doubled. If this failed, patients were considered to have relapsed, which occurred in 22 per cent taking the lower dose and 20 per cent on the higher dose, with fewer side-effects in the former. Marder *et al.* found that lower doses carried a greater risk of relapse, but these were not 'serious' and were eliminated once the clinician was permitted to double the dose at the onset of a prodrome (the survival curves of the dosage groups were not different under targeted conditions). The study by Gaebel *et al.* (1993) found the rate of two year relapse under maintenance and targeted pharmacotherapy was 23 per cent compared to 48 per cent under targeted conditions alone ($p < 0.001$). Overall these data suggest two conclusions: first, using pharmacotherapy alone, in maintenance and targeted forms, relapse can be reduced to between 12–23 per cent over two years; and second this can be achieved with a low dose regime. A cognitively oriented intervention would therefore have some further work to do to reduce relapse still further if it were to be combined with this 'ideal' form of pharmacotherapy.

Opportunities for cognitive early intervention do not rest on this consideration alone, however. There is first of all the problem of medication non-adherence (Hoge, 1990). Studies of clients' attitudes to medication show that the prevailing view is ambivalent: a necessary evil (Pan and Tantam, 1989). This resistance is linked partly to the experience of dysphoria and other drug side-effects (Hogan *et al.*, 1985) and to a perception that treatment is coercive and disempowering.

Non-adherence has been associated with youth (Davis *et al.*, 1977), compulsory detention (Buchanan, 1992) and to its excessive use among Black groups (Sashidharan, 1993). Cognitive and pharmacological early intervention approaches that are essentially client driven may find favour with those who are disaffected by prescriptive approaches. In the wider arena of psychosocial interventions, a titration of drug dose against family intervention has been reported (Falloon *et al.*, 1985; Hogarty *et al.*, 1988); a cognitive approach to early intervention, if successful, may similarly offer options that allow medication to be used more sparingly than at present, thus maximising its efficacy and attractiveness.

Collaborative early intervention

Collaborative early intervention described here is an attempt to confer, in a practical sense, empowerment in relation to relapse by placing the individual in the 'driving seat', determining when and if and how intervention should take place. We are presently in the midst of a trial of this approach but we are able to present indirect evidence that the impact of collaborative early intervention is a positive one.

Table 10.6 shows a comparison of thirty-five patients taking part in our early intervention project two years prior to and post trial entry (i.e. non first episodes). This shows a sharp decline in rates of readmission including compulsory admission and time spent in hospital. We believe the style of service provision is facilitating the engagement with services of a difficult client group who were selected as young, high relapse risk and predominantly inner city resident. We are also collecting data on a group of clients who have spent two years in the early intervention programme, comparing them with a case matched control group on their ability to discriminate and clarify their prodrome, their understanding of the significance of these symptoms and their attribution of these symptoms, and fear and control of relapse (Davis and Birchwood, in preparation).

Cognitive early intervention

There are as yet no studies which have attempted to evaluate cognitive early interventions using single cases or group studies. As we have seen, there is little as yet in the way of theory to guide such an approach. Stress-vulnerability is a general theory which would offer stress management intervention linked to the cues or stressors and to clients' cognitive and emotional stress responses. If the model outlined in Figure 10.3 is correct, then once in prodrome, cognitive and attributional processes would come into play that might exacerbate stress (e.g. catastrophic thoughts about relapse) as well as driving delusional thought through an externalising attribution process.

205

Table 10.6 Analysis of admissions and days in admission 2 years pre- and post-trial entry (Those entering the trial after a first admission are excluded)

	Pre-trial entry	*Post-trial entry*
No. (%) of patients admitted	26 (74%)	9 (26%)
Total no. of admissions for group	31	10
No. of compulsory admissions	13	1
Days in hospital	2781	729

n = 35 patients

Since prodromes are neither regular nor prolonged occurrences, developing these interventions will be fraught with difficulty (in contrast to cognitive therapy for psychotic symptoms or panic disorder). This will necessitate the use of considerable rehearsal as a prelude to in vivo management of the kind described for KF. There are immense opportunities here, particularly as it holds out the hope of engaging a client group who are traditionally resistant and for whom the approach outlined in this chapter will have face validity.

IMPLICATIONS AND CLINICAL APPLICATIONS

The clinical application of early signs monitoring offers considerable opportunity for improving care. However, if the encouraging results of the early intervention studies employing targeted medication are to be realised in clinical practice, careful thought must be given to the identification of individual 'relapse signatures', the design of monitoring methodology and the nature of the service response to secure these advances for the well-being of patients.

The relationship between early signs of decompensation and actual psychotic relapse remains unclear. There is unlikely to be a simplistic relationship and the evidence suggests that false positives and negatives will occur. We have discussed a number of means to improve the specificity of early signs information using additional information relating to idiosyncratic signs for a given individual.

Experienced staff, engaged in long-term clinics supporting patients often have years of regular contact with a client, and can provide useful information concerning certain key changes which in themselves might go unnoticed but, for a given individual, may be highly predictive of relapse. The fuller 'relapse signature' that is thus obtained can be incorporated into the early signs monitoring procedure and used as a hypothesis to predict specific idiosyncratic signs which will occur at a subsequent relapse of a given individual. Any additional early signs information observed at this relapse can be added to the signature, thereby increasing the accuracy of prediction with each relapse.

The strategy of close monitoring by highly trained personnel is impractical in routine care. On the other hand, the use of close monitoring by staff for particular target groups with a high relapse risk is limited by the ability to reliably select high potential relapsers. The methodology adopted by Birchwood et al. (1989), harnessing the experiences of patients and their carers in a routine service setting, may be possible to apply clinically. This offers the potential for documenting information relating to early signs of relapse for a substantial group of patients, with relatively limited input of professional time. However, it is still probable that a substantial group of patients, who retain very little insight or lose insight very early in decompensation, may be unable or unwilling to entertain self-monitoring, and are also least likely to consent to observation by another. There are no easy solutions to these problems, although education about the illness may, in some cases, improve insight and permit key people in the individual's life to monitor and recognise specific early warning signs, and to initiate preventative strategies such as seeking professional help promptly if relapse is predicted.

Notwithstanding its potential therapeutic value, the notion of self-monitoring does raise a number of concerns about sensitising patients and carers to disability, promoting the observations as critical responses, burdening individuals and carers further with requests for repetitive information at frequent intervals, or increasing the risk of self-harm in an individual who becomes demoralised by an impending relapse. There is no real evidence that self-monitoring is likely to increase the risk of self-harm; indeed, florid and uncontrolled relapse may be more dangerous and more damaging. Engaging patients and carers more actively in the management of the illness may also promote a sense of purposeful activity and have therapeutic benefits per se. The repetitive nature of the procedure may be self-defeating in the long term and indeed wasteful in well-stabilised patients. Instituting monitoring at times of stress may be a reasonable alternative to continuous monitoring. Those individuals who develop expertise in monitoring through a number of relapses may develop and sharpen the signature in the minds of professionals and carers alike. Despite the many limitations, if early signs monitoring fulfils even part of its promise, it may for many patients with recurrent episodes, promote learning and lead to increased opportunity for combined efforts to control exacerbations due to stress.

For the group of patients who routinely attend clinical appointments, information from monitoring by patients and carers has an identified route of access. If this route were formalised it might be possible to ensure clear responses from the service. However, not all patients attend services and the move away from an institutional model is likely to further devolve care away from centralised services. The difficulty in accessing traditional psychiatric services was well documented by Creer and Wing (1974), and

Johnstone *et al.* a decade later (1984), describe patchy access to care with particular problems for relocated patients and families. The implementation of case management for the long-term mentally ill may ensure constant service links at a distance, but the utilisation of psychiatric services during critical periods will necessarily require information concerning early signs of relapse to be adequately assessed and harnessed (Shepherd, 1990).

The nature of the service response to information concerning early signs of decompensation is still an open question. Most clinical trials have employed pharmacological interventions upon recognition of early signs of decompensation (Hirsch and Jolley, 1989). Within defined cohorts (as in clinical trials) the use of targeted medication has not been sufficient to cope with individual variation. In the clinical setting, where there is a very wide range of maintenance therapy and where the dose and duration of targeting is likely to vary considerably between individuals, targeted medication would be required to be individually tailored. The implementation of strategies that are already recognised by patients and carers as useful would often be entirely appropriate. Indeed, the work of McCandless-Glincher *et al.* (1986) is particularly encouraging since it suggests that very nearly all patients recognise loss of well-being and the majority institute some change in behaviour at their own initiative in response to this, including engaging in diversionary activities, seeking professional help or resuming and increasing neuroleptic medication. In the face of this information, individuals might be encouraged to employ self-management strategies, e.g. stress management procedures or symptom control strategies (Breier and Strauss, 1983) to initiate preventative actions in terms of increasing the frequency of day centre attendance, requesting brief admission, or enlisting professional support to assist in symptom management. This may require radical service change in the direction of developing a more responsive and flexible service than currently exists. The resultant service envisaged would need to be proactive rather than reactive, and responsive to the needs and concerns of individuals and their carers, particularly if these alternative preventative strategies are to be viable.

In summary, routinely monitoring early signs to identify individual relapse signatures opens the possibility for individuals to recognise and act on symptoms suggestive of reduced well-being and to initiate early intervention strategies to prevent relapse. However, if the promising results of the research studies are to be systematically applied and incorporated into routine clinical practice a viable system of monitoring needs to be established in order to access information routinely and accurately. The service structure also needs to be adapted in order to facilitate this and to be able to respond flexibly and promptly when relapse is predicted. It is to this end that the authors' research efforts are devoted.

REFERENCES

American Psychiatric Association (1987) *Diagnostic and Statistical Manual of Mental Disorders*, 3rd edition, revised, Washington DC: APA.

Birchwood, M. and Tarrier, N. (eds) (1992) *Innovations in the Psychological Management of Schizophrenia*, Chichester: Wiley.

Birchwood, M., Smith, J. and Cochrane, R. (1992) 'Specific and non-specific effects of educational intervention for families living with schizophrenia: A comparison of three methods', *British Journal of Psychiatry* 160: 806–14.

Birchwood, M., Smith, J., Macmillan, F., Hogg, B., Prasad, R., Harvey, C. and Bering, S. (1989) 'Predicting relapse in schizophrenia: The development and implementation of an early signs monitoring system using patients and families as observers', *Psychological Medicine* 19: 649–56.

Breier, A. and Strauss, J. S. (1983) 'Self control in psychiatric disorders', *Archives of General Psychiatry* 40: 1141–5.

Brewin, C. (1988) *Cognitive Foundations of Clinical Psychology*, Hove: Lawrence Erlbaum Associates.

Buchanan, A. (1992) 'A two year prospective study of treatment compliance in patients with schizophrenia', *Psychological Medicine* 22: 787–97.

Carpenter, W. I., Hanlon, T. E., Heinrichs, D. W., Summerfelt, A. T., Kirkpatrick, B., Levine, J. and Buchanan, R. W. (1990) 'Continuous versus targeted medication in schizophrenic outpatients: Outcome results', *American Journal of Psychiatry* 147: 1138–48.

Chadwick, P. and Birchwood, M. (1994) 'The omnipotence of voices. A cognitive approach to auditory hallucinations', *British Journal of Psychiatry* 164: 190–201.

Chadwick, P. and Lowe, C. F. (1990) 'The measurement and modification of delusional beliefs', *Journal of Consulting and Clinical Psychology* 58: 225–32.

Chapman, J. (1966) 'The early symptoms of schizophrenia', *British Journal of Psychiatry* 112: 22–251.

Clements, D. and Turpin, G. (1992) 'Vulnerability theories' in M. Birchwood and N. Tarrier (eds) *Innovations in the Psychological Management of Schizophrenia*, Chichester: Wiley.

Creer, C. and Wing, J. (1974) *Schizophrenia at Home*, Surbiton: National Schizophrenia Fellowship.

Davis, E. and Birchwood, M. (in preparation) 'Clarifying the relapse signature in people with psychosis: The impact of prodromal monitoring'.

Davis, J. M., Estess, F. M., Simonton, S. C. and Gonda, T. A. (1977) 'Effects of payment mode on clinical attendance and rehospitalisation', *American Journal of Psychiatry* 134: 576–8.

Derogatis, L., Lipman, R. and Covi, L. (1973) 'SCL-90: An outpatient psychiatric rating scale – preliminary report', *Psychopharmacology Bulletin* 9, 13–17.

Donlon, P. T. and Blacker, K. H. (1975) 'Clinical recognition of early schizophrenic decompensation', *Disorders of the Nervous System* 36: 323–30.

Falloon, I. R. H., Boyd, J. L. and McGill, C. W. (1985) 'Family management in the prevention of morbidity of schizophrenia', *Archives of General Psychiatry* 42: 887–96.

Foulds, G. W. (1976) *The Hierarchical Nature of Personal Illness*, London: Academic Press.

Gaebel, V., Frick, W. and Kopcke, M. (1993) 'Early neuroleptic intervention in schizophrenia', *British Journal of Psychiatry* 163: 8–12.

Heinrichs, D., Cohen, B. and Carpenter, W. (1985) 'Early insight and the management of schizophrenic decompensation', *The Journal of Nervous and Mental Disease* 173: 133–8.

Herz, M. and Melville, C. (1980) 'Relapse in schizophrenia', *American Journal of Psychiatry* 137: 801–12.

Herz, M. I., Szymanski, H. V. and Simon, J. (1982) 'Intermittent medication for stable schizophrenic outpatients', *American Journal of Psychiatry* 139: 918–22.

Hirsch, S. R. and Jolley, A. G. (1989) 'The dysphoric syndrome in schizophrenia and its implications for relapse', *British Journal of Psychiatry* 156: 46–50.

Hogan, T. P., Awed, A. G. and Eastwood, M. R. (1985) 'Early subjective response and prediction of outcome to neuroleptic drug treatment in schizophrenia', *Canadian Journal of Psychiatry* 30: 246–8.

Hogarty, G. E., McEvoy, J. P., Munetz, M., DiBarry, A. L., Bartone, P., Cather, R., Cooley, S. J., Ulrich, R. F., Carter, M. and Madonia, M. J. (1988) 'Dose of fluphenazine, familial expressed emotion and outcome in schizophrenia', *Archives of General Psychiatry* 45: 797–805.

Hogarty, G. E., Anderson, C. M., Reiss, D. J., Kornblith, S. J., Greenwald, D. P., Ulrich, R. F. and Carter, M. (1991) 'Family psychoeducation, social skills training and maintenance chemotherapy in the after care treatment of schizophrenia: II Two year effects of a controlled study on relapse and adjustment', *Archives of General Psychiatry* 48: 340–7.

Hoge, S. K. (1990) 'A prospective multi-centre study of patients' refusal of anti-psychotic medication', *Archives of General Psychiatry* 47, 949–56.

Johnstone, E. C., Owens, D. G. C., Gold, A., Crow, T. and Macmillan, J. F. (1984) 'Schizophrenic patients discharged from hospital: A follow up study', *British Journal of Psychiatry* 145: 586–90.

Jolley, A. G., Hirsch, S. R., McRink, A. and Wilson, L. (1989) 'Trial of brief intermittent neuroleptic prophylaxis for selected schizophrenic outpatients: Clinical outcome at one year', *British Medical Journal* 298: 985–90.

Jolley, A. G., Hirsch, S. R., Morrison, G., McRink, A. and Wilson, L. (1990) 'Trial of brief intermittent neuroleptic prophylaxis for selected schizophrenia outpatients: Clinical and social outcome at two years', *British Medical Journal* 301: 837–42.

Kane, J. (ed.) (1984) *Drug Maintenance Strategies in Schizophrenia*, Washington DC: American Psychiatric Press.

Kumar, S., Thara, R. and Rajkumar, S. (1989) 'Coping with symptoms of relapse in schizophrenia', *European Archives of Psychiatry and Neurological Sciences* 239: 213–15.

Loebel, A., Lieberman, J. and Jose, M. (1992) 'Duration of psychosis and outcome in first episode schizophrenia', *American Journal of Psychiatry* 149: 1183–8.

McCandless-Glincher, L., McKnight, S., Hamera, E., Smith, B. L., Peterson, K. and Plumlee, A. A. (1986) 'Use of symptoms by schizophrenics to monitor and regulate their illness', *Hospital and Community Psychiatry* 37: 929–33.

McGlashan, T. H. (1988) 'A selective review of recent North American follow-up studies of schizophrenia', *Schizophrenia Bulletin* 14: 515–42.

Maher, B. A. (1988) 'Anomalous experiences and delusional thinking: The logic of explanations', in T. F. Oltmanns and B. A. Maher (eds) *Delusional Beliefs*, New York: Wiley.

Malla, A. K. and Norman, R. (1994) 'Prodromal symptoms in schizophrenia', *British Journal of Psychiatry* 164: 487–93.

Marder, S. R., Van Putten, T., Mintz, J., Lebell, M., McKenzie, J. and Faltico, G. (1984) 'Maintenance therapy in schizophrenia: New findings', in J. Kane (ed.) *Drug Maintenance Strategies in Schizophrenia*, Washington DC: American Psychiatric Press.

Marder, S. R., Van Putten, T., Mintz, J., McKenzie, J., Lebell, M., Faltico, G. and

May, R. P. (1987) 'Low and conventional dose maintenance therapy with fluphenazine decanoate: Two year outcome', *Archives of General Psychiatry* 44: 518–21.

Marder, S. R., Mintz, J., Van Putten, T., Lebell, M., Wirsching, W. and Johnstone-Cronk (1991) 'Early prediction of relapse in schizophrenia: An application of receiver operating characteristic (ROC) methods', *Psychopharmacology Bulletin* 27: 79–82.

Meuser, K., Bellack, A., Wade, J., Sayers, S. and Rosenthal, K. (1992) 'An assessment of the educational needs of chronic psychiatric patients and their relatives', *British Journal of Psychiatry* 160: 668–73.

Oltmanns, T. F. and Maher, B. A. (eds) (1988) *Delusional Beliefs*, New York: Wiley.

Overall, J. E. and Gorham, D. R. (1962) 'The brief psychiatric rating scale', *Psychological Reports* 10: 799–812.

Pan, R. and Tantum, D. (1989) 'Clinical characteristics, health beliefs, and compliance with maintenance treatment: A comparison between regular and irregular attenders at a depot clinic', *Acta Psychiatrica Scandinavica* 7: 564–70.

Roberts, G. (1991) 'Delusional belief systems and meaning in life: A preferred reality', *British Journal of Psychiatry* 159 (suppl. 14): 19–28.

Sashidharan, S. (1993) 'Afro-Caribbeans and schizophrenia: the ethnic vulnerability hypothesis examined', *International Review of Psychiatry* 5: 129–44.

Shepherd, G. (1990) 'Case management', *Health Trends* 22: 59–61.

Smith, J. and Birchwood, M. (1990) 'Relatives and patients as partners in the management of schizophrenia', *British Journal of Psychiatry* 156: 654–60.

Strauss, J. S. (1991) 'The person with delusions', *British Journal of Psychiatry* 159 (suppl. 14): 57–61.

Subotnik, K. L. and Nuechterlein, K. H. (1988) 'Prodromal signs and symptoms of schizophrenic relapse', *Journal of Abnormal Psychology* 97: 405–12.

Tarrier, N., Barrowclough, C. and Bamrah, J. (1991) 'Prodromal signs of relapse in schizophrenia', *Social Psychiatry and Psychiatric Epidemiology* 26: 157–61.

Weiner, B. (1985) 'Spontaneous causal thinking', *Psychological Bulletin* 97: 74–84.

Weiner, B. (1986) *An Attribution Theory of Motivation and Emotion*, New York: Springer-Verlag.

Wing, J. K., Cooper, J. and Sartorius, N. (1974) *The Description and Classification of Psychiatric Symptomology: An Instruction Manual for the PSE and CATEGO Systems*, London: Cambridge University Press.

11

FAMILY INTERVENTIONS
AND SCHIZOPHRENIA

Nicholas Tarrier

INTRODUCTION

Interest in research on family intervention and family management has been considerable, and has led to some, although patchy, service development. This interest has not been without its controversy, and opinions on the value of family management have varied between viewing it as a major breakthrough in the care of people suffering from schizophrenia to it being a trivial irrelevance. The aim of this chapter is to summarise the research on family management by:

1. briefly examining some of the background from which family management developed,
2. reviewing the efficacy of family management on a range of outcome measures,
3. examining the attempts to disseminate family management through training programmes, and finally
4. to comment, or speculate, on future developments.

BACKGROUND

When initially described, schizophrenia was thought to follow an inevitably deteriorating course; later clinical observation and longitudinal studies carried out in Europe and the USA (e.g. Ciompi, 1980; Harding *et al.*, 1987) have suggested that there can be much variation in the long-term natural history of schizophrenia, and the course over the short and medium term is frequently episodic. The development of neuroleptic medication four decades ago was heralded as a major advance in the management of schizophrenia, since the use of these drugs considerably reduced the positive symptoms of schizophrenia. Furthermore, the prophylactic use of neuroleptics increased the possibility of community tenure and reduced the need for hospitalisation. However, the inadequacies of neuroleptic medication have now become apparent. For example, many patients will fail to comply with their medication, especially when used prophylactically, and of those who do, 30 to 50 per cent will relapse in the short term (Falloon *et al.*, 1978; Hogarty *et al.*, 1979).

The vulnerability-stress model of schizophrenia

The above points emphasise the variability within the disorder, the aetiology of which still remains an enigma. In 1977, Zubin and Spring published a very influential paper outlining a vulnerability-stress model of schizophrenia (Zubin and Spring, 1977). This, they emphasised, was a second order model which attempted to accommodate a range of differing aetiological explanations of schizophrenia. The model was refined by Nuechterlein and his colleagues (Nuechterlein and Dawson, 1984; Nuechterlein, 1987) and puts forward a psychobiological formulation of schizophrenia and its course which suggests that a range of biological, psychological and psychosocial factors interact and determine the course and outcome of schizophrenia (see Figure 11.1). The principle of this formulation, that psychological and social stressors and mediators can influence the course of schizophrenia, lent impetus to management strategies to modify these factors and hence bring about positive change in the course of the disorder.

Expressed emotion

In the early 1950s, a series of research studies carried out by Brown and his colleagues at the MRC Social Psychiatry Unit in London investigated the outcome of patients discharged from psychiatric hospitals (Brown, 1985; Leff and Vaughn, 1985). The initial finding, that patients diagnosed as suffering from schizophrenia who returned to live with their parents and close family did worse than those who lived alone or in hostel accommodation (Brown *et al.*, 1958), stimulated an attempt to investigate the nature of the home environment (Brown, 1985). This resulted in the development of the measure of Expressed Emotion (EE). Although what EE actually represents is still the subject of much debate (see Kavanagh, 1992), it was initially formulated as an index of the emotional climate within the home environment and attempted to assess the quality of the relationship between patient and relative. The nature of this emotional climate was viewed as potentially important in the developing course of schizophrenia, and assuming this was true, then such a measure as EE could predict outcome. The initial studies of Brown and colleagues (Brown *et al.*, 1962; 1972) and the later study of Vaughn and Leff (1976) demonstrated an association between EE and relapse. In these studies, patients were recruited during hospitalisation for an acute episode of schizophrenia. During this hospitalisation their relatives were interviewed using a semi-structured interview known as the Camberwell Family Interview (CFI). The CFI was usually audio-taped and elicited information relating to: household composition and time budget; psychiatric history of the patient; current

213

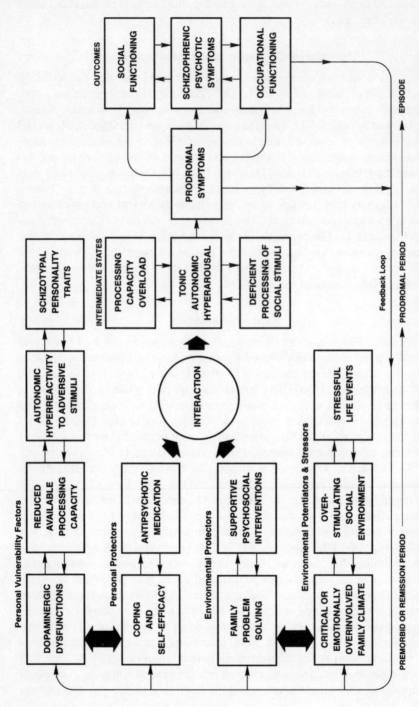

Figure 11.1 A schematic articulation of the vulnerability–stress model (reprinted by permission of Nuechterlein, 1987)

problems and symptoms; relationships between family members; and general information about activities of household members. From this interview, a number of dimensions were rated (see Chapter 2 of Leff and Vaughn, 1985 for details of the CFI). During the initial studies, the interview and the rating of EE scales were refined: the present established method of categorising EE is through the rating of the following scales:

1. Critical comments: this is a frequency count of the number of criticisms the relative makes about the patient during the interview. A critical comment needs to include an expression of dissatisfaction and a critical tone in the voice of the respondent.
2. Hostility: which is an expression of rejection of the patient and is indicated by the presence of a generalised negative comment or a rejecting comment. Hostility is rated on a four-point scale, with a score of zero indicating absence of hostility, a score of one indicating generalisation of a negative comment, two indicating the presence of rejection, and three indicating the presence of both generalisation and rejection.
3. Marked emotional overinvolvement (EOI), which includes assessment of: exaggerated emotional responses; self-sacrificing and devoted behaviour; extremely overprotective behaviour; and examples of dramatisation and emotional display during the interview. EOI is rated on a six-point global scale, from a score of zero indicating no EOI to a score of five indicating marked EOI.
4. Warmth: this refers to the warmth expressed by the relative about the patient during the interview and is rated on a six-point global scale where zero represents no warmth, up to a score of five which represents a high degree of warmth.
5. Positive remarks: these refer to statements that express praise, approval or appreciation of the behaviour or personality of the patient. This scale is expressed in a frequency count (see Chapter 3 of Leff and Vaughn, 1985 for extensive details of the EE scales).

The three dimensions of EE which are considered important are: the frequency of critical comments, the presence of hostility, and the magnitude of EOI. If any of the following three thresholds are reached: six or more critical comments, hostility present (i.e. a score of one or more), and a score of three or more on EOI, then the relative is rated as high on EE. If none of these thresholds is achieved then, by default, the relative is rated as low EE. There have been some minor modifications to these thresholds over time. For example, initial studies utilised a threshold of seven or more critical comments and a score of four or more on EOI; and because hostility is frequently associated with high levels of criticism, some workers have felt that rating hostility has not increased the predictive power and have excluded it from the rating. These minor differences do not appear to have had any effect on the robustness of EE.

In the EE studies, once discharged from hospital, the clinical condition of patients has been assessed over a follow-up period. Relapse rates between patients returning to live with high EE relatives and those returning to live with low EE relatives have then been compared. Well over twenty prospective studies have now been published and these have recently been reviewed by Kavanagh (1992). The median relapse rate in a high EE environment is 48 per cent, compared with 21 per cent in a low EE environment over the first year after discharge. Kavanagh (1992) concludes that the predictive power of EE, with regard to relapse, is remarkably robust and this effect does not appear to be due to a confounding with other variables.

The results of EE research have stimulated much interest and some controversy, and prompted researchers both to examine correlates of EE and to construct explanatory models. Briefly, research has investigated the following areas:

1. Behavioural correlates of EE. Laboratory interaction studies have found that high EE critical relatives make more critical remarks, and high EE emotionally overinvolved relatives are more intrusive during interactions (Valone *et al.*, 1983; Miklowitz *et al.*, 1984; Strachan *et al.*, 1986; Hahlweg *et al.*, 1989). High EE relatives also talk more and listen less effectively (Kuipers *et al.*, 1983). Naturalistic studies of the relative-patient interaction have yet to be performed, probably due to the immense methodological and logistic difficulties of such studies. Other studies have also indicated that living with a high EE relative is associated with lower levels of social functioning (Barrowclough and Tarrier, 1990).

2. The patient's psychophysiological reactions to EE. These studies have indicated that interaction with a high EE relative is associated with higher levels of physiological arousal in the patient (see Tarrier and Turpin, 1992 for a review). The association of elevated electrodermal activity in the presence of relatives rated as high EE has been advanced as evidence for the mediating role of arousal in schizophrenic relapse. We are currently analysing data on the association between the patient's electrodermal responses and relative's verbal behaviour during a 15 minute interaction, which we hope will elucidate the relationship between the patient's physiological responsiveness and relative's EE (Tarrier *et al.*, n.d. a).

3. Causal attributions and EE. An attributional model has been advanced to explain why individual relatives differ in their responses and attitudes to schizophrenic patients (Barrowclough *et al.*, 1994). Barrowclough *et al.* utilised a modified version of the Leeds Attributional Coding System (Stratton *et al.*, 1986) to assess spontaneous causal attributions made by the relative about negative events associated with the patient and the illness. The results of the study support the attributional model. High EE relatives made more attributions about the illness than did low EE relatives. Within the high EE group there were differences in the type of beliefs that the relative held. The attributions of relatives with marked EOI were similar to

low EE relatives, with problems attributed to factors more external to, and uncontrollable by, the patient. Relatives who were high EE on criticism gave more causes internal to the patient, whilst the relatives who were high EE on hostility also tended to perceive the causes to be controllable by, and personal to, the patient. The study also found that attributional variables were better predictors of patient relapse at nine-month follow-up than were EE variables. This last finding has the potential to influence greatly the development of behavioural family management methods towards a more cognitive approach which will target beliefs and cognitions of relatives.

FAMILY MANAGEMENT AND FAMILY INTERVENTIONS

Perhaps the greatest influence of EE has been in stimulating the develop-ment of family interventions. These interventions were mainly aimed at reducing the relapse rates in schizophrenic patients. In these studies, EE has been used as an index of high risk of relapse, as in the studies of Falloon and colleagues and Hogarty and colleagues (Falloon et al., 1982; 1985; Hogarty et al., 1986; 1991) or as an important focus of the interven-tion in studies where there has been an explicit attempt to change relatives' EE status from high to low, as in the studies of Leff and colleagues and Tarrier and colleagues (Leff et al., 1982; 1985; Tarrier et al., 1988; 1989). To date seven studies have been published which have compared a family intervention to a control intervention with high EE families.

Three trials of family intervention have taken place in the UK, two of which have been carried out by Julian Leff and colleagues at the Institute of Psychiatry in London. These workers appear to have been strongly influenced by the research on EE, which had emanated from this research group, and eclectic approaches to family therapy. The first trial compared a family intervention consisting of education for relatives about schizo-phrenia, relatives' groups, and individual psychotherapy (Leff et al., 1982; 1985). The intervention lasted nine months and was compared to routine care carried out by the local mental health services. Their second trial attempted to examine which of the components of their intervention package were effective. Accordingly, a comparison was made between education and relatives' groups and education and individual family therapy (Leff et al., 1989; 1990).

The third UK study was carried out by Tarrier and Barrowclough and colleagues in Salford (Tarrier et al., 1988; 1989). This group was strongly influenced by the behaviour therapy movement, especially from Barrowclough's experience in the learning disability field. Their design attempted to compare interventions of increasing complexity. They argued that relatives needed to become rehabilitative agents and, to assume this role, relatives needed management skills both to reduce and dissipate

217

stress in the home environment and to encourage positive levels of functioning in the patient. Three types of intervention were compared with
NHS routine care. First, a short two-session education programme was
presented which provided relatives with information about schizophrenia
and general advice on how best to manage the patient at home. Second, an
extended nine-month intervention was carried out which consisted of the
short education programme, four sessions on stress management and nine
sessions on goal setting aimed at increasing the patient's functioning. This
intervention was termed 'Symbolic' as it was carried out through discussion
and verbal advice. The third intervention was identical to the Symbolic in
content, except that it included actions such as role playing, monitoring
and teaching of active stress management strategies, guided practice in
achieving goals and objectives, and active participation from the therapists
rather than the sole use of verbal advice. Hence this intervention was
termed 'Enactive'. On the basis of past research on teaching parents skills
for managing their learning disabled child, it was reasoned that skills would
be learnt more proficiently, and change in family interactions would occur
more systematically, if advice was practised rather than just presented
verbally. So the three interventions, Education, Symbolic and Enactive,
represented an increasingly more intense and focused form of family
intervention. Patients living with low EE families were also recruited into
the study and a comparison was made between the education programme
and routine care with these families.

Two studies have been completed in the USA. The first by Falloon and
colleagues was carried out in California (Falloon et al., 1982; 1985). Falloon
and his colleagues were influenced by the research on EE and also by their
prior work on social skills training (Wallace et al., 1980), which they
now applied to the family setting using behavioural methods to improve
communication within the family, and a problem solving format to enhance
the use of these communication skills. Their trial compared a family
intervention package consisting of an education programme for relatives,
communication training and problem solving, to a control group who
received an identical programme carried out with the individual patient
rather than the family. So the family unit was the focus of the intervention
in the experimental treatment, while the patient alone was the focus in the
control treatment.

The second North American study was carried out by Hogarty and
colleagues in Pittsburgh (Hogarty et al., 1986; 1991). This group had a
research tradition of intervention studies with schizophrenia, having
published the results of two very large trials which evaluated the effectiveness of medication, active versus placebo (Hogarty et al., 1973) and depot
versus oral (Hogarty et al., 1979), and social work intervention with
patients and their families. Hogarty and his colleagues then progressed to
a large study examining the efficacy of family intervention, social skills

218

training, a combination of both family intervention and social skills training, and medication alone with patients living with high EE relatives. The family intervention was termed Psychoeducation and, as the name suggests, consisted of a large educational component with 'survival skills' workshops being held for relatives. There was an influence from their earlier work with families in this intervention. The social skills training intervention focused on the patient's skills, both in dealing with his or her family, and in the wider community setting.

One study was carried out in Hamburg, Germany and differs from the others in that it was largely psychodynamic in content and consisted of separate groups for relatives and patients (Kottgen *et al.*, 1984; Dulz and Hand, 1986).

The final study was carried out in Sydney, Australia by Vaughan and colleagues (Vaughan *et al.*, 1992). These workers had a behavioural tradition and adapted their intervention from the work of Hogarty and colleagues. This intervention was of much shorter duration than the others, being of ten sessions over three months instead of extending over nine to twelve months as in the other controlled trials. It aimed to reduce relatives' levels of EE, and, with this aim, the intervention was carried out solely with the relatives and the research intervention team had no contact with the patient. Because the behaviour and characteristics of the relative were viewed of paramount importance the research team did not liaise at all with the clinical team who were caring for the patient.

The above studies are all characterised by the recruitment of patients with a relative or relatives rated as high EE while the patient has been suffering an acute psychotic episode, with the vast majority of patients being hospitalised at the time of recruitment. The intervention usually commenced on their discharge and the patient was followed up after nine or twelve months. Excepting the Sydney study, the interventions took place over this follow-up period.

Outcomes

The intervention studies have used a range of outcome measures, but the outcome of primary interest has been relapse. A number of investigators have called for the use of a wide range of outcome measures (e.g. Barrowclough and Tarrier, 1984), both because this reflects comprehensive evaluation and because measures other than relapse may better reflect levels of functioning and quality of life. The emphasis on relapse as an outcome measure has probably occurred for a number of reasons: because medical research has historically been interested in relapse and morbidity rather than social functioning or quality of life; because the original EE research investigated relapse rates; because relapse appears a simple measure, both conceptually and practically (although it probably is not); and because relapse usually reflects rehospitalisation, which is expensive and hence of interest in the newer more economically minded climate. Some investigators have made more strenuous efforts than others to measure a range of outcomes, which can be classified as follows: relapse; social functioning; family functioning; burden of care; and economic cost.

Relapse

The percentage relapse rates for the seven published studies are presented in Table 11.1. All studies present relapse rates of nine to twelve months. It can be seen from Table 11.1, that four out of six studies (Leff *et al.*, 1982; Falloon *et al.*, 1982; Hogarty *et al.*, 1986; Tarrier *et al.*, 1988) demonstrate significant reductions in relapse rates for families receiving the family intervention at nine to twelve months.

Neither the Hamburg study (Kottgen *et al.*, 1984), nor the Sydney study (Vaughan *et al.*, 1992), were able to demonstrate significant benefits from their interventions. It should be noted that both these studies used interventions which differed markedly from those implemented by the successful trials. (The Hamburg study used a group psychoanalytic-oriented approach, while the Sydney study provided intervention solely with relatives and did not have any contact with the patient's clinical team). The second study of Leff and colleagues compared two parts of the original intervention (relatives groups and family intervention), but was not able to show a superiority of one over the other. Furthermore, Tarrier and colleagues were unable to demonstrate a superiority of their Enactive intervention over their Symbolic intervention, as they had predicted, neither was their short education programme found to be significantly better than routine care. Hogarty and colleagues found that, at twelve months, family intervention and social skills training were approximately equivalent, but in combination, the intervention prevented more relapses in families who completed treatment. Relapses were fewer in the family intervention group if treatment drop-outs were excluded.

Five studies have included a two-year follow-up which demonstrated that although relapses increased in the second year a significant benefit was still maintained. Schizophrenia is a disorder which frequently starts in late adolescence or early adulthood and continues for the rest of the patient's life; hence, two years as a follow-up period is a very short time. Tarrier and colleagues (Tarrier *et al.*, 1994) have followed up their patient cohort through examination of the psychiatric notes for a longer period, assessing relapse at both five years and at eight years. Because of the earlier results which did not demonstrate a difference between Enactive and Symbolic treatments, or between education and routine care, the groups have been collapsed into three groups: family intervention, high EE control and low EE control. The relapse results are presented in Figure 11.2 and show the

Table 11.1 Relapse rates in percentages for high EE households from published
Family Intervention Studies

Study	Relapse rates	
	9 or 12 months	*24 months*
	%	%
Camberwell Study 1		
(Leff *et al.*, 1982; 1985)		
Family intervention	8	20
Routine treatment	50	78
Camberwell Study 2		
(Leff *et al.*, 1989)		
Family therapy	8	
Relatives' groups	17	
California-USC Study		
(Falloon *et al.*, 1982; 1985)		
Family interventions	6	17
Individual intervention	44	83
Hamburg Study		
(Kottgen *et al.*, 1984)		
Group psychodynamic		
interventions	33	
Control group	43	
Pittsburg Study		
(Hogarty *et al.*, 1986; 1987)		
Family intervention	23 (19)	(32)
Social skills training	30 (20)	(42)
Combined FI & SST	9 (0)	(25)
Control group	41	66
Salford Study		
(Tarrier *et al.*, 1988; 1989)		
Family intervention	12 (5)	33 (24)
Education programme	43	57
Routine treatment	53	60
Sydney Study		
(Vaughan *et al.*, 1992)		
Relatives' counselling	41	
Control group	65	

NB: Percentages in parentheses represent 'treatment takers' only and exclude those who did
not complete the intervention programme.

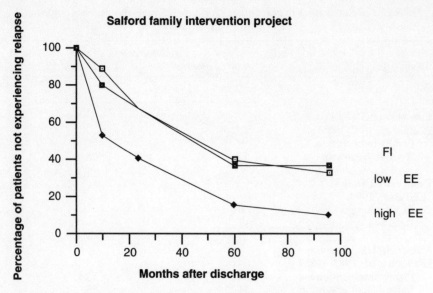

Figure 11.2 Percentage of patients not experiencing relapse following family intervention compared to low and high EE groups

percentage of patients in each group who were well at each follow-up point: nine months, two years, five years and eight years.

These results indicate that although there is an accumulating increase in the number of patients who relapse over the extended follow-up period, the difference between the family intervention group and the high EE control group is maintained for up to eight years. However, over two-thirds of patients who received family intervention with their families do eventually relapse.

Social functioning

Both the California study (Falloon *et al.*, 1984) and the Salford study (Barrowclough and Tarrier, 1990) systematically measured social functioning in the index patients. Both studies found patients in the family intervention group showed significant improvements in social functioning. In the Salford study, the patients' social functioning was assessed using Birchwood *et al.*'s (1990) Social Functioning Scale (SFS). The changes in the total score are represented in Figure 11.3; again, groups have been collapsed into the family intervention group and the high EE control group. As can be seen, although the changes are significant, they are quite small. If the changes in the patient's social functioning are graphed by dividing patients into those whose relatives remained high EE at nine-month follow-up and those whose relatives changed from high to low EE at follow-up, the

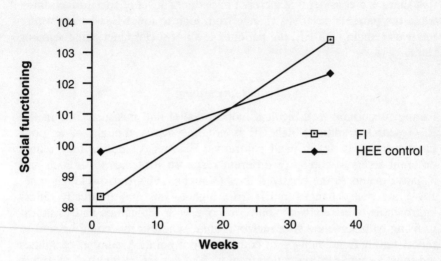

Figure 11.3 Changes in social functioning with family intervention

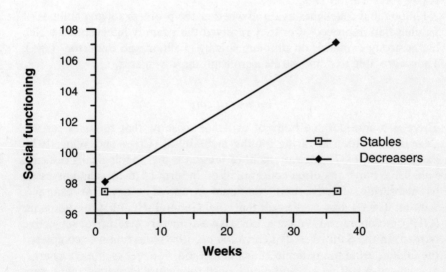

Figure 11.4 Patients' social functioning and changes in relatives' EE

difference is quite dramatic (see Figure 11.4). In Figure 11.4 it can be seen that there is a considerable increase in patients' level of social functioning when the patients' relatives change from high to low EE, whereas where relatives remain high EE, the patients' level of social functioning remains static.

Family functioning

Family functioning is difficult to conceptualise and measure. Within the EE research tradition, high EE is not necessarily thought of as poor functioning, it is not in itself pejorative. Expressed emotion may reflect different styles of coping or different response strategies to difficult and negative events in the relatives' lives (Vaughn, 1986; Barrowclough et al., 1994). As such, changes in EE from high to low may indirectly reflect improvements in relatives' ability to cope with difficulties and to adjust to living with someone with schizophrenia. Whether this could be said to reflect family functioning is of course a moot point. A number of studies did show a significant reduction from high to low EE in relatives receiving the family intervention (Leff et al., 1982; 1989; Hogarty et al., 1986; Tarrier et al., 1988). These reductions in EE were also associated with decreases in relapse (Hogarty et al., 1986; Leff et al., 1989). It should also be noted that there is doubt about the stability of EE in some families. Approximately one-third of relatives rated as high EE when the patient is in hospital will show a change to low EE if reassessed sometime after discharge (Dulz and Hand, 1986; Tarrier et al., 1988).

Falloon and colleagues assessed whether the problem solving abilities of families had improved after they received their family intervention which had a strong emphasis on problem solving (Falloon and Pederson, 1985). They were able to demonstrate significant improvements.

Burden of care

There is a considerable body of evidence to show that relatives carry a substantial burden in caring for the mentally ill (Creer and Wing, 1974; Fadden et al., 1987). Measurement of burden is methodologically difficult. Subjective burden is often conceptualised in term of distress and assessed by measuring affective and emotional symptomatology. For example, Tantum (1989) has suggested that the General Health Questionnaire (GHQ, Goldberg and Williams, 1988) is a satisfactory measure of subjective burden. In the Salford study (Tarrier et al., 1988), the relatives completed the GHQ during the patients' index admission, two weeks after discharge, at four-and-a-half month and nine-month follow-up. However, there were no significant changes over the follow-up periods for the intervention or control groups, nor were there significant differences between the groups

(Tarrier *et al.*, n.d. b). These data suggest that the family intervention had no impact on relatives' subjective burden. Positive results were reported by Falloon (Falloon and Pederson, 1985), who found significant reductions in symptomatology of relatives in the family management group, as measured by the Hopkins Symptom Check List. Brooker *et al.* (1992) evaluated the effectiveness of community psychiatric nurses (CPNs) trained in the Tarrier and Barrowclough intervention and did find a significant reduction in GHQ scores in relatives of families receiving family intervention, contrary to the negative results of Tarrier and colleagues reported from the Salford project.

Economic cost

There is increasing attention to the economics of health care which make some attempt to examine the costs of family intervention imperative. Falloon and colleagues (Cardin *et al.*, 1986) undertook a detailed analysis of all direct and indirect costs to the patients, families, health, welfare and community agencies associated with their intervention. A cost–benefit analysis of the twelve-month data showed the total costs for family management were 19 per cent less than for the individually managed patients. A much less ambitious cost analysis of the Salford project was undertaken by Tarrier *et al.* (1991), and only direct costs were analysed. The treatment of patients who received family intervention showed an overall saving of 36.4 per cent over the high EE control group and a saving of 26.2 per cent on mean costs per patient. These costings included the cost of the psychologists' time who carried out the family intervention. In both the California and Salford studies, reducing inpatient stay was a big factor in reducing costs. The potential of family interventions for reducing relapse and hence hospitalisations in the short term represents a large financial saving which far outweighs the costs of the extra resources in staff time required to carry out the intervention.

DISSEMINATION AND TRAINING

Despite the successful results reported for family interventions, the point has often been made that these results were the product of enthusiastic and highly trained specialist research teams, and the case for family interventions working in a normal service setting remains unproven. There is some truth in this argument, although the Salford project was performed by psychologists attempting to run a District service with a research-funded evaluation team. The potential for family interventions to become standard practice requires two conditions: first, the availability of quality training in family intervention methods, and second, radical organisational change to accommodate family and psychosocial management as the core management approach for psychosis.

225

Some progress has been achieved in training. The School of Nursing at Manchester University, UK, set up a project in 1988 to train community psychiatric nurses (CPNs) in family management methods and to evaluate the effectiveness of this training. This project was stimulated by the research results reporting the benefits of family intervention and also by concern about the 'drift' in the role and activity of CPNs. Community psychiatric nurse services had been established in the mid 1950s for the aftercare and follow-up of psychotic patients receiving the newly introduced neuroleptics (Simmons and Brooker, 1986). Evidence suggested that CPNs were spending considerably less time with psychotic patients than non-psychotic affective disordered patients (Wooff *et al.*, 1988) and that schizophrenic patients 'constituted a mere 27 per cent of all total CPN caseloads throughout the UK' (White, 1990). The advances in therapeutic interventions appear not to have been reflected in CPN training and the lack of skills in psychosocial interventions had resulted in CPNs 'drifting' away from contact with patients with psychoses. As a result, a training scheme was devised which aimed to train CPNs in family intervention and provide them with clinical supervision in the hope that the provision of these skills and clinical supervision would re-kindle interest in working with psychotic patients.

In the initial trial (Brooker *et al.*, 1992b), nine CPNs were recruited from three regional Health Authorities through advertisement. Each selected CPN was matched with a colleague from the same health authority on a number of variables such as: length of experience as a CPN; amount of post-qualification training; age and sex. The aim of the study was for each CPN to recruit three schizophrenic patients and their families into their caseload, making a total of fifty-four families. Initially, 87 per cent of the target was achieved; however, seventeen of these families dropped out during one-year follow-up. The thirty families who completed the trial represented 64 per cent of the recruited sample. All CPNs, both experimental and control, were trained in clinical assessment methods and the nine experimental CPNs attended a training course in family management derived from that used in the Salford project (see Barrowclough and Tarrier, 1992). The course was of six months' duration and consisted of didactic and workshop teaching, and clinical supervision throughout the six months. The continuous clinical supervision was considered an essential constituent of the course and was led by clinical psychologists experienced in the area. Evaluation of the patients and families indicated that there were small but significant improvements in patients' symptomatology. Depression, anxiety, delusions and physical retardation improved in patients managed by the CPNs who were receiving training, whereas only delusions improved in the control group. There was a trend towards a reduction in neuroleptic medication for patients in the experimental group that was not evident in the control group. Furthermore, there was evidence for significant improvements in personal and social functioning in the experimental group but not the control group. There was also evidence that relatives of patients in the experimental group showed a significant decrease in the presence of minor psychological symptoms as measured by the General Health Questionnaire while there was no change in the control group. Such differences may indicate a decrease in the perceived or subjective burden of care in relatives who received family intervention compared to those who did not. Interestingly, this result is in contrast to that of Tarrier and colleagues who reported no changes in GHQ scores for relatives who participated in the family intervention. An evaluation of knowledge about schizophrenia held by the relatives using the KASI evaluation method (see Barrowclough *et al.*, 1987) found that relatives in the experimental group significantly increased their functional knowledge about schizophrenia whereas the control group did not (Brooker *et al.*, 1992a).

In a subsequent study, Brooker and colleagues (Brooker *et al.*, 1994) carried out a within-subject design trial of CPN training, in which ten CPNs recruited six patients and their families, of which three patients and families received family intervention and the other three acted as controls. After six months follow-up data were collected, the control families were then offered active family intervention, and 65 per cent of the group accepted. Seventy-eight per cent of families in the intervention group and 96 per cent of control families remained in the study until follow-up. The family intervention in this study was taught by Falloon and his colleagues. The patients who had received the intervention showed a significant improvement in positive and negative symptoms and a significant increase in social functioning. There was also evidence of a dramatic decline in hospital usage when mean hospital days per patient were compared between the twelve months prior to the intervention and a comparable period post-intervention. The experimental group demonstrated a decline from 18.4 days per annum, before treatment, to 1.8 days per annum, after treatment. In the untreated controls this figure increases from a baseline of 23.5 days per annum to 73.5 days.

Both studies carried out by Brooker and his colleagues in Manchester indicate the positive benefits of training CPNs in family intervention, even though two different types of intervention were used, taught by different groups of workers. In an Australian study of family intervention training, Kavanagh and his colleagues (Kavanagh *et al.*, 1993), trained mental health workers in a cognitive–behavioural approach to family intervention. However, despite the considerable efforts by the training team, the training appeared to have little impact upon clinical practice with few of the trainees actually engaging families for any length of time. Trainees received didactic and workshop training of approximately 30 to 35 hours' duration; they were then asked to participate in a controlled evaluation of family intervention by acting as trial therapists. Initially, 160 therapists received training but only 44 of these elected to take part in the treatment trial and 28 of these saw only one family. In fact, 57 per cent of the families in the study were seen by six therapists. Therapists reported particular difficulty in integrating the family work with their other duties and interests. Only 4 per cent of the sample reported that their knowledge of cognitive–behavioural approaches was a significant problem, but in a written test most therapists failed to demonstrate even the minimum recall of the material they had been taught (ibid.). The authors report that in families receiving intervention, 13 per cent of patients receiving family intervention had experienced a marked exacerbation of symptoms compared to 27 per cent in the group who received an individual intervention (ibid.). Despite this they conclude 'as a demonstration that the structured family intervention could be disseminated into routine community health practice, the project clearly was of limited success' (p. 7).

There are two possible reasons why the training programme of Kavanagh and colleagues yielded such poor results compared to the comparative success of Brooker and colleagues. Successful training requires continuity and progressive clinical supervision. Time-limited didactic and workshop teaching is unlikely to result in skill acquisition in the absence of guided practice. Without supervision within a structured teaching programme trainees will abandon the new approach very quickly. The second important factor is the necessity for health service management commitment for the training and practice of the new approach. In Kavanagh's programme there appears to have been little in the way of management commitment to the reorganisation of workloads so that family intervention could be given a high priority. It appears that, for most trained therapists in this study, family work was just one more activity that they had to complete in an already overloaded schedule. It is perhaps not surprising that very few therapists attempted to implement what they had been taught without management prioritising their family work and clinical supervision to shape their practice.

An ongoing project funded by The Jules Thorn Charitable Trust (The Thorn Initiative) is dedicated to evaluating the training of CPNs in problem-oriented case management, which will include training in three modules: family intervention, psychological management of psychotic symptoms, and case management. The Thorn Initiative is taking place on two sites, the University of Manchester and the Institute of Psychiatry and Maudsley Hospital, London. The training effectiveness is being extensively evaluated, with the assessment of knowledge and skills acquired by the nurses being assessed by academic measures, and evidence of practical skills assessed through clinical casework and tape recordings of interventions. Trainees also assess the clinical effectiveness of their work through the use of standardised clinical assessments and monitoring of problems and goals. An objective clinical assessment is also being performed by an independent evaluator on a sample of the patients and their relatives. Initial results from the first cohort of eleven students trained in Manchester reveal that patients show a significant decrease in positive symptoms and a significant increase in social functioning (Lancashire *et al.*, 1995).

FUTURE DEVELOPMENTS

There are a number of areas in which development is probable. The issue of dissemination of skills and the establishment of family intervention into common clinical practice has been discussed above. Another important area is that of engagement of families into treatment. Despite the proven success of family interventions, there is considerable evidence that a sizeable number of families either refuse family intervention or drop out at a very early stage (Smith and Birchwood, 1990; Tarrier, 1991). The percentage of families refusing intervention ranges from 7 per cent to 21 per cent (median 13 per cent), and the percentage withdrawing from treatment ranges from 7 per cent to 14 per cent (median 9.5 per cent). Some treatments, such as relatives' groups run by Leff and colleagues, have reported refusal rates of 50 per cent. Furthermore, patients who become treatment refusers and treatment drop-outs appear to be particularly vulnerable to relapse, with 67 per cent of this group relapsing over nine months in the Salford study (Tarrier, 1991). The difficulty of engaging and maintaining families in treatment is a crucial issue that needs to be addressed. Explanatory models of adherence and health behaviour have emphasised a cost–benefit, decision-making perspective and the adoption of such a conceptualisation to engagement and maintenance in family intervention may well be productive (ibid.).

There is also a risk that family interventions are not critically appraised and improved. Recent work on causal attributions and beliefs held by relatives (Barrowclough *et al.*, 1994) has suggested a psychological explanation of relatives' response to living with a schizophrenic family member which may suggest further refinements to intervention programmes (Barrowclough and Tarrier, 1992). It can be hypothesised that causal beliefs are functional: they are attempts to limit or control difficult situations. Barrowclough *et al.* (1994) have outlined the following examples of how beliefs held by the relative can determine coping strategies. If a relative believes that a problem lies within the patient and that they can control their own behaviour without exceptional effort, then such beliefs will result in efforts to persuade or coerce the patient to behave normally. It is suggested that such coping behaviour on the part of the relative will be stressful to the vulnerable schizophrenic patient. Other beliefs that attribute the patient's behaviour to external factors beyond their control would mediate different sets of coping behaviour on the part of the relative. If the patient is viewed as suffering from a legitimate illness which is having a severely negative and upsetting effect on the relative, then the coping response is to attempt to ameliorate problems by taking control and doing things for the patient. Some aspects of EOI are understandable in this context.

The direct investigation of beliefs held by the relatives and their behavioural consequences, rather than an indirect measure such as EE, may result in more focused cognitive–behavioural family interventions which are more effective, both in maintaining change over longer periods of time and in producing change in those families with entrenched problems who have been resistant to the behavioural family interventions. Lastly, the cognitive focused approach should accommodate some of our understanding as to why some relatives are very difficult to engage and maintain in treatment.

ACKNOWLEDGEMENT

The Salford Family intervention project was funded by a project grant (No. 5062) from the North West Regional Health Authority. I am indebted to: Dr Barrowclough for many of the ideas expressed in this chapter; to Dr Brooker for information relating to the CPN training studies; to the Thorn Nurse Project for information relating to the CPN training study; and to Dr Nuechterlein for permission to use Figure 11.1.

REFERENCES

Barrowclough, C. and Tarrier, N. (1984) 'Psychosocial interventions with families and their effects on the course of treatment', *Psychological Medicine* 14: 629–42.
—— (1990) 'Social functioning in schizophrenic patients. I: The effects of expressed emotion and family intervention', *Social Psychiatry and Psychiatric Epidemiology* 25: 125–9.
—— (1992) *Families of Schizophrenic Patients: Cognitive–Behavioural Intervention*, London: Chapman and Hall.
Barrowclough, C., Tarrier, N., Watts, S., Vaughn, C., Bamrah, J. S. and Freeman, H. L. (1987) 'Assessing the functional knowledge about schizophrenia: A preliminary report', *British Journal of Psychiatry* 151: 1–8.
Barrowclough, C., Johnston, M. and Tarrier, N. (1994) 'Attributions, expressed emotion and patient relapse: An attributional model of relatives' response to schizophrenic illness', *Behavior Therapy* 25: 67–88.
Birchwood, M., Smith, J., Cochrane, R., Wetton, S. and Copestake, S. (1990) 'The social functioning scale: The development and validation of a scale of social adjustment for use in family intervention programmes with schizophrenic patients', *British Journal of Psychiatry* 157: 853–9.
Brooker, C., Barrowclough, C. and Tarrier, N. (1992a) 'Evaluating the impact of training community psychiatric nurses to educate relatives about schizophrenia', *Journal of Clinical Nursing* 1: 19–25.
Brooker, C., Tarrier, N., Barrowclough, C., Butterworth, A. and Goldberg, D. (1992b) 'Training community psychiatric nurses for psychosocial intervention: Report of a pilot study', *British Journal of Psychiatry* 160: 836–44.

Brooker, C., Falloon, I. R. H., Butterworth, C. A., Goldberg, D., Graham-Hole, V. and Hillier, V. (1994) 'The outcome of training community psychiatric nurses to deliver psychosocial intervention', *British Journal of Psychiatry* 165: 222-30.

Brown, G. W. (1985) 'The discovery of expressed emotion: induction or deduction', in J. P. Leff and C. E. Vaughn *Expressed Emotion in Families*, New York: Guildford Press.

Brown, G. W., Carstairs, G. M. and Topping, G. (1958) 'Post hospital adjustment of chronic mental patients', *Lancet* ii: 685–9.

Brown, G. W., Mock, E. M., Carstairs, G. M. and Wing, J. K. (1962) 'Influence of family life on the course of schizophrenia', *British Journal of Preventative and Social Medicine* 16: 55–68.

Brown, G. W., Birley, J. T. L. and Wing, J. K. (1972) 'Influence of family life on the course of schizophrenia: A replication', *British Journal of Psychiatry* 121: 241–58.

Cardin, V. A., McGill, C. W. and Falloon, I. R. H. (1986) 'An economic analysis: Costs, benefits and effectiveness', in I.R.H. Falloon (ed.) *Family Management of Schizophrenia*, Baltimore: John Hopkins University Press.

Ciompi, L. (1980) 'The natural history of schizophrenia in the long term', *British Journal of Psychiatry* 136, 413–20.

Creer, C. and Wing, J. K. (1974) *Schizophrenia at Home*, Surrey: National Schizophrenia Fellowship.

Dulz, B. and Hand, I. (1986) 'Short term relapse in young schizophrenics: can it be predicted and affected by family (CFI), patient and treatment variables? An experimental study', in M. J. Goldstein, I. Hand and K. Hahlweg (eds) *Treatment of Schizophrenia: Family Assessment and Intervention*, Berlin: Springer-Verlag.

Fadden, G., Bebbington, P. and Kuipers, L. (1987) 'Caring and its burden', *British Journal of Psychiatry* 151: 660–7.

Falloon, I. R. H. (ed.) (1986) *Family Management of Schizophrenia*, Baltimore: John Hopkins University Press.

Falloon, I. R. H. and Pedersen, J. (1985) 'Family management in the prevention of morbidity of schizophrenia: The adjustment of the family unit', *British Journal of Psychiatry* 147: 156–63.

Falloon, I. R. H., Watt, D. C. and Shepherd, M. (1978) 'A comparative controlled trial of pimozide and fluphenazine decanoate in the continuation therapy of schizophrenia', *Psychological Medicine* 7: 59–70.

Falloon, I. R. H., Boyd, J. L., McGill, C. W., Razani, J., Moss, H. B. and Gilderman, A. M. (1982) 'Family management in the prevention of exacerbations of schizophrenia', *New England Journal of Medicine* 306: 1437–40.

Falloon, I. R. H., Boyd, J. L. and McGill, C. W. (1984) *Family Care of Schizophrenia*, New York: Guildford Press.

Falloon, I. R. H., Boyd, J. L., McGill, C. W., Williamson, M., Razani, J., Moss, H. B., Gilderman, A. M. and Simson, G. M. (1985) 'Family management in the prevention of morbidity of schizophrenia: Clinical outcome of a two year longitudinal study', *Archives of General Psychiatry* 42: 887–96.

Goldberg, D. and Williams, P. (1988) *A User's Guide to the General Health Questionnaire*, Windsor: NFER-Nelson.

Goldstein, M. J., Hand, I. and Hahlweg, K. (eds) (1988) *Treatment of Schizophrenia: Family Assessment and Intervention*, Berlin: Springer-Verlag.

Hafner, H., Gattaz, W. and Jangerik, W. (eds) *Searches for the Cause of Schizophrenia*, Berlin: Springer-Verlag.

Hahlweg, K., Goldstein, M. J., Nuechterlein, K. H., Magana, A. B., Mintz, J., Doane, J. A., Miklowitz, D. J. and Snyder, K. S. (1989) 'Expressed emotion and patient–relative interaction in families of recent onset schizophrenia', *Journal of Consulting and Clinical Psychology* 57: 11–18.

231

Harding, C., Brooks, G. W., Ashikaga, T., Strauss, J. S. and Breier, A. (1987) The Vermont longitudinal study of persons with severe mental illness: II Long term outcome of subjects who retrospectively met DSM III criteria for schizophrenia', *American Journal of Psychiatry* 144: 727–35.

Hogarty, G. E., Goldstein, S. C. and Collaborative Study Group (1973) 'Drug and sociotherapy in the aftercare of schizophrenic patients: One year relapse rates', *Archives of General Psychiatry* 28: 54–64.

Hogarty, G. E., Schooler, N. R., Ulrich, R. F., Mussare, F., Ferro, P. and Herron, E. (1979) 'Fluphenazine and social therapy in the aftercare of schizophrenic patients', *Archives of General Psychiatry* 36: 1283–94.

Hogarty, G. E., Anderson, C. M., Reiss, D. J., Kornblith, S. J., Greenwald, D. P., Javan, C. D. and Madonia, M. (1986) 'Family psychoeducation, social skills training and maintenance chemotherapy in the aftercare treatment of schizophrenia. I: One year effects of a controlled study on relapse and expressed emotion', *Archives of General Psychiatry* 43: 633–42.

Hogarty, G. E., Anderson, C. M., Reiss, D. J., Kornblith, S. J., Greenwald, D. P., Ulrich, R. F. and Carter, M. (1991) 'Family psychoeducation, social skills training, and maintenance chemotherapy in the aftercare treatment of schizophrenia. II. Two year effects of a controlled study on relapse and adjustment', *Archives of General Psychiatry* 48: 340–7.

Kavanagh, D. (1992) 'Recent developments in expressed emotion and schizophrenia', *British Journal of Psychiatry* 160: 601–20.

Kavanagh, D., Clark, D., Piatkowska, O., O'Halloran, P., Manicavasagar, V., Rosen, A. and Tennant, C. (1993) 'Application of cognitive–behavioural family interventions for schizophrenia in multidisciplinary teams: what can the matter be?', *Australian Psychologist* 28:1–8.

Kottgen, C., Soinnichsen, I., Mollenhauer, K. and Jurth, R. (1984) Results of the Hamburg Camberwell family Interview study, I–III. *International Journal of Family Psychiatry* 5: 61–94.

Kuipers, L., Sturgeon, D., Berkowitz, R. and Leff, J. P. (1983) 'Characteristics of expressed emotion: its relationship to speech and looking in schizophrenic patients and their relatives', *British Journal of Clinical Psychology* 22: 257–64.

Lancashire, S., Haddock, G., Tarrier, N., Baguley, I., Butterworth, T. and Brooker, C. (1995) 'The impact of training community psychiatric nurses to use psychosocial interventions with people who have serious mental health problems: The Thorn Nurse Training Project'.

Leff, J. P. and Vaughn, C. E. (1985) *Expressed Emotion in Families*, New York: Guildford Press.

Leff, J. P., Kuipers, L., Berkowitz, R., Eberlein-Fries, R. and Sturgeon, D. (1982) 'A controlled trial of intervention with families of schizophrenic patients', *British Journal of Psychiatry* 141: 121–34.

Leff, J. P., Kuipers, L., Berkowitz, R. and Sturgeon, D. (1985) 'A controlled trial of social intervention in the families of schizophrenic patients', *British Journal of Psychiatry* 146: 594–600.

Leff, J. P., Berkowitz, R., Shavit, A., Strachan, A., Glass, I. and Vaughn, C. E. (1989) 'A trial of family therapy versus relatives' groups for schizophrenia', *British Journal of Psychiatry* 154: 58–66.

Leff, J. P., Berkowitz, R., Shavit, A., Strachan, A., Glass, I. and Vaughn, C. E. (1990) 'A trial of family therapy versus relatives' groups for schizophrenia: two year follow up', *British Journal of Psychiatry* 157: 571–7.

Miklowitz, D. J., Goldstein, M. J., Falloon, I. R. H., *et al.* (1984) 'Interactional correlates of expressed emotion in families of schizophrenics', *British Journal of Psychiatry* 144: 482–7.

Nuechterlein, K. H (1987) 'Vulnerability models: state of the art', in H. Hafner, W. Gattaz and W. Jangerik (eds) *Searches for the Cause of Schizophrenia*, Berlin: Springer-Verlag.

Nuechterlein, K. H. and Dawson, M. E. (1984) 'A heuristic vulnerability-stress model of schizophrenic episodes', *Schizophrenia Bulletin* 10: 300–12.

Simmons, S. and Brooker, C. (1986) *Community Psychiatric Nursing: A Social Perspective*, London: Heinemann.

Smith, J. and Birchwood, M. (1990) 'Relatives and patients as partners in the management of schizophrenia: The development of a service model', *British Journal of Psychiatry* 150: 645–52.

Strachan, A. M., Leff, J. P., Goldstein, M. J., Doane, J. A. and Burtt, C. (1986) 'Emotional attitudes and direct communication in the families of schizophrenics: A cross national replication', *British Journal of Psychiatry* 149: 279–87.

Stratton, P., Heard, D., Hanks, H. G. I., Munton, A. G., Brewin, C. R. and Davidson, C. (1986) 'Coding causal beliefs in natural discourse', *British Journal of Social Psychology* 25: 299–313.

Tantam, D. (1989) 'Family factors in psychiatric disorders', *Current Opinion in Psychiatry* 2: 296–302.

Tarrier, N. (1991) 'Some aspects of family interventions in schizophrenia. I: Adherence to intervention programmes', *British Journal of Psychiatry* 159: 475–80.

Tarrier, N. and Turpin, G. (1992) 'Psychosocial factors, arousal and schizophrenic relapse: The psychophysiological data', *British Journal of Psychiatry* 161: 3–11.

Tarrier, N., Barrowclough, C., Vaughn, C. E., Bamrah, J. S., Porceddu, K., Watts, S. and Freeman, H.(1988) 'The community management of schizophrenia: A controlled trial of a behavioural intervention with families to reduce relapse', *British Journal of Psychiatry* 153: 532–42.

Tarrier, N., Barrowclough, C., Vaughn, C. E., Bamrah, J. S., Porceddu, K., Watts, S. and Freeman, H. (1989) 'The community management of schizophrenia: A controlled trial of a behavioural intervention with families to reduce relapse: a two year follow up', *British Journal of Psychiatry* 154: 625–8.

Tarrier, N., Lowson, K. and Barrowclough, C. (1991) 'Some aspects of family interventions in schizophrenia. II: Financial considerations', *British Journal of Psychiatry* 159: 481–4.

Tarrier, N., Barrowclough, C., Porceddu, K. and Fitzpatrick, E. (1994) 'The Salford Family Intervention Project: Relapse rates of schizophrenia at five and eight years', *British Journal of Psychiatry* 165: 829–32.

Tarrier, N., Barrowclough, C. and Intili, R. (n.d. a) *Expressed Emotion, Arousal and the Verbal Behaviour of Relatives of Schizophrenic Patients*. Project funded by the National Health and Medical Research Council, Australia.

Tarrier, N., Barrowclough, C., Porceddu, K. and Watts, S. (n.d. b) *Distress in the Relatives of Schizophrenic Patients as Measured by the GHQ: The Effect of Family Intervention*. Unpublished data.

Valone, K., Norton, J. P., Goldstein, M. J. and Doane, J. A. (1983) 'Parental expressed emotion and affective style in an adolescent sample at risk for schizophrenia spectrum disorders', *Journal of Abnormal Psychology* 92: 399–407.

Vaughan, K., Doyle, M., McConaghy, N., Blaszczynski, A., Fox, A. and Tarrier, N. (1992) 'The Sydney intervention trial: A controlled trial of relatives' counselling to reduce schizophrenic relapse', *Social Psychiatry and Psychiatric Epidemiology* 27: 16–21.

Vaughn, C. E. (1986) 'Patterns of emotional response in the families of schizophrenic patients', in M. J. Goldstein, I. Hand and K. Hahlweg (eds) *Treatment of Schizophrenia: Family Assessment and Intervention*, Berlin: Springer-Verlag.

Vaughn, C. E. and Leff, J. P. (1976) 'The influence of family and social factors on the course of psychiatric illness: A comparison of schizophrenic and depressed neurotic patients', *British Journal of Psychiatry* 129: 125–37.
Wallace, C. J., Nelson, C. J., Liberman, R. P., Aitchison. R. A., Lukoff, D., Elder, J. and Ferris, C. (1980) 'A review and critique of social skills training with schizophrenic patients', *Schizophrenia Bulletin* 6: 42–64.
White, E. (1990) *The Third National Quinquennial Survey of Community Psychiatric Services*, Leeds: CPNA Publications.
Wooff, K., Goldberg, D. and Fryers, T. (1988) 'The practice of community psychiatric nursing and mental health social work in Salford', *British Journal of Psychiatry* 152: 783–92.
Zubin, J. and Spring, B. (1977). 'Vulnerability: a new view of schizophrenia', *Journal of Abnormal Psychology* 86: 103–26.

12

NEUROLEPTIC MEDICATION AND THE PSYCHOSOCIAL TREATMENT OF PSYCHOTIC SYMPTOMS: SOME NEGLECTED ISSUES

Jennifer C. Day and Richard P. Bentall

INTRODUCTION

Since the early 1950s, neuroleptic medication has been the mainstay of the psychiatric treatment of psychotic symptoms. Indeed, this type of medication is still widely regarded to be the treatment of choice for psychotic patients (Lieberman, 1993). Neuroleptics are often credited with the reduction in the number of hospital beds occupied by psychiatric patients over the last three decades (see, for example, Croyden-Smith, 1982), despite historical evidence that this reduction has been the result of broad changes in mental health policy and has not been much influenced by the introduction of new treatments (Warner, 1985). So central is the role of neuroleptic medication in the day-to-day management of psychosis that, in response to the perceived shortcomings of community care, some authors have advocated the introduction of Community Treatment Orders which would compel patients to comply with this kind of therapy (see Bean and Mounser, 1992, for discussions of some of the practical and ethical issues surrounding this proposal). It is therefore abundantly clear that, for the foreseeable future at least, most patients who receive psychosocial treatments for their psychotic symptoms will also be receiving neuroleptic drugs.

Yet the implications that neuroleptic drugs have for psychosocial treatments have rarely been considered in either the psychological or pharmacological literature, despite the obvious importance of this issue for therapists working via either modality (Bentall and Day, 1994). In this chapter we will raise some broad concerns about the inter-relationship between psychological and pharmacological variables in determining outcome for patients who have a diagnosis of 'schizophrenia'. Much of what we will say will be speculative for the simple reason that very little has been written on this topic before now. Before moving to this kind of speculation, however, we will present a brief review of the clinical literature on neuroleptics for the benefit of readers who do not have a background in medicine or psychopharmacology.

THE EFFICACY OF NEUROLEPTIC DRUGS

The first neuroleptic (literally 'to clasp the neurone') drug to be developed was chlorpromazine, which was synthesised as an antihistamine in France. The anti-psychotic properties of this drug were discovered empirically by Delay *et al.* (1952); this discovery was not based on a priori knowledge of the mechanism of drug action or of the pathophysiology of psychosis. Since that time many other neuroleptic compounds have been synthesised belonging to different chemical groups and having varied pharmacological action (see Table 12.1 for a list of widely used drugs listed according to their generic and proprietary names, together with typical daily dose ranges). Although most of these drugs can be given orally, since the 1970s it has been common practice to give neuroleptics in the form of a 'depot' injection, usually at intervals of a week or more, in the hope of improving compliance. In this kind of preparation, the drug is dissolved in an oily base and injected intramuscularly, so that it is gradually released into the bloodstream over a prolonged period of time. This drug form is preferred by many prescribers as compliance with treatment can be more easily monitored, although administration can lead to a number of problems, such as injection site reactions (Starmark *et al.*, 1980) and is, arguably, a potentially humiliating experience for the client.

In 1963, Carlsson and Lindqvist demonstrated the association between dopamine receptor blockade and the anti-psychotic action of the drugs, showing a positive correlation between the clinical potency of neuroleptics and dopamine metabolism. Since that time, the exact role of abnormalities in the dopaminergic pathways in producing psychotic symptoms has been the subject of extensive research which has often yielded conflicting findings so that, at the time of writing, the status of the 'dopamine hypothesis' of schizophrenia might best be described as equivocal (see Sunahara *et al.*, 1993 and Van Kammen, 1991, for relatively up-to-date reviews of the literature).

Neuroleptics differ in respect of their affinity for various receptors in the central nervous system (CNS). In addition to dopamine receptors, they are known to block muscarinic (cholinergic), alpha-adrenergic and trypta-minergic (serotonergic) receptors, and they differ in their specificity for different sites in the brain, particularly in the nigrostriatal and mesolimbic systems. Current research is aimed at identifying drugs which act mainly in the mesolimbic and mesocortical structures in the hope that this will bring about beneficial effects on mood and emotion (Lieberman, 1993).

Table 12.1 List of commonly used oral drugs and daily dose ranges
(based on British National Formulary 1993 guidelines)

Generic (trade names)	Anti-psychotic dose ranges/day (mg)
Phenothiazines	
Aliphatic	
Chlorpromazine (Laragactil)	75–1000
Piperidine	
Thioridazine (Melleril)	50–800
Pericyazine (Neulactil)	75–300
Piperazine	
Perphenazine (Fentazin)	12–24
Trifluoperazine (Stelazine)	10 (no max. stated)
Fluphenazine (Moditen)	5–20
Thioxanthenes	
Flupenthixol (Depixol)	6–18
Butyrophenones	
Haloperidol (Haldol, Serenace, Dozic)	5–200
Droperidol (Droleptan)	5–80
Benperidol (Anquil)	0.25–1.5
Diphenylbutyropiperidines	
Pimozide (Orap)	2–20
Substituted Benzamides	
Sulpiride (Dolmatil, Sulpitil)	200–2400
Dibenzoxazepine	
Loxapine (Loxapac)	20–250
Dibenzazepine derivative	
Clozapine (Clozaril)	25–450
Benzisoxazole derivative	
Risperidone (Rispidol)	6–16

Unfortunately, because of their lack of specificity for particular brain sites, many of the currently available neuroleptics have a large number of side-effects. These include extrapyramidal side-effects (Parkinsonian symptoms such as tremor, drooling mouth, slowing of movements) caused by dopamine blockade in the nigrostriatal pathway of the basal ganglia; sedation and effects on sensory input mediated in the brain stem; and endocrine effects and effects on appetite and body weight thought to be mediated by blockade of 5HT receptors in the hypothalamus. These effects will be described in more detail below.

The efficacy of neuroleptic drugs at reducing psychotic symptomatology and the probability of relapse has been established in a number of double blind placebo controlled trials (Davis, 1975; Leff and Wing, 1971). Some controlled studies have employed barbiturates as a comparison treatment in order to control for the effects of sedation, thus ensuring that the observed effects are specifically anti-psychotic (Klein and Davis, 1969). It is widely acknowledged that the response to neuroleptic drugs is not immediate and that days or weeks may pass before any anti-psychotic effect is evident. Although it is impossible to predict the time course of action for an individual patient, an immediate sedative/anxiolytic effect is typically seen, followed by an effect on psychotic symptoms after one to two weeks, although the maximal effect may not be reached for several weeks thereafter.

It has been commonly believed that the therapeutic efficacy of neuroleptic drugs is specific for patients diagnosed as 'schizophrenic'. However, disputes about the diagnostic borderlines of 'schizophrenia' and other conditions such as 'manic-depressive psychosis' (Bentall, 1993; Farmer et al., 1993; McGorry et al., 1992; see Chapter 1) must make this claim contentious. Clinical studies have indicated that patients diagnosed as schizophrenic sometimes benefit from other types of compounds such as lithium (Delva and Letemendia, 1982) or benzodiazapines (Beckman and Haas, 1980), whereas patients diagnosed as suffering from an affective psychosis have sometimes been shown to benefit from neuroleptics (Brockington et al., 1978). In a particularly interesting study, Johnstone et al. (1988) randomly assigned psychotic patients to four groups who were given the neuroleptic pimozide plus lithium, pimozide plus placebo lithium, lithium plus placebo pimozide, or placebo pimozide plus placebo lithium, irrespective of diagnosis. The effects of the drugs were subsequently observed to be *symptom-specific* but not *diagnosis-specific*, so that, irrespective of diagnosis, delusions and hallucinations tended to respond to the neuroleptic compound whereas abnormally elevated mood tended to respond to lithium. This finding is consistent with previous studies which have indicated that the main impact of neuroleptics tends to be on positive symptoms rather than negative symptoms. (It should also be noted that the benefits experienced by positive symptom patients may not always reflect the direct impact of a drug on symptoms. In an early study [Bellack, 1958], it was observed that patients given promazine experienced a reduction in the anxiety consequent on their auditory hallucinations, even though the hallucinations themselves remained unaffected. Similarly, in a recent study which we have conducted with a large group of patients receiving neuroleptics [Day et al., submitted], we observed a number of patients who reported being less bothered by their symptoms as a consequence of neuroleptic medication, even though the symptoms persisted.)

There remains some debate about the optimal strategy for prescribing

238

neuroleptics. Maintenance treatment (continuous medication over a period of many years) is the most common neuroleptic treatment regime. However, some authors have advocated an intermittent regime in which patients are drug-free for long periods and receive medication only at times of stress or following the appearance of prodromal symptoms. Although a United States study comparing this kind of regime with maintenance therapy yielded promising results (Carpenter *et al.*, 1987), subsequent studies in both Britain and North America have revealed that, despite apparent advantages in the short term, relapse rates are higher over the long term following intermittent therapy (Herz *et al.*, 1991; Jolley *et al.*, 1990). Moreover, Herz *et al.* (1991) found no difference in the amount and severity of side-effects experienced by patients undergoing the two types of treatment.

Very high doses of neuroleptics (sometimes several times the recommended maximum given in the British National Formulary) are occasionally employed by clinicians working with treatment resistant patients. However, such high dosages cannot be justified on therapeutic grounds. A meta-analysis of the relevant literature has revealed that the therapeutic benefits of high dose neuroleptic regimes are no greater than those conferred by low dose regimes, but that patients treated with high dosages have a greater risk of side-effects (Bollini *et al.*, 1994). Moreover, high dose neuroleptics may have adverse effects on the social functioning of patients (Hogarty *et al.*, 1988). In the light of this kind of evidence the Royal College of Psychiatrists in Great Britain has recently issued a consensus statement which advocated the avoidance of high dose neuroleptic medication whenever possible, and which recommended a number of alternatives that prescribers might consider before resorting to high dose treatment of non-responding patients (Royal College of Psychiatrists, 1993).

Despite the well-established therapeutic effects of neuroleptics, it is clear that not even all patients who experience positive symptoms benefit from neuroleptic treatment (Brown and Herz, 1989), and some patients may even do worse on neuroleptics (Bowers and Swigar, 1988). The exact proportion of patients who fail to benefit is hard to estimate, but an indication can be gained from relapse rates. In studies carried out in Britain and the United States, it has been estimated that approximately 40 per cent of patients receiving maintenance neuroleptic therapy relapse over a period of one year, whereas the relapse rate in non-medicated patients is approximately two-thirds (Hogarty, 1984; Johnstone *et al.*, 1992). Brown and Herz (1989), in a review of the literature on psychotic patients who fail to benefit from neuroleptics, concluded that non-responding is a stable trait, so that patients who are shown not to benefit following extensive trials with a range of compounds are unlikely to benefit from similar treatment in the future. Despite this observation, many non-responding patients are maintained on inappropriately high doses despite no obvious symptom relief, often because clinicians fear that reducing the dosage will result in an exacerbation of the patients' symptomatology.

Recently, a number of new neuroleptic drugs have been introduced (in the case of remoxipride and risperidone) or re-introduced (in the case of clozapine, which was briefly marketed in the 1970s but discontinued because of potentially fatal side-effects) onto the market, and these are reported to have a novel action on the CNS. There is evidence that these drugs can sometimes benefit patients who are suffering from negative symptoms or who have not responded to more conventional neuroleptic compounds (Kane *et al.*, 1988). In the case of clozapine, despite claims of its novel action, blockade of dopamine D_2 receptors is still an attribute of the drug. Furthermore, anxieties caused by potential adverse and possibly fatal haematological reactions limit its use. Similarly, recent reports by the Committee on the Safety of Medicines indicate that fatalities due to blood dyscrasias have occurred in patients prescribed remoxipride, and this drug has now been withdrawn by the manufacturers. For these reasons, and also due to the comparative expense of newer agents (caused partly by the need for frequent blood tests), traditional neuroleptics such as chlorpromazine and haloperidol are still the most commonly used anti-psychotic drugs in the UK.

There are few set rules when considering neuroleptic treatment for a particular patient, and the selection and monitoring of a drug's effects largely depends on subjective decisions of the prescriber. It is not possible to select a drug to match a patient's characteristics as there is no clear relationship between plasma levels and drug response (May *et al.*, 1981; Van Putten *et al.*, 1991) and the clinical use of neuroleptics therefore remains very much a matter of trial and error.

ADVERSE EFFECTS OF NEUROLEPTIC DRUGS

So far we have focused on the positive effects of neuroleptic medication. However, any attempt to understand the interaction between pharmacological and psychosocial treatments of psychotic symptoms must also take into account their adverse effects, which are numerous and at times severe. As a number of authors have pointed out, these side-effects are so extensive that they have confounded attempts to identify biological and psychological causes of psychotic disorders (Blanchard and Neale, 1992).

Although all neuroleptics can produce most of these side-effects, some drugs are more likely to produce particular groups of side-effects than others (see Table 12.2 for side-effect profiles of the most widely used compounds). For example, the butyrophenones such as haloperidol are more likely to produce extra-pyramidal side-effects than other neuroleptics, and thioridazine is associated with a high rate of sexual side-effects

Table 12.2 Side-effect profiles of commonly used neuroleptic drugs

Drug	EPSE	A.Ch.	Cardiac	Hypotension	Sedation
Chlorpromazine	**	***	**	***	***
Thioridazine	**	***	*	***	**
Trifluoperazine	***	?	*	*	*
Sulpiride	*	*	?	?	*
Haloperidol	***	*	*	*	*
Flupenthixol	**	***	?	?	*
Fluphenazine	***	**	*	*	**
Clozapine	*	***	***	*	***

Notes:

EPSE = Extrapyramidal side-effects
A.Ch. = Anticholinergic side-effects
The number of stars (*) indicates relative potency of drugs. There is generally a lack of well-controlled studies so this table is intended only as a guide.
? indicates lack of data.

compared with other drugs due to its high alpha-adrenergic affinity. For this reason it should be possible to minimise side-effects by carefully monitoring the patient and, if necessary, changing to a drug which is tailored to the individual.

In clinical practice, however, there are a number of reasons why it may be difficult to establish whether or not a symptom reported by a patient is an adverse effect of medication. In some cases it may be possible that the symptom is part of the underlying disorder. Moreover, some side-effects (for example, constipation) are similar to the kinds of everyday complaints widely reported by healthy non-medicated individuals. A further complication is that many patients are prescribed more than one type of medication, making it difficult to establish a causal relationship between a particular drug and a particular adverse response.

Neurological effects

Neuroleptic drugs produce a number of neurological effects, the most common of which are of the extra-pyramidal type. With the exception of the acute dystonias (prolonged muscle spasms), which are more common in men, women are most susceptible to these kinds of adverse reactions. There are four main adverse reactions in this category:

241

Parkinsonian side-effects

Parkinsonian side-effects include changes in gait, tremor, rigidity, hyper-salivation, akinesia (slowing of movements), dysphagia (difficulty swallowing), and characteristic facies (a dazed or expressionless appearance which is often wrongly attributed to the underlying condition). It is not possible to differentiate between drug-induced Parkinsonism and classical idiopathic Parkinsonism. Parkinsonian effects are usually evident after five to eighty days of neuroleptic treatment and are reversible with the administration of anti-cholinergic drugs such as procyclidine. Various estimates have been given for the prevalence of drug-induced Parkinsonism, mostly ranging between 15 and 25 per cent of patients (Ayd, 1961; Kennedy et al., 1971).

Acute dystonic reactions

Acute dystonic reactions are characterised by dramatic muscular spasms (or sustained tonic contractions of muscles or muscle groups), usually affecting the head and neck. Examples include the oculogyric crisis in which muscles of the eye contract, causing the eyes to remain fixed in an upward stare, and spasmodic torticollis in which muscles of the neck contract to cause a prolonged unnatural posture. These reactions are extremely distressing to those who experience them. They usually occur within the first five days of neuroleptic treatment, are more common in males and are quickly reversed by administration of intramuscular or intravenous anti-cholinergics. Younger individuals tend to be more susceptible to acute dystonias and the prevalence level of this kind of reaction in neuroleptic treated patients has been estimated at about 10 per cent (Swett, 1975).

Akathisia

The term akathisia is derived from the Greek for 'unable to sit'. Patients suffering this side-effect experience an inner subjective restlessness which is often, but not always, accompanied by motor restlessness. In some cases, patients will constantly stand up and sit down in order to relieve inner discomfort. In severe cases they may shift continually from foot to foot or run from side to side. This adverse behavioural effect can be extremely distressing for a patient but it can also be mistaken for a worsening of psychotic symptoms, resulting in an inappropriate increase in the neuro-leptic dosage. The prevalence rate for this type of side-effect amongst treated patients has usually been estimated at approximately 20 per cent (Ayd, 1961; Braude et al., 1983), although some authors have suggested that as many as 75 per cent of patients may be affected at some time during their treatment (Van Putten et al., 1984).

Tardive dyskinesia

Tardive dyskinesia is a late developing movement disorder which is often irreversible (Jeste and Wyatt, 1979). It is characterised by involuntary oro-buccal movements such as tongue protrusion, fly-catching tongue, lip-smacking movements and lateral jaw movements. The aetiology and treatment of tardive dyskinesia remain matters of debate. Widely differing estimates have been made for the number of neuroleptic treated patients who eventually suffer from tardive dyskinesia, ranging from 0.5 per cent to 65 per cent (Simpson et al., 1982). The onset of the disorder is associated with increasing age, female gender and neuroleptic dosage (Kane and Smith, 1982; Muscettola et al., 1993). There is no proven treatment and withdrawing neuroleptics may exacerbate the condition. Tardive dyskinesia causes considerable concern for health professionals although not all patients feel a high level of distress as a result of this side-effect (Rosen et al., 1982; see below).

Effects on convulsive threshold

In addition to the well-known neurological side-effects, neuroleptics often produce other kinds of adverse reactions. They may lower the convulsive threshold and thereby precipitate seizures, both in patients with a previous history of seizures and in those previously seizure-free. This is most likely to occur in patients given high doses of low potency neuroleptics, or following rapid dose changes (Toone and Fenton, 1977).

Anti-cholinergic effects

As all neuroleptic drugs block muscarinic receptors in the CNS, anti-cholinergic side-effects are quite common, including dry mouth, constipation, blurred vision and urinary retention. These reactions are a particular problem in patients with pre-existing physical disorders such as glaucoma or prostatic hypertrophy. Some drugs such as thioridazine and chlorpromazine are more likely to cause anti-cholinergic effects due to their intrinsic selectivity for these receptors. Paradoxically, clozapine has a high affinity for muscarinic receptors but is associated with nocturnal hypersalivation. Overall, the prevalence of these kinds of side-effects has been estimated at about 40 per cent amongst treated patients (Lingjaerde et al., 1987).

Cardiovascular effects

The most common drug-induced cardiovascular effect of neuroleptics is postural hypotension, which is related to a drug's capacity to antagonise alpha-adrenergic receptors. Other cardiac effects include non-specific electrocardiograph abnormalities, cardiac conduction defects and arrhythmias. There is an increase in sudden unexpected death due to cardiac arrest in patients taking neuroleptic medication compared to matched non-medicated controls (Thorogood et al., 1992).

Hormonal effects

Neuroleptics also induce hormonal and metabolic effects, mainly resulting in adverse consequences for sexual function and body weight. The sexual effects are primarily due to alpha-adrenoceptor blockade and include orgastic dysfunction and reduced libido in both sexes, and erectile dysfunction, ejaculatory dysfunction and priapism (permanent erection) in males (Segraves, 1988; Sullivan and Lukoff, 1990). The sparse research which exists on this topic almost certainly underemphasises the adverse sexual effects for females. This may be because women's sexuality is seen as not as important by researchers (being predominantly male), because changes in women's sexual functioning may be less physically obvious, and also because women may be less willing to discuss their sexual experiences with prescribers.

Due to antagonism of dopamine receptors in the pituitary, neuroleptics elevate prolactin levels, often resulting in amenorrhoea (absence of menstruation in females), gynaecomastia (swollen and tender chest, which may occur in both males and females) and galactorrhoea (milk production, also in both sexes). Weight gain is also a common side-effect of neuroleptic medication. Low potency neuroleptics such as chlorpromazine and thioridazine are more associated with weight gain than higher potency drugs, and the gain in weight can be as much as 22 kg (Gordon and Grotte, 1964). The mechanism of this side-effect is not understood but it is thought that neuroleptics stimulate carbohydrate craving (Robinson et al., 1975).

Haematological effects

The most feared haematological consequence of neuroleptic medication, particularly the phenothiazines, is agranulocytosis (reduction in the white blood cell count) which has a 30 per cent mortality rate (Edwards, 1986). It is reversible on discontinuation of the drug, but due to its rarity and the commonality of its early symptoms (such as sore throat), it is often not recognised until it is well advanced. Agranulocytosis usually occurs within the first three months of treatment but may occur later. The claimed incidence rate varies from one in 3,000 to one in 250,000 patients (Dukes, 1992). However, the incidence rises to one to two in 100 for clozapine (Shopshin and Feiner, 1983), which is the reason for strict monitoring of blood in patients prescribed this drug.

Hepatic effects

Neuroleptic drugs are predominantly metabolised in the liver and it is therefore not surprising that hepatic effects have been reported. Hepatotoxicity was associated with chlorpromazine when it was first prescribed but fortunately has become a more rare reaction with the passage of time. Jaundice, which is particularly associated with the phenothiazines, may occur usually within the first two to four weeks of treatment and is thought to be an allergic reaction. Minor abnormalities as revealed by liver function tests have also been reported (Dickes *et al.*, 1957).

Allergic reactions

Neuroleptic drugs have also been implicated in a number of skin reactions, including erythematous reaction (a red rash), morbilliform reaction (a measles-type rash), urticaria (itchy skin), exfoliative dermatitis (in which the skin flakes off) and photosensitivity reactions (which may require patients to use a sunblock to avoid sun burn even in winter months). Chlorpromazine is the most likely drug to cause these reactions. After large doses of chlorpromazine over many years, a purple-blue pigmentation may accumulate in the skin and eyes (lenticular and corneal deposits and pigmentary retinopathy), in the latter case leading to visual impairment. These effects are usually reversible on withdrawal of the drug. In some cases a hypersensitivity syndrome is observed which includes bronchospasm (contraction of the airways), gastrointestinal symptoms, urticaria and cholestatic jaundice; again the phenothiazines have been particularly implicated in this kind of reaction (Edwards, 1986).

Miscellaneous effects

The neuroleptics may affect mineral and fluid balance, with water retention and oedema occurring rarely. Polyuria (excessive urination) and polydipsia (excessive drinking) are associated with the neuroleptics and are possibly caused by drug-induced dry mouth and/or direct stimulation of the hypothalamic thirst centre (Lawson *et al.*, 1985).

Neuroleptic malignant syndrome is a particularly serious consequence of neuroleptic medication and is characterised by muscular rigidity, fever, fluctuating consciousness, hyperthermia, dyskinesia and autonomic dysfunction. Its presence can be mistaken for serious bacterial infection leading to inappropriate treatment with antibiotics. The condition is confirmed by the occurrence of raised serum creatinine phosphokinase and leucocytosis. Approximately 0.5 to 1 per cent of patients experience this kind of reaction and the associated fatality rate is about 20 per cent (Caroff, 1980). High potency drugs such as haloperidol are more likely to be implicated. Once the condition has been diagnosed the drug must be stopped and intensive monitoring of essential functions must be carried out, usually in an intensive care unit. Drugs used to treat this condition include dantrolene sodium (used for malignant hyperthermia) and bromocriptine (a dopamine agonist). The condition can persist for five to ten days after discontinuation of neuroleptics, although this period may be prolonged (at least several weeks) if a depot preparation has been administered.

Behavioural effects

Finally, neuroleptics exert a number of psychological effects including blunting of affect. In 1951, Laborit and Huguenard argued that chlorpromazine causes sedation not in the same way as barbiturates or anaesthetics but by inducing indifference (described by the authors as the 'ataractic' effect of medication). In this context, it is interesting to note that very few investigators have concerned themselves with the impact of neuroleptic medication on positive life achievements. However, Crow *et al.* (1986), in the large Northwick Park trial of neuroleptic versus placebo medication, examined this very issue. Despite being more vulnerable to relapse, patients receiving placebo medication made significantly more life achievements than patients receiving medication.

Side-effects are usually monitored unsystematically by prescribing clinicians. Rogers *et al.* (1993) found that few of the 361 patients they surveyed who had been taking neuroleptics had been informed about side-effects by the doctors and nurses who had prescribed and administered their medication. In part, this no doubt reflects the fact that clinicians fear that informing patients about side-effects will reduce compliance. However, there is no empirical evidence which indicates that informing patients about side-effects impairs adherence to neuroleptic regimens. Indeed, Seltzer *et al.* (1980), despite finding that fear of side-effects was associated with non-compliance, observed that educating patients about the side-effects of neuroleptics reduced fear without compromising compliance. More recently, Kleinman *et al.* (1989) found that informing patients about the risk of tardive dyskinesia had no impact on compliance rates.

In recent years a number of investigators have developed instruments which allow the measurement of the adverse effects of neuroleptics. The most comprehensive scale so far developed for this purpose is the UKU side-effect rating scale (Lingjaerde *et al.*, 1987). This 48-item scale has been extensively tested, has been shown to have good validity and reliability and has also been used in a longitudinal investigation of patients' side-effects. The main disadvantage of the scale is that it is intended for administration by a suitably qualified investigator (typically a psychiatrist) and the necessary interview can take 30 to 60 minutes. For this reason it may be impractical to use the UKU routinely in the clinical setting.

A number of questionnaire instruments for the assessment of adverse neuroleptic effects have also been published. However, most of these assess a very limited range of the side-effects experienced by patients. For example, Mindham (1976) and Simpson and Angus (1970) have described brief scales designed to measure extrapyramidal side-effects and Barnes (1989) has described a three-item scale designed to assess drug-induced akathisia. Recently, the present authors have developed a 51-item self-rated questionnaire based on the UKU scale (Day *et al.*, 1995) which is more comprehensive in the range of symptoms covered. This questionnaire, known as LUNSERS (Liverpool University Neuroleptic Side-Effect Rating Scale), was found to have good psychometric properties and to correlate well with the UKU and with medication dosage. In order to further validate the scale, 'red herring items' referring to symptoms which were not known neuroleptic side-effects (e.g. chilblains) were included in the questionnaire but patients did not give abnormal responses on these items. These findings indicate that most psychotic patients can accurately report the side-effects which they are experiencing. This is an important observation as it has sometimes been assumed that psychotic patients' responses to questionnaires cannot be trusted (Platt, 1986).

PATIENTS' EXPERIENCES OF NEUROLEPTICS

Patients' subjective experiences of neuroleptic medication is a neglected area of research (Awad and Hogan, 1994). This neglect undoubtedly reflects, to some degree, the reluctance of some clinicians to take seriously the patient's perspective when planning treatment interventions. A few months before completing this chapter, the authors attended a debate on the value of neuroleptics. The two main speakers in the debate were distinguished psychiatrists who had achieved international reputations for their work. One was almost completely opposed to neuroleptic therapy whereas the other made (what to us sounded like) extravagant claims for the drugs. During the ensuing discussion, one of us observed that patients hold widely differing views about the value of neuroleptics, and that often these views have developed over many years of experience with medication. We suggested that patients' opinions about the personal benefits of neuroleptics should therefore be listened to very carefully and should be taken into account as treatment progresses.

The distinguished psychiatrist who was opposed to neuroleptics was the first to answer. He said that he agreed that it was important to take into account the patient's perspective, but that we should remember that neuroleptics have profound effects on the central nervous system, one consequence of which is the patient's inability to recognise the harmful effects of the drugs. Next to answer was the distinguished psychiatrist who was in favour of the widespread use of neuroleptic therapy, who also agreed that it was important to take into account the patient's perspective, but who went on to point out that many schizophrenic patients lack insight into their illness, and are therefore incapable of deciding whether medication is of benefit. We were surprised to see two intelligent and caring clinicians, who were completely opposed to each other in their views about treatment, apparently united by a common lack of respect for their patients' opinions.

In one of the few published surveys of patients' experiences of psychiatric services, Rogers *et al.* (1993) observed that, of the patients they questioned who had experienced neuroleptic therapy, 56.8 per cent felt the medication to be helpful but 27.7 per cent rated the medication as either 'harmful' or 'very harmful'. Davidhizar (1987) also observed that patients' attitudes towards neuroleptics varied widely, and noted that some held both strongly negative and strongly positive opinions about the medication at the same time. In a more complex study, Finn *et al.* (1990) attempted to measure the subjective utility ratings for neuroleptics of patients and prescribers. In their study, no difference was observed between the distress caused by psychotic symptoms and the distress caused by side-effects of neuroleptics as reflected in the patients' ratings and also the ratings of a group of psychiatrists. However, the psychiatrists saw side-effects as significantly less bothersome than symptoms when taking into account costs to society. An interesting finding was that, although psychiatrists were generally accurate at judging the overall distress caused to patients by symptoms and side-effects, they misjudged the distress associated with particular side-effects. For example, the distress caused to patients by akathisia, dystonia and orthostatic hypotension was overestimated by the psychiatrists, whereas the distress resulting from constipation, painful urination and weight gain was underestimated.

A recent qualitative study carried out by the present authors indicated that patients' attitudes towards neuroleptics are highly varied and cannot be simply reduced to a single dimension of 'for versus against medication' (Day *et al.*, submitted). Using Q-methodology (a factor-analytic technique which allows the identification of prototypical subjective viewpoints), it was observed that patients with a diagnosis of schizophrenia expressed a range of attitudes and opinions towards their medication. Three distinctive viewpoints were identified. Some patients expressed attitudes which suggested that they were 'unreflectively compliant'; these patients (who were generally older) expressed great trust in the judgement of medical professionals and fear of the consequences of discontinuing medication. A second group of patients was sceptical about the value of medication and expressed the need for personal autonomy in decision-making about treatment. For this group, side-effects were not an important issue and did not seem to contribute to their negative appraisal of the drugs. Finally, a third group of patients expressed opinions consistent with having formed a balanced appraisal of the pros and cons of medication. Qualitative data collected in this study also suggested a discrepancy between carers' attitudes to compliance and their attitudes about neuroleptics. Health professionals tended to attribute non-compliance to negative personality traits such as lack of insight or a rejection of care, but had a negative attitude to the drugs when considering them from a personal level (e.g. when commenting on whether they would be prepared to take neuroleptics themselves).

Psychological factors and neuroleptic response

It is clear that psychological variables are implicated in patients' responses to neuroleptic medications. Such variables may have a direct effect, in the sense that they may play a causal role in symptoms and may be the point of action of the medication, or they may have an indirect effect, in the sense that they may influence whether patients take their medications and thereby benefit from them. The indirect role of psychological variables, traditionally considered under the rubric of 'compliance', will be considered under a separate heading below.

There has been only limited research into direct psychological mediators of drug response. However, a number of researchers have attempted to compare medicated and non-medicated patients, or the same patients when drug-free and when receiving medication, in order to explore relationships between the clinical effects of neuroleptics and cognitive abnormalities presumed to be directly responsible for schizophrenic symptoms. In a review of the relevant literature, Spohn and Strauss (1989) found evidence that chronic schizophrenic patients given neuroleptic medication become less disordered in their thinking, show a reduction of deficits in sustained attention and improvements in their span of apprehension, and become less distractible. However, no evidence was found that neuroleptics lead to an improvement in reaction time. Integrating these kinds of findings, a number of researchers have suggested that neuroleptic medication results in improvements in controlled or effortful cognitive processes but has relatively little impact on more basic automatic or perceptual processes (Earl-Boyer *et al.*, 1991; Harvey and Pedley, 1989; Killian *et al.*, 1984; Oltmanns *et al.*, 1979).

A second intriguing line of evidence about possible mediators of neuroleptic response has emerged from studies of the role of psychosocial factors in psychotic breakdowns. Considerable evidence, collected over many years, indicates that there is a relationship between life stressors and variations in psychotic symptoms over time. (There is less clear-cut evidence that psychotic patients have experienced more stressors in their lives than the general population or people suffering from other kinds of psychiatric disorders; see Norman and Malla, 1993a, b for a review of this literature.) These kinds of findings have usually been interpreted in terms

249

of a diathesis-stress model in which some kind of biological abnormality is assumed to make psychosis-prone individuals highly sensitive to adverse life events (Nuechterlein and Dawson, 1984; Zubin and Spring, 1977). As Norman and Malla (1993a) point out, virtually all of the research on the relationship between stressors and psychotic breakdown has been carried out on medicated patients. One exception was a study by Leff *et al.* (1973), who observed a relationship between stressors and relapse in medicated patients but not in patients receiving placebo therapy. This observation can be interpreted as indicating that non-medicated patients are so sensitive to stress that even apparently trivial events precipitate relapse.

Further evidence of a relationship between medication and sensitivity to stress was collected by Leff and his colleagues in studies of the impact of familial stress on the course of psychotic disorders (see Chapter 11 in the present volume). In a well-known investigation, Vaughn and Leff (1976) found that patients exposed to a critical or overcontrolling family environment were more likely to relapse over a nine-month follow-up period. An interesting interaction between medication and stressful family environment was observed in this study: whereas those living in high Expressed Emotion (EE) environments were much more likely to relapse if on medication, no significant difference was observed between the relapse rates of medicated and non-medicated patients living in low EE environments. The clear implication of this observation was that the medication protected patients against chronic stress. In a subsequent two-year follow-up of the same cohort of patients, Leff and Vaughn (1981) observed that the advantage of medication for those living in high EE environments had disappeared whereas those living in low EE environments now benefited from drugs. Leff and Vaughn interpreted this finding as indicating that adverse life events would provoke a relapse even in patients living in a benign environment unless they received medication. However, Johnstone (1993) has recently questioned Leff and Vaughn's two-year follow-up findings on methodological and statistical grounds.

Whichever way Leff and Vaughn's data are interpreted, the available evidence clearly indicates that medicated patients are less vulnerable to the adverse effects of stress than non-medicated patients. These observations, together with the results of the studies of the relationship between medication and cognitive abnormalities described above, support the suggestion by Schooler and Spohn (1992) that neuroleptics achieve their positive effects, at least in part, by redressing attentional abnormalities and thereby increasing patients' ability to cope with adverse events.

Compliance with neuroleptic medication

Given the wide range of opinions which patients express about neuroleptic medication it is perhaps unsurprising that compliance with neuroleptic therapy in people with a diagnosis of schizophrenia has frequently been described as poor (Kane, 1985, cites a rate of compliance of between 30 and 50 per cent). There is a well-established association between non-compliance with neuroleptic medication and frequent rehospitalisation (Green, 1988). It might therefore be argued that, if compliance with neuroleptics could be improved, there would be a reduction in both distress caused to patients and their families, and in the financial costs to services by prevention or shortening of hospital admissions.

These observations are particularly important when considered in the context of the recent debates about the potential value of Community Treatment Orders. In this context it is interesting to note that patients' subsequent attitudes towards coercive treatment vary substantially from very positive to very negative, and that a negative response to coercion is sometimes associated with poor clinical response (Hiday, 1992). Given that a sizeable minority of voluntary psychiatric patients (certainly in the UK) feel that they have been coerced into going into hospital (their legal status notwithstanding) and that this perception is associated with negative attitudes towards psychiatric services and staff (Rogers et al., 1993), a collaborative, coercion-free alliance between patients and prescribers of psychiatric drugs is always likely to be preferable to forced treatment (Piatkowska and Farnill, 1992).

A number of investigators have studied demographic factors associated with non-compliance. Non-compliant patients in comparison with compliant patients tend to be younger (Davis et al., 1977; Myers, 1975; Raynes and Patch, 1971), are equally represented in both sexes (Baekeland and Lundwall, 1975), are more likely to come from a poor socioeconomic background and to be socially isolated (Altman et al., 1972; Astrup et al., 1962; Davis et al., 1957; Mason et al., 1963; Seltzer et al., 1980; Winkelman, 1964). A relationship between lack of 'insight' (denial of illness) and non-compliance has also been observed in a number of studies (Bartko et al., 1988; Lin et al., 1979; Marder et al., 1983; Nelson et al., 1975). However, this relationship has not been found by all investigators who have studied this issue (McEvoy et al., 1989). Moreover, a central difficulty faced by researchers attempting to link neuroleptic compliance with insight is the problem of defining insight. Although there have been recent attempts to develop measures of insight in psychotic patients which have suggested that it is relatively independent of severity of psychopathology, as defined by clinical measures (Amador et al., 1991; David et al., 1990), the concept of insight remains relatively unanalysed in these studies. Patients' accounts of their experiences leading to hospitalisation might be seen as one of a number of possible theories. From this perspective, lack of insight might be viewed as simply having a theory which is different to that of the relevant mental health professionals and at variance with the prevailing scientific paradigm of the psychiatric establishment.

In a large study carried out in the USA, Hoge *et al.* (1990) observed that non-compliance with neuroleptics was associated with negative attitudes towards hospitalisation and treatment, frequent seclusion and restraint, lengthy hospitalisation, and lack of health-care insurance (presumably indicative of poor-quality psychiatric care). When a subgroup of the non-compliant patients were asked why they refused their medication, their responses were categorised into four types: due to side-effects (35 per cent); denial of mental illness (21 per cent); avowed ineffectiveness of medication (12 per cent); and 'other responses that overtly reflect psychotic or idiosyncratic thought processes' (30 per cent). Interestingly, psychiatrists attributed non-compliance with medication to side-effects in only 7 per cent of cases, blamed interpersonal issues between patients and clinicians in 11 per cent of cases, and felt that psychotic or idiosyncratic factors were important in 49 per cent of cases. The psychiatrists and their non-compliant patients disagreed about the patients' reasons for non-compliance in the majority of cases.

A number of investigators have attempted to identify specific predictors of non-compliance. Van Putten and his colleagues (Van Putten *et al.*, 1981) found that dysphoric reaction (an adverse subjective response in which the individual feels severely uncomfortable and attributes this to the medication) shortly after administration of a neuroleptic was a predictor of poor compliance and poor clinical outcome. There was evidence that dysphoric patients tended to be less symptomatic and showed less impairment on the Continuous Performance Test (CPT), a measure of sustained attention widely used in schizophrenia research. Given that psychotic patients often perform poorly on the CPT, and that CPT performance has been observed to improve following treatment with neuroleptic medication (Spohn and Strauss, 1989), the implication of this observation is that neuroleptics may be appropriate only for patients suffering from this specific attentional deficit. Clearly, this hypothesis deserves further scrutiny by researchers.

Hogan *et al.* (1983) attempted to develop an attitude scale predictive of non-compliance. Items included in the scale were derived from comments patients made about their medication. The final scale was found to have good psychometric properties and discriminated well between compliant and non-compliant patients as defined by therapist ratings. Hogan *et al.* found that the maximum variability in responses to the questionnaire was accounted for by items reflecting how patients felt on medication (e.g. "my thoughts are clearer while on medication"), rather than what they knew or believed about medication.

It seems likely that the quality of the communications between patients and prescribers has a major impact on compliance with medication. Diamond (1985) argued that clinicians should strive to understand and respect the patients' subjective viewpoint and in particular those symbolic aspects of medication which may influence patients' attributions about treatment. For example, when a medication is prescribed, this may be taken by the patient as evidence that the physician is a caring individual, or it may be interpreted as a threat to the patient's need for self-determination. Direct evidence of an association between compliance and the quality of the relationship between clinicians and patients is available from several studies. Irwin *et al.* (1971) observed that compliance rates were higher when prescribers believed that medication had an essential role in the treatment of psychosis, as opposed to when prescribers felt ambivalent about the benefits of medication. More recently, in a study of psychodynamic therapy with schizophrenic patients which failed to find any evidence of a superior outcome for patients receiving this form of treatment (Frank and Gunderson, 1990), many patients were observed to develop a poor alliance with their therapists, as measured by standardised rating scales. However, a good therapeutic alliance was found to predict compliance with medication and a better clinical outcome with less medication over a follow-up period of two years.

Given these observations, there would seem to be many opportunities for psychosocial therapists to influence the outcome of psychotic disorders by manipulating variables known to affect compliance. A number of studies have addressed this issue. For example, Kelly and Scott (1990) found that education of patients and their families significantly improved medication compliance. Eckman and Liberman (1990) have described a short training scheme for mental health professionals designed to enable them to teach compliance-related skills to patients. In a controlled trial, Boczkowski *et al.* (1985) found that simple behavioural techniques (for example, self-monitoring of pill taking; tailoring pill taking to personal routines and habits) were superior to education when attempting to improve neuroleptic compliance amongst outpatients with a diagnosis of schizophrenia.

The results from these studies, although interesting, are limited by the small numbers of subjects taking part. A more serious objection which can be made to some of this research concerns the assumption that improving compliance with neuroleptic medication is always beneficial. Simple compliance may not be a desirable goal when attempting to improve patients' response to medication for several reasons that are outlined below.

First, compliance is a concept which is difficult to define and even more difficult to measure. Some studies have found poor correlations between different indices of compliance (Boczkowski *et al.*, 1985). Pill counts have been used to assess compliance but, in other areas, have been found to compare poorly with biochemical indicators (Pullar *et al.*, 1989) and are obviously inappropriate when patients are mainly receiving depot medication. Although urinary assays for phenothiazine medications are available (Forrest and Forrest, 1960) they have been found to overestimate compliance with long half-life medications (Babiker, 1986) and cannot be used with some compounds. These observations suggest that data obtained by means of traditional compliance measures should be treated with some degree of caution.

Second, it is worth stating that compliance is only appropriate if an optimum dose of medication tailored to an individual's needs is prescribed and carefully monitored. Given the evidence in the literature that a proportion of patients actually become worse on neuroleptics (Bowers and Swigar, 1988) and that a further proportion of patients are non-responders (Brown and Herz, 1989), it is possible that enhanced compliance with an inappropriate medication regime will increase adverse effects and produce little therapeutic benefit in some patients.

Third, the concept of compliance as usually stated is paternalistic – it assumes that the clinician knows best and that the patient has little role in decision-making. Some authors use the term 'adherence' in an attempt to assert the autonomy of the patient but it is doubtful whether a simple terminological change of this sort, on its own, can adequately address this problem. Others have argued that it is necessary to develop a patient-centred approach to understanding compliance which, in addition to emphasising the therapeutic costs and benefits of drugs, also emphasises the patient's concern with self-regulation (Conrad, 1985). Interestingly, a number of authors have suggested that adherence to neuroleptics can be enhanced by the development of a truly collaborative relationship between clinician and patient (Corrigan *et al.*, 1990; Eisenthal *et al.*, 1979; Frank and Gunderson, 1990; Piatkowska and Farnill, 1992).

Clearly, there is a need to develop a patient-centred approach to adherence to neuroleptics. It is likely that psychosocial therapists will be able to contribute significantly to developments in this area. Research on this problem should focus not only on those variables which we have described and which seem to influence patients' attitudes and behaviour with respect to psychiatric drugs, but also on the accurate targeting of medication. Single-subject research methodologies (Morley, 1989), which have long been used to monitor and evaluate psychological treatments, could obviously be applied for this purpose. For example, the kind of questionnaire measures which have been used to measure treatment response following the cognitive–behavioural interventions, described in other chapters of this book, could be used to measure positive symptoms and neuroleptic side-effects over a period of a few weeks following the administration of a neuroleptic. Information collected over this period could then be used to decide whether the dosage should be changed, or whether a new neuroleptic should be tried. Further monitoring would then reveal whether any change of medication had been effective. Monitoring of this sort should enable prescribers to feel comfortable that they are administering pharmacotherapy in a way which is tailored to the particular needs of the patient. Perhaps more importantly, it is likely that patients will feel reassured about the value of their treatment if they can see a record of the benefits achieved over a period of time.

INTERACTION BETWEEN DRUG AND
PSYCHOSOCIAL THERAPY

We arrive at long last at the question which will be of most concern to
psychosocial therapists (and the question which we will be able to answer
with least certainty) – is there an interaction between neuroleptic medication and psychosocial therapies? As indicated at the outset, there has been
a lamentable lack of interest in this question, for reasons which have been
very well summarised by Karasu:

> Ironically, there has been both tremendous need for and, at the same
> time, great resistance to the development of integrated treatment
> models for pharmacotherapy and psychotherapy. The overall paucity
> of guidelines for their conjoint use (simultaneous, intermittent, or
> sequential) has been created and compounded by a host of inter-
> related ideological, administrative, moral, scientific, and clinical
> factors and their manifestations. These include the following:
> 1. Deeply rooted conceptual antagonisms inherent in developing a
> comprehensive psychobiological view, including conflicting organic
> (e.g. neurochemical) versus psychogenic (e.g. psychodynamic or
> psychosocial) orientations towards the etiology of mental illness
> and goals of treatment. 2. The reinforcement of these concepts by
> parochialism, rigid cultism, over-allegiance to one's own affiliation,
> and deficient training and learning experiences. ... 3. Lack of
> resources or availability of institutions administratively, economically,
> or practically able to offer broad exposure or extensive experience
> with a diversity of modalities. 4. Ethical and regulatory barriers to
> psychopharmacological investigation and treatment.
>
> (Karasu, 1982, pp. 1102–3)

As Karasu notes, highly complex interactions are possible when psychological
and medical therapies are combined. Falloon and Liberman (1983), in one of
the few published discussions of the problems of combining drug and psychosocial therapies in the treatment of psychotic symptoms, have similarly
noted that it is too simple to assume that a combination of drugs and psychotherapy will always be superior to either treatment alone. For example,
psychosocial therapies may add nothing to the beneficial effects of medication, drugs may add nothing to the beneficial effects of psychosocial therapies,
psychosocial interventions may impair the effects of medication or vice
versa, or drugs and psychosocial therapies may have additive, even syner-
gistic effects. In a review of relevant literature available at that time, Falloon
and Liberman (1983) concluded that, although there was some evidence that
medical and psychosocial therapies could act together for the benefit of
patients, the precise interaction observed depended on the kind of psychosocial intervention employed and the dose of medication prescribed.

255

Some empirical studies have produced evidence that patient characteristics may also be important determinants of the effects of combining drug and psychosocial treatments. For example, Goldberg *et al.* (1977) studied relapse rates in patients diagnosed as schizophrenic who received medication and psychotherapy. Patients in this study who were asymptomatic at the time of receiving psychotherapy experienced some protection from relapse whereas, in the case of those patients who were symptomatic at the time of treatment, the psychotherapy appeared to hasten relapse. More recently, Harris (1989) reported an investigation in which he sought evidence of an interaction between medication dose and response to a behavioural intervention (a token economy). In this study, although patients on high dose medication responded poorly to the token regime in comparison with those on low dose medication, this difference seemed to reflect the fact that the most impaired patients were more likely to be given high dose medication rather than a direct causal interaction between drugs and response to psychological treatment. More detailed analyses revealed that highly impaired patients did not show improved response to the token system following an increase in their medication, but that medication increases did not adversely affect their response to the programme either.

In the absence of hard clinical data, judgements about how best to combine drug and psychosocial therapies in clinical practice can be no more than educated guesses supported by inferences from research on the effects of medication and psychosocial therapies alone. Few would agree with those commentators who have attributed the apparent failure of psychodynamic therapies with psychotic patients to the unwillingness of psychiatrists to withdraw patients from neuroleptics (Karon, 1984). However, the observation that neuroleptics, like the symptoms they are used to treat, can reduce the ability of patients to make positive life achievements. Crow *et al.* (1986) suggest the common sense hypothesis that, all other things being equal, low dosages of medication will facilitate patients' attempts to engage in psychological therapies whereas high dosages will prevent patients from benefiting from psychosocial treatments. This suggestion is supported by the results of a large study of the treatment of patients with a diagnosis of schizophrenia carried out in Turku, Finland (Alanen *et al.*, 1986), in which it was observed that the best outcomes were obtained when low dose medication was combined with psychotherapy. Moreover, the provision of supportive psychotherapy led to a lower probability of relapse once medication was withdrawn. In the light of these observations, it is not surprising that many clinicians regard a combination of low dose neuroleptic medication and psychosocial therapy as the treatment of choice for most (but not all) psychotic patients (Falloon and Fadden, 1993).

Clearly, further research is required in this area. It will be particularly important to study interactions between medication dosage and the newer, increasingly well-established cognitive and family interventions for psychotic patients which have been the focus of many of the chapters in this book.

CONCLUSIONS

In this chapter we have tried to draw together the limited available information on the ways in which neuroleptic medication and psychosocial therapies may work together in the effective treatment of psychotic disorders. In the course of this review we have also tried to provide a brief overview of neuroleptic therapy for those psychosocial therapists who work with psychotic patients but who do not have a background in medicine or psychopharmacology.

We have tried to be fair in our appraisal of neuroleptic treatment. We do not share the sincerely held view of some authors that these drugs invariably do more harm than good (Breggin, 1991), but equally we do not believe that they are a panacea for psychosis or that they are of benefit to all patients. Rather, the evidence that we have reviewed on side-effects and patients' subjective experiences following neuroleptic therapy shows clearly that, for many, the balance between the costs and benefits of this kind of treatment will be a fine one. It is possible that some patients are currently receiving neuroleptics without obvious gain, and that others may be on dosages which cannot be justified on scientific or clinical grounds. If these suspicions are correct, the solution to this problem does not lie in the complete abandonment of neuroleptic therapy, or in psychosocial therapists pleading ignorance and leaving difficult decisions to their medically qualified colleagues. Rather, new ways must be found to ensure that medication is appropriately targeted at those patients who can most benefit from it, and at appropriate dosages.

We have identified at least four ways in which psychosocially orientated clinicians and researchers can contribute towards the development of treatment strategies which optimally combine medical and psychosocial elements. First, further studies must be carried out in order to identify those psychological characteristics of patients that predict neuroleptic response. Second, new strategies must be developed to encourage those patients who benefit from neuroleptics to take them appropriately. Third, the relationship between neuroleptic dosage and response to psychosocial interventions must be carefully studied. Finally, methods must be developed to monitor patients' responses to neuroleptic therapy (including symptoms, side-effects and subjective experiences) on a day-to-day basis, leading to a practical system for titrating drug dosage against clinical change.

Studies in each of these areas will require a sophisticated understanding of both psychological and psychopharmacological processes and will undoubtedly necessitate the development of close but flexible collaborative relationships between biological investigators and psychosocial researchers.

ACKNOWLEDGEMENT

We are grateful to the Department of Health for supporting Jennifer C. Day with a Pharmacy Practice Research Award which has enabled her to carry out research into psychological aspects of neuroleptic medication in the Department of Clinical Psychology at Liverpool University.

REFERENCES

Alanen, Y. O., Rakkolainen, V., Laakso, J., Rasimus, R. and Kaljonen, A. (1986) *Towards Needs-specific Treatment of Schizophrenic Psychoses*, New York: Springer-Verlag.

Altman, H., Brown, M. L. and Sletten, I. W. (1972) '"And . . . silently steal away"; A study of elopers', *Diseases of the Nervous System* 33: 52–8.

Amador, X. F., Strauss, D. H., Yale, S. A. and Gorman, J. M. (1991) 'Awareness of illness in schizophrenia', *Schizophrenia Bulletin* 17: 113–32.

Astrup, C., Fossum, A. and Holmboe, R. (1962) *Prognosis in Functional Psychoses*, Springfield, Ill..

Awad, A. G. and Hogan, T. P. (1994) 'Subjective response to neuroleptics and the quality of life: Implications for treatment outcome', *Acta Psychiatrica Scandinavica* 89, Supplement 380: 27–32.

Ayd, F. J. (1961) 'A survey of drug-induced extrapyramidal reactions', *Journal of the American Medical Association* 175: 1054–60.

Babiker, I. E. (1986) 'Non-compliance in schizophrenia', *Psychiatric Developments* 4: 329–37.

Baekeland, F. and Lundwall, L. (1975) 'Dropping out of treatment: A critical review', *Psychological Bulletin* 82: 735–83.

Barnes, T. R. E. (1989) 'A rating scale for drug induced akathisia', *British Journal of Psychiatry* 154: 672–6.

Bartko, G., Herczeg, I. and Zador, G. (1988) 'Clinical symptomatology and drug compliance in schizophrenic patients', *Acta Psychiatrica Scandinavica* 77: 74–6.

Bean, P. and Mounser, P. (1992) *Discharged from Mental Hospitals*, London: Macmillan.

Beckman, H. and Haas, S. (1980) 'High dose diazepam in schizophrenia', *Psychopharmacology* 71: 79–82.

Bellack, L. (1958) *Schizophrenia: A Review of the Syndrome*, New York: Logos Press.

Bentall, R. P. (1993) 'Deconstructing the concept of schizophrenia', *Journal of Mental Health* 2: 223–38.

Bentall, R. P. and Day, J. C. (1994) 'Psychological factors and neuroleptic therapy: Some neglected issues', *International Review of Psychiatry* 6, 217–25.

Blanchard, J. J. and Neale, J. M. (1992) 'Medication effects: Conceptual and methodological issues in schizophrenia research', *Clinical Psychology Review* 12: 345–61.

Boczkowski, J. A., Zeichner, A. and Desanto, N. (1985) 'Neuroleptic compliance among chronic schizophrenic outpatients', *Journal of Consulting and Clinical Psychology* 53: 666–71.

Bollini, P., Pampallona, S., Orza, M. J., Adams, M. E. and Chalmers, T. C. (1994) 'Antipsychotic drugs: Is more worse? A meta analysis of the published randomized controlled trials', *Psychological Medicine* 24: 307–16.

Bowers, M. B. and Swigar, M. E. (1988) 'Psychotic patients who become worse on neuroleptics', *Journal of Clinical Psychopharmacology* 8: 417–21.

Bradley, P. B. and Hirsch, S. R. (eds) *The Psychopharmacology and Management of Schizophrenia*, Oxford: Oxford University Press.

Braude, W. M., Barnes, T. R. E. and Gore, S. M. (1983) 'Clinical characteristics of akathisia: A systematic investigation of acute psychiatric inpatient admissions', *British Journal of Psychiatry* 143: 139–50.

Breggin, P. (1991) *Toxic Psychiatry*, London: Fontana.

Brockington, I. F., Kendell, R. E., Kellett, J. M., Curry, S. H. and Wainwright, S. (1978) 'Trials of lithium, chlorpromazine and amitriptyline in schizoaffective patients', *British Journal of Psychiatry* 133: 162–8.

Brown, W. A. and Herz, L. R. (1989) 'Response to neuroleptic drugs as a device for classifying schizophrenia', *Schizophrenia Bulletin* 15: 123–8.

Carlsson, A. and Lindqvist, M. (1963) 'Effect of chlorpromazine or haloperidol on formation of 3-methoxytyramine and normetanephrine in mouse brain', *Acta Pharmacologica et Toxicologica* 20: 140–4.

Caroff, S. N. (1980) 'The neuroleptic malignant syndrome', *Journal of Clinical Psychiatry* 41: 79–83.

Carpenter, W. T., Heinrichs, D. W. and Hanlon, T. E. (1987) 'A comparative trial of pharmacologic strategies in schizophrenia', *American Journal of Psychiatry* 144: 1466–70.

Conrad, C. (1985) 'The meaning of medications: Another look at compliance', *Social Science and Medicine* 20: 29–37.

Corrigan, P. W., Liberman, R. P. and Engel, J. D. (1990) 'From non-compliance to collaboration in the treatment of schizophrenia', *Hospital and Community Psychiatry* 41: 1203–11.

Crow, T. J., MacMillan, J. F., Johnson, A. L. and Johnstone, E. C. (1986) 'The Northwick Park study of first episodes of schizophrenia II: A controlled trial of prophylactic neuroleptic treatment', *British Journal of Psychiatry* 148: 120–7.

Croyden-Smith, A. (1982) *Schizophrenia and Madness*, Herts: Allen and Unwin.

David, A. S., Buchanan, A., Reed, A. and Almeida, O. (1990) 'The assessment of insight in psychosis', *British Journal of Psychiatry* 161: 599–602.

Davidhizar, R. E. (1987) 'Beliefs, feelings and insight of patients with schizophrenia about taking medication', *Journal of Advanced Nursing* 12: 177–82.

Davis, J. A., Freeman, H. E. and Simmons, O. G. (1957) 'Rehospitalization and performance level among former mental patients', *Social Problems* 5: 37–44.

Davis, J. M. (1975) 'Overview: maintenance therapy in psychiatry – I. Schizophrenia', *American Journal of Psychiatry* 132: 1237–45.

Davis, K. L., Estess, F. M., Simonton, S. C. and Gonda, T. A. (1977) 'Effects of payment mode on clinical attendance and rehospitalization', *American Journal of Psychiatry* 134: 576–8.

Day, J. C., Wood, G., Dewey, M. and Bentall, R. P. (1995) 'A self-rating scale for measuring neuroleptic side-effects: Validation in a group of schizophrenic patients', *British Journal of Psychiatry* 166, 650–3.

Day, J. C., Bentall, R. P. and Warner, S. (submitted) 'Schizophrenic patients' subjective perspectives on neuroleptic medication: A social constructionist investigation using Q methodology'.

Delay, J., Deniker, P. and Harl, J. M. (1952) 'Utilisation en thérapeutique psychiatrique d'une phénothiazine d'action centrale élective', *Annales Médico-Psychologiques* 2: 112–17.

Delva, N. J. and Letemendia, F. J. J. (1982) 'Lithium treatment in schizophrenia and schizo-affective disorders', *British Journal of Psychiatry* 141: 387–400.

Diamond, R. (1985) 'Drugs and the quality of life: The patients' point of view', *Journal of Clinical Psychiatry* 46: 29–35.

Dickes, R., Schenker, V. and Deutsch, L. (1957) Serial liver function and blood studies in patients receiving chlorpromazine', *New England Journal of Medicine* 256: 1–7.

Dukes, M. N. G. (ed.) (1992) *Meyler's Side-effects of Drugs*, Amsterdam: Elsevier.

Earl-Boyer, E. A., Serper, M. R., Davidson, M. and Harvey, P. D. (1991) 'Continuous performance tests in schizophrenic patients: Stimulus and medication effects on performance', *Psychiatry Research* 41: 47–56.

Eckman, T. A. and Liberman, R. P. (1990) 'A large-scale field test of a medication management skills training program for people with schizophrenia', *Psychosocial Rehabilitation Journal* 13: 31–5.

Edwards, J. G. (1986) 'The untoward effects of anti-psychotic drugs: Pathogenesis and management', in P. B. Bradley and S. R. Hirsch (eds) *The Psychopharmacology and Management of Schizophrenia*, Oxford: Oxford University Press.

Eisenthal, S., Emery, R., Lazare, A. and Udin, H. (1979) '"Adherence" and the negotiated approach to patienthood', *Archives of General Psychiatry* 36: 393–8.

Falloon, I. R. H. and Fadden, G. (1993) *Integrated Mental Health Care: A Comprehensive Community-based Approach*, Cambridge: Cambridge University Press.

Falloon, I. R. H. and Liberman, R. P. (1983) 'Interactions between drug and psychosocial therapy in schizophrenia', *Schizophrenia Bulletin* 9: 543–54.

Farmer, A. E., Jones, I., Williams, J. and McGuffin, P. (1993) 'Defining schizophrenia: Operational criteria', *Journal of Mental Health* 2: 209–22.

Finn, S. E., Bailey, J. M., Scultz, R. T. and Faber, R. (1990) 'Subjective utility ratings of neuroleptics in treating schizophrenia', *Psychological Medicine* 35: 843–8.

Forrest, I. S. and Forrest, F. M. (1960) 'Urine color test for the detection of phenothiazine compounds', *Clinical Chemistry* 6: 11–15.

Frank, A. F. and Gunderson, J. G. (1990) 'The role of therapeutic alliance in the treatment of schizophrenia', *Archives of General Psychiatry* 47: 228–36.

Goldberg, S. C., Schooler, N. R., Hogarty, G. E. and Roper, M. (1977) 'Prediction of relapse in schizophrenic outpatients treated by drug and sociotherapy', *Archives of General Psychiatry* 34: 171–84.

Gordon, H. L. and Grotte, C. (1964) 'Weight changes during and after hospital treatment', *Archives of General Psychiatry* 10: 187–91.

Green, J. H. (1988) 'Frequent rehospitalisation and non-compliance with treatment', *Hospital and Community Psychiatry* 39: 963–6.

Harris, G. T. (1989) 'The relationship between neuroleptic drug dose and the performance of psychiatric patients in a maximum security token economy program', *Journal of Behavior Therapy and Experimental Psychiatry* 20: 57–67.

Harvey, P. D. and Pedley, M. (1989) 'Auditory and visual distractibility in schizophrenia: Clinical and medication status correlations', *Schizophrenia Research* 2: 295–300.

Herz, M. I., Glazer, W. M., Mostert, M. A., Sheard, M. A., Szymanski, H. V., Hafez, H., Mirza, M. and Varna, J. (1991) 'Intermittent vs maintenance medication in schizophrenia', *Archives of General Psychiatry* 48: 333–9.

Hiday, V. A. (1992) 'Coercion in civil commitment: Process, preferences and outcome', *Journal of Law and Psychiatry* 15: 339–77.

Hogan, T. P., Awad, A. G. and Eastwood, R. (1983) 'A self-report scale predictive of drug compliance in schizophrenics: Reliability and discriminative validity', *Psychological Medicine* 13: 177–83.

Hogarty, G. E. (1984) 'Depot neuroleptics: The relevance of psychosocial factors – a United States perspective', *Journal of Clinical Psychiatry* 45: 36–42.

Hogarty, G. E., McEvoy, J. P., Munetz, M., DiBarry, A. L., Bartone, P., Cather, R., Cooley, S. J., Ulrich, R. F., Carter, M. and Madonia, M. J. (1988) 'Dose of fluphenazine, familial expressed emotion and outcome in schizophrenia', *Archives of General Psychiatry* 45: 797–805.

Hoge, S. K., Appelbaum, P. S., Lawlor, T., Beck, J. C., Litman, R., Greer, A., Gutheil, T. G. and Kaplan, E. (1990) 'A prospective, multi-center study of patients' refusal of antipsychotic medication', *Archives of General Psychiatry* 47: 949–56.

Irwin, D. S., Weitzel, W. D. and Morgan, D. W. (1971) 'Phenothiazine intake and staff attitudes', *American Journal of Psychiatry* 127: 1631–5.

Jeste, D. V. and Wyatt, R. J. (1979) 'In search of treatment of tardive dyskinesia: Review of the literature', *Schizophrenia Bulletin* 5: 251–93.

Johnstone, C. D., Crow, T. J., Owens, D. G., Done, D. J., Baldwin, E. J. and Charlette, A. (1992) 'The Northwick Park functional psychosis study', *Psychological Medicine* 22: 331–46.

Johnstone, E. C., Crow, T. J., Frith, C. D. and Owens, D. G. C. (1988) 'The Northwick Park functional psychosis study: Diagnosis and treatment response', *Lancet* ii: 119–25.

Johnstone, L. (1993) 'Family management of "schizophrenia": Its assumptions and contradictions', *Journal of Mental Health* 2: 255–69.

Jolley, A. G., Hirsch, S. R., Morrison, E., McRink, A. and Wilson, L. (1990) 'Trial of brief intermittent neuroleptic prophylaxis for selected schizophrenic outpatients: clinical and social outcome at two years', *British Medical Journal* 301: 837–42.

Kane, J. M. (1985) 'Compliance issues in outpatient treatment', *Journal of Clinical Psychopharmacology* 5: 22S-27S.

Kane, J. M. and Smith, J. M. (1982) 'Tardive dyskinesia: Prevalence and risk factors, 1959-1979', *Archives of General Psychiatry* 39: 473–81.

Kane, J., Honigfeld, G., Singer, J. and Meltzer, H. (1988) 'Clozapine for the treatment-resistant schizophrenic', *Archives of General Psychiatry* 45: 789–96.

Karasu, T. (1982) 'Psychotherapy and pharmacotherapy: Towards an integrative model', *American Journal of Psychiatry* 139: 1102–13.

Karon, B. P. (1984) 'The fear of reducing medication, and where have all the patients gone'? *Schizophrenia Bulletin* 10: 613–17.

Kavanagh, D. J. (ed.) (1992) *Schizophrenia: An Overview and Practical Handbook*, London: Chapman and Hall.

Kelly, G. R. and Scott, J. E. (1990) 'Medication compliance and health education among chronic outpatients with mental disorders', *Medical Care* 28: 1181–97.

Kennedy, P. F., Hershon, H. I. and McGuire, R. J. (1971) Extrapyramidal disorders after prolonged phenothiazine therapy', *British Journal of Psychiatry* 118: 509–18.

Killian, G. A., Holzman, P. S., Davis, J. M. and Gibbons, R. (1984) 'Effects of psychotropic medication on selective cognitive and perceptual measures', *Journal of Abnormal Psychology* 93: 58–70.

Klein, D. F. and Davis, J. M. (1969) *Diagnosis and Drug Treatment of Psychiatric Disorders*, Baltimore: Williams and Wilkins.

Kleinman, I., Schacter, D. and Koritar, E. (1989) 'Informed consent and tardive dyskinesia', *American Journal of Psychiatry* 146: 902–4.

Laborit, H. and Huguenard, P. (1951) 'L'hibernation artificielle par moyens pharmacodynamiques et physiques', *Presse Médicale* 59: 1329.

Lawson, W. B., Karson, C. N. and Bigelow, L. B. (1985) 'Increased urine volume in chronic schizophrenic patients', *Psychiatry Research* 14: 323.

Leff, J. and Vaughan, C. (1981) 'The role of maintenance therapy and relatives' expressed emotion in relapse of schizophrenia. A two-year follow up', *British Journal of Psychiatry* 139: 102–4.

Leff, J. P. and Wing, J. K. (1971) 'Trial of maintenance therapy in schizophrenia', *British Medical Journal* 3: 599–604.

Leff, J. P., Hirsch, S. R., Gaind, R., Rohde, P. and Steven, B. (1973) 'Life events and maintenance therapy in schizophrenic relapse', *British Journal of Psychiatry* 123: 659–80.

Lieberman, J. A. (1993) 'Understanding the mechanism of action of atypical antipsychotic drugs. A review of compounds in use and development', *British Journal of Psychiatry* 163: 7–18.

Lin, I. F., Spiga, R. and Fortsch, W. (1979) 'Insight and adherence to medication in chronic schizophrenics', *Journal of Clinical Psychiatry* 40: 430–2.

Lingjaerde, O., Ahlfors, V. G., Dech, P., Dencker, S. J. and Elgen, K. (1987) 'The UKU side-effect rating scale for psychotropic drugs and a cross sectional study of side-effects in neuroleptic treated patients', *Acta Psychiatrica Scandinavica Supplementum* 334: 76.

McEvoy, J. P., Freter, S., Everett, G., Geller, J. L., Appelbaum, P., Apperson, L. J. and Roth, L. (1989) 'Insight and the clinical outcome of schizophrenic patients', *Journal of Nervous and Mental Disease* 177: 48–51.

McGorry, P. D., Singh, B. S., Connell, S., McKenzie, D., van Riel, R. J. and Copolov, D. L. (1992) 'Diagnostic concordance in functional psychosis revisited: A study of the inter-relationships between alternative concepts of psychotic disorder', *Psychological Medicine* 22: 367–78.

Marder, S. R., Mebane, A., Chien, C.-p., Winslade, W. J., Swann, E. and Van Putten, T. (1983). 'A comparison of patients who refuse and consent to neuroleptic treatment', *American Journal of Psychiatry* 140: 470–2.

Mason, A. S., Forrest, I. S., Forrest, F. W. and Butler, H. (1963) 'Adherence to maintenance therapy and rehospitalization', *Diseases of the Nervous System* 24: 103–4.

May, P. R. A., Van Putten, T., Jenden, D. J., Yale, C. and Dixon, W. J. (1981) 'Chlorpromazine levels and the outcome of treatment in schizophrenic patients', *Archives of General Psychiatry* 38: 202–7.

Mindham, R. H. S. (1976) 'Assessment of drug-induced extrapyramidal reactions and of drugs given for their control', *British Journal of Clinical Pharmacology*, Supplement 3: 395–400.

Morley, S. (1989) 'Single case research', in G. Parry and F. N. Watts (eds) *Behavioural and Mental Health Research: Handbook of Skills and Methods*, Hove: Lawrence Erlbaum.

Muscettola, G., Pampallona, S., Barbato, G., Casiello, M. and Bollini, P. (1993) 'Persistent tardive dyskinesia: Demographic and pharmacological risk factors', *Acta Psychiatrica Scandinavica* 87: 29–36.

Myers, E. D. (1975) 'Age, persistence and improvement in an outpatient group', *British Journal of Psychiatry* 127: 157–9.

Nelson, A., Gold, B., Hutchinson, R. and Benezra, E. (1975) 'Drug default among schizophrenic patients', *American Journal of Hospital Pharmacy* 32: 1237–42.

Norman, R. M. G. and Malla, A. K. (1993a) 'Stressful life events and schizophrenia I: A review of the research', *British Journal of Psychiatry* 162: 161–6.

Norman, R. M. G. and Malla, A. K. (1993b) 'Stressful life events and schizophrenia II: Conceptual and methodological issues', *British Journal of Psychiatry* 162: 166–74.

Nuechterlein, K. H. and Dawson, M. E. (1984) 'A heuristic vulnerability-stress model of schizophrenia', *Schizophrenia Bulletin* 10: 300–12.

Oltmanns, T. F., Ohayon, J. and Neale, J. M. (1979) 'The effect of medication and diagnostic criteria on distractibility in schizophrenia', *Journal of Psychiatric Research* 14: 81–91.

Parry, G. and Watts, F. N. (eds) (1989) *Behavioural and Mental Health Research: Handbook of Skills and Methods*, Hove: Lawrence Erlbaum.

Piatkowska, O. and Farnill, D. (1992) 'Medication – compliance or alliance? A client centred approach to increasing adherence', in D. J. Kavanagh (ed.) *Schizophrenia: An Overview and Practical Handbook*, London: Chapman and Hall.

Platt, S. (1986) 'Evaluating social functioning: A critical review of scales and their underlying concepts', in P. B. Bradley and S. R. Hirsch (eds) *The Psychopharmocology and Management of Schizophrenia*, Oxford: Oxford University Press.

Pullar, T., Kumar, S., Tindall, H. and Feely, M. (1989) 'Time to stop counting the tablets?', *Clinical Pharmacology and Therapeutics* 46: 163–8.

Raynes, A. E. and Patch, V. D. (1971) 'Distinguishing features of patients who discharge themselves from a psychiatric ward', *Comprehensive Psychiatry* 12: 473–9.

Robinson, R., McHugh, P. and Follstein, M. (1975) 'Measurement of appetite disturbance in psychiatric disorders', *Journal of Psychiatric Research* 12: 59–68.

Rogers, A., Pilgrim, D. and Lacey, R. (1993) *Experiencing Psychiatry: Users' Views of Services*, London: Macmillan, in association with MIND Publications.

Rosen, A. M., Mukherjee, S. and Olarte, S. (1982) 'Perception of tardive dyskinesia in outpatients receiving maintenance neuroleptics', *American Journal of Psychiatry* 139: 372.

Royal College of Psychiatrists (1993) *Consensus Statement on the Use of High Dose Anti-psychotic Medication, Report Number CR26*, London: Royal College of Psychiatrists.

Schooler, C. and Spohn, H. E. (1992) 'Social dysfunction and treatment failure in schizophrenia', *Schizophrenia Bulletin* 8: 85–98.

Segraves, R. T. (1988) 'Sexual side-effects of psychiatric drugs', *International Journal of Psychiatry in Medicine* 18: 243–51.

Seltzer, A., Roncari, I. and Garfinkel, P. (1980) 'Effect of patient education on medication compliance', *Canadian Journal of Psychiatry* 25: 638–45.

Shopshin, B. and Feiner, N. F. (1983) 'Letter to the editor', *Psychopharmacology Bulletin* 19: 563–4.

Simpson, G. M. and Angus, J. W. S. (1970) 'A rating scale for extrapyramidal side-effects', *Acta Psychiatrica Scandinavica, Supplementum* 212: 11–19.

Simpson, G. M., Pi, E. H. and Stramek, J. J. (1982) 'Management of tardive dyskinesia: Current update', *Drugs* 23: 382.

Spohn, H. E. and Strauss, M. E. (1989) 'Relation of neuroleptic and anticholinergic medication to cognitive functions in schizophrenia', *Journal of Abnormal Psychology* 98: 367–80.

Starmark, J. E., Forsman, A. and Wahlstrom, J. (1980) 'Abscesses following prolonged intramuscular administration of perphenazine enantate', *Acta Psychiatrica Scandinavica*, 62: 154–7.

Sullivan, G. and Lukoff, D. (1990) 'Sexual side-effects of antipsychotic medication: Evaluation and interventions', *Hospital and Community Psychiatry* 41: 1238–41.

Sunahara, R. K., Seeman, P., Van Tol, H. H. M. and Niznik, H. B. (1993) 'Dopamine receptors and antipsychotic drug response', *British Journal of Psychiatry Supplement* 163: 31–8.

Swett, C. (1975) 'Drug induced dystonia', *American Journal of Psychiatry* 132: 532–4.

Thorogood, N., Cowen, P., Mann, J., Murphy, M. and Vessey, M. (1992) 'Fatal myocardial infarction and use of psychotropic drugs in young women', *Lancet* 340: 1067–8.

Toone, B. K. and Fenton, G. W. (1977) 'Epileptic seizures induced by psychotropic drugs', *Psychological Medicine* 7: 265–70.

Van Kammen, D. P. (1991) 'The biochemical basis of relapse and drug response in schizophrenia: Review and hypothesis', *Psychological Medicine* 21: 881–95.

Van Putten, T. and May, P. R. (1978) 'Subjective response as a predictor of outcome in pharmacotherapy', *Archives of General Psychiatry* 35: 477–80.

Van Putten, T., May, P. R., Marder, S. R. and Wittman, L. A. (1981) 'Subjective response to antipsychotic drugs', *Archives of General Psychiatry* 38: 187–90.

Van Putten, T., May, P. R. A. and Marder, S. R. (1984) 'Akathisia with haloperidol and thiothixene', *Archives of General Psychiatry* 41: 1036–9.

Van Putten, T., Marder, S. R., Wirshing, W. C., Aravagiri, M. and Chabert, N. (1991) 'Neuroleptic plasma levels', *Schizophrenia Bulletin* 17: 197–216.

Vaughn, C. and Leff, J. P. (1976) 'Influence of family and social factors on the course of psychiatric illness', *British Journal of Psychiatry* 129: 125–37.

Warner, R. (1985) *Recovery from Schizophrenia. Psychiatry and Political Economy*, New York: Routledge and Kegan Paul.

Winkelman, N. W. (1964) 'A clinical and socio-cultural study of 200 psychiatric patients started on chlorpromazine 10.5 years ago', *American Journal of Psychiatry* 120: 861–9.

Zubin, J. and Spring, B. (1977) 'Vulnerability: A new view of schizophrenia', *Journal of Abnormal Psychology* 86: 26-266.

264

13

IMPLICATIONS FOR SERVICES AND FUTURE RESEARCH

Gillian Haddock and Peter D. Slade

The aim of this book was to provide a comprehensive coverage of the current research and literature regarding cognitive–behavioural interventions for people with psychotic symptoms. There now appears to be little doubt that these approaches are useful and effective ways to assist in the remediation of, and reduce the distress associated with, persistent and enduring psychotic symptoms. Despite this, there are a number of issues which still need to be addressed if these approaches are to become accepted into mainstream services for people with psychotic symptoms.

TREATMENT

The majority of authors who have contributed to this book have evaluated their work and a number of common themes have emerged. For example, early work in psychosis (e.g. operant procedures) emphasised the importance of behaviours which ultimately aimed to distract the individual from the particular symptom which was targeted. Indeed, as pointed out by Turkington and Kingdon (see Chapter 6), many psychiatric and nursing texts recommend that discussing delusions and hallucinations with patients may lead to a worsening of these symptoms. In contrast, the majority of authors in this book emphasise the importance of focusing on the symptom and its related phenomena of emotions and cognitions, as an important process of therapy. This does not usually result in a worsening of the symptoms, but is an important step in reducing the occurrence of the symptom.

Many authors have also noted that the content of patients' experiences may have some relevance or meaning, and that the elucidation of this may be an important step towards their remediation. For example, Romme and Escher (see Chapter 8) showed that the content of patients' voices was related to unresolved life stresses, and that it was important to resolve the life stresses in order to reduce the impact and severity of distressing voices. Alternatively, it may not be the symptom itself which causes most distress to the patient. For example, Chadwick and Birchwood (1994; and see

265

Chapter 4) have demonstrated that patients' distress about their voices may not be related to the voice content but may be related to their beliefs about their origin and content. With regard to delusional experiences, again, the content of the belief must be explored in order to employ cognitive–behavioural techniques of belief modification and reality testing. It is only by examining the belief itself, the relationship to the person's thoughts and exploring the information they hold as evidence for their belief that these approaches can be utilised. In addition, the function of a particular belief may have relevance to the types of interventions employed. A person experiencing grandiose beliefs may find that evidence which is contrary to his or her belief results in a lowering of self-esteem or depression. In a psychiatric population who are at risk for suicide (Falloon and Talbot, 1981) an increase in depression must be treated with caution. It is important to assess this possibility before employing techniques aimed at reducing belief conviction. These observations reinforce the notion that the nature of patients' experiences must be explored, by focusing on the symptoms, in order that a formulation of the meaning and role of the symptom can be made. This formulation can then direct the intervention devised by the therapist.

A further commonality in the approaches relates to the flexibility which is necessary to carry out psychological interventions with psychotic patients. Many authors have noted that the experiences of patients with psychotic symptoms are complex and are part of a range of other difficulties which they experience. For example, the number of sessions which is required to carry out the approaches may depend on the particular needs and difficulties of the patient. Some authors have used up to twenty sessions (Haddock *et al.*, 1993; see Chapter 3) over a four-month time period in their treatment approach, and Yusupoff and Tarrier (Chapter 5; and see also Tarrier *et al.*, 1993) have increased the number of sessions in their second intervention study from ten to twenty sessions. In addition, with regard to time needed to carry out these approaches, it is important to note that the therapist must be flexible in the length of time spent with patients. The cognitive deficits associated with experiencing psychotic symptoms may make long sessions inadvisable, and therapists may want to tailor their interventions over a larger number of sessions which last for a shorter amount of time.

A number of authors have noted the importance of low self-esteem and depression in patients experiencing persistent psychotic symptoms (Tarrier, 1987; Kingdon and Turkington, 1994). Again, these findings have been highlighted during this volume, and techniques designed to reduce depression and low self-esteem are seen to be an important part of comprehensive packages of care for psychotic patients. In addition, techniques aimed to reduce anxiety and distress from symptoms is seen as an important part of treatment and in some cases this is the main aim of treatment rather than to reduce symptom occurrence. For example, Romme and colleagues (Romme and Escher, 1989; see Chapter 8) have shown that many people may experience voices which they do not believe to be a problem, and do not always result in anxiety and distress or contact with psychiatric services. They believe that if patients can be taught coping strategies to reduce the distress caused by the symptoms, that there is no reason for the symptom to be eliminated. Indeed, they report that some voice hearers value their symptoms and report that they do not wish to remove them.

FUTURE RESEARCH QUESTIONS

Although results from these studies are promising and support the notion that psychological treatments have a useful contribution to make in the treatment of individuals suffering from persistent psychotic symptoms despite neuroleptic medication, there are still important areas regarding the nature of psychotic symptoms and their psychological treatment which have not been addressed in these studies.

We do not know whether psychological treatments would be more effective if they were delivered when the symptoms first began. Many of the authors have highlighted the importance of belief modification, not just for people experiencing delusions but also for those experiencing persistent auditory hallucinations (Chadwick and Birchwood, 1994). If beliefs regarding psychotic symptoms are an important maintaining factor, then intervention to manage these beliefs at an early stage in their development is likely to have more impact than an intervention delivered after they have been established for many years, as the individual has had less time to incorporate the beliefs into their lives over a long period. Studies examining the effect of these strategies on patients at first presentation to services are still in their infancy, although a recent study by Drury (1994) has attempted to implement a cognitive–behavioural approach with a sample of acute in-patients, some of which were experiencing a first episode of psychosis. Patients were allocated to either an intensive cognitive–behavioural treatment group or an equally intensive programme of activities. Results indicated that the length of hospital stay for the group of patients who received cognitive–behaviour therapy was approximately half that of the control group, and the time to a 50 per cent reduction in symptoms was half that of the control groups. There were no differences in initial symptomatology or demographic variables between the two groups of patients studied. This study is an important one as it indicates that psychological treatments can be effective for inpatients early in their psychiatric career and they can have a massive impact on the time spent in hospital. Although the long-term benefits of this to patients are not clear, it could be speculated that a shorter hospital admission may reduce the likelihood of institutionalisation and reduce the likelihood of loss of contact with family or social networks. From a service perspective, the financial costs of providing hospital inpatient services are very high, and if this can be reduced then the financial saving could well be used to maintain people in the community effectively.

Likewise, we do not know what impact psychological treatments would have if they were delivered without neuroleptic medication. The majority of reported studies are with patients who have been taking neuroleptic medication for a number of years. Studies examining the treatment of hallucinations in patients not receiving neuroleptic medication are few. A recent case study (Morrison, 1994) was able to demonstrate a reduction in severity of auditory hallucinations, which was maintained over a short follow-up period, with a woman who had been experiencing persistent and distressing auditory hallucinations but who had refused neuroleptic medication. Although, at present, it is not possible to suggest that psychological treatments could be offered as alternatives to neuroleptic medication, it is clear that in order to assess the benefits of psychological treatment correctly studies designed to investigate this are warranted. This is particularly important for those patients who are not able to tolerate neuroleptic medication due to the side-effects they produce and for those patients who refuse to comply with a medical approach to their illness.

In addition, many studies reported in this book contain a number of different elements of psychological techniques. It may be important to separate out individual techniques to assess their efficacy in order that treatments can be streamlined and be offered using the most cost-effective methods. Related to this, due to the diversity of symptoms presented by patients who receive a diagnosis of a psychotic illness, it may be important to determine whether particular types of patients or particular types of symptoms respond differently to specific types of treatments. For example, some authors clearly believe that treatments should be developed which address a particular type of symptom rather than address a broad diagnostic category such as schizophrenia (Bentall, 1990; Haddock *et al.*, 1993; Chadwick and Birchwood, 1994; also see Chapters 3 and 4 of this book). Research is needed to further elucidate those elements of therapy which have most impact on particular symptoms and which patients respond optimally to them.

Finally, studies on psychological techniques in the treatment of psychotic symptoms are in their infancy, and there have not been any large well-controlled studies assessing their efficacy. To demonstrate convincingly that these approaches produce benefits which significantly affect the lives of the sufferer means that the number of subjects included in the studies needs to be increased and comparable control groups should be included to account for any contact-time effects.

IMPLICATIONS FOR SERVICES AND TRAINING

Despite the above caution, it is clear that any benefits to people who have such distressing and enduring psychotic symptoms may be significant and should be offered as routine to sufferers presenting to mental health services. It is unlikely that this will happen until the benefits have been demonstrated to be cost-effective as well as clinically effective. This also has an implication for who carries out this type of approach. Psychologists are few and far between in health services and only a small proportion of them work with people who have psychotic symptoms. One important aspect of future research will be to demonstrate which aspects of these approaches can be carried out by other health professionals, as part of an overall mental health service. It has already been demonstrated that Community Psychiatric Nurses (CPNs) can be trained to carry out behavioural family management interventions with high Expressed Emotion families. This has resulted in reduced relapse rates for the family member who has a diagnosis of schizophrenia (Brooker *et al.*, 1992). A current study being carried out at the University of Manchester and the Institute of Psychiatry is attempting to train CPNs in a combination of approaches relating to the psychological management of psychosis. The training involves family management approaches, individual symptom management and clinical case management. The aim of the training is to provide CPNs with skills to reduce relapse and reduce the severity and impact of persistent symptoms within a framework of case management. Initial data from a small cohort in Manchester, suggest that CPNs can be trained in these methods and that this does have a beneficial effect on patients' symptoms and their social functioning (Lancashire *et al.*, 1995). This research highlights the importance of the settings in which psychological treatments are delivered and the importance of good case management. As the needs of patients with severe and enduring mental health problems are diverse, it is necessary to provide a comprehensive assessment of those needs, devise a comprehensive programme of intervention which will address those needs (only one of which may be psychological management of symptoms) and provide continuous monitoring of the effectiveness of those interventions. The framework of clinical case management is one in which all of these aims are met (Onyett, 1992).

PROSPECTS FOR PREVENTION

It is generally agreed that prevention can be carried out at three broad levels: primary, secondary and tertiary levels. Primary prevention refers to attempts at intervention which are focused on the period prior to the development of a disorder. It generally involves trying to alter 'risk factors'. Thus in the case of coronary heart disease, for example, primary prevention directs its efforts towards changing diet, decreasing smoking and increasing exercise and fitness levels, as these factors have been shown to increase the risk of the general population developing the disorder. Secondary prevention refers to attempts to inhibit the development of a full-blown disorder and involves early recognition and intervention with vulnerable individuals. For example, with regard to coronary heart disease, this usually requires regular monitoring of blood pressure and the appropriate use of beta-blockers. Tertiary prevention essentially refers to the direct treatment of a disorder in order to reduce or minimise its most disabling effects.

Possible applications to psychotic disorders

In the case of psychotic disorders, there is general agreement amongst researchers that the disorders emerge as a result of an underlying vulnerability, which may be biological and have a genetic component. The nature of this basic vulnerability has not been established in relation to schizophrenia, although many authors have speculated on its nature. For example, there is evidence for biochemical (Owen and Cross, 1992) and neuroanatomical (Roberts and Bruton, 1990) abnormalities in patients with a diagnosis of schizophrenia which may contribute to a vulnerability to develop psychotic disorders, although the evidence in support of a common biological basis for psychosis is equivocal (Bentall, 1990). These observations suggest that primary prevention could potentially take place in a number of areas, e.g. in genetic engineering or in manipulating biochemistry. Despite this, the search for a common vulnerability factor which is common to schizophrenia and other psychotic disorders has remained elusive, which suggests that primary prevention in psychosis, with regard to altering a vulnerability marker, is currently not a viable option. Despite this, it has been shown that environmental factors can play an important part in the development of a psychotic disorder. For example, research examining the concept of Expressed Emotion (Brown *et al.*, 1972) in patients already experiencing psychotic disorders has shown that it can play an important part in the developing course of the illness. Although it is not likely that Expressed Emotion plays a part in the cause of schizophrenia, it is possible that reducing Expressed Emotion before the onset of an illness may influence the subsequent development of a disorder favourably. As this would involve interventions aimed at the whole population this is unlikely to be achieved except through general education. In addition, research into the effects of stress and life events has revealed that psychotic symptoms are more likely to occur following sleep deprivation, during hostage situations (Siegel, 1984) and other arousing circumstances (Slade, 1974). General awareness of these factors in the general population may serve to reduce the occurrence of psychotic symptoms, although it is uncertain whether this would affect the development of psychosis in particularly vulnerable individuals. Further research in this area is warranted.

270

Secondary prevention

As outlined above, a commonly endorsed notion of psychosis is a stress-diathesis model (Zubin and Spring, 1977; Nuechterlein and Dawson, 1984) where it is assumed that a vulnerability to develop schizophrenia or other psychotic disorders interacts with environmental factors to produce symptoms of illness when there is persistent or extreme stress. In highly vulnerable individuals, only a small amount of environmental stress is required to precipitate the onset of psychosis, whereas a large degree of stress is required in those individuals with a small degree of vulnerability. If it were possible to identify those individuals who are most at risk for developing psychosis it may be possible to target them and their families with specific interventions to reduce Expressed Emotion, increase coping strategies and to reduce the likelihood of engaging in stressful situations. It may also be possible to improve or correct deficits in cognitive functioning which result from a vulnerability to psychosis (Green, 1992) and hence improve an individual's resistance to the effects of extreme or persistent stress. Although this approach is attractive, the lack of progress in identifying markers which indicate the presence of a vulnerability limits its applicability, although some authors have attempted to identify psychosis-prone individuals using questionnaires designed to assess psychotic-like experiences. One concept which has received some attention over the last twenty years is that of schizotypy (e.g. Claridge, 1985; Claridge and Broks, 1984) which emerged as a result of the notion that psychotic experiences may lie on a continuum with normality, rather than as indicators of 'abnormality'. Questionnaires have been developed which aim to identify those individuals who demonstrate psychotic-like experiences but have not developed any concrete diagnostic signs of illness (Chapman and Chapman, 1980; Bentall et al., 1989; Launay and Slade, 1981). Although a number of questionnaire studies have been carried out, it has not been demonstrated, as yet, that the presence of schizotypy predicts the development of psychotic illness later in life or that, if this were the case, that it is possible to intervene to reduce schizotypal traits and prevent the onset of psychosis.

Other authors have attempted to remediate the cognitive deficits which are often associated with a diagnosis of schizophrenia or psychotic disorder (Brenner et al., 1992). For example, patients with a diagnosis of schizophrenia often perform poorly on tests of cognitive functioning, and it is not possible to distinguish reliably between patients with organic brain damage and patients with schizophrenia on tests measuring a wide range of cognitive functioning (Heaton et al., 1978). If it were possible to identify those individuals whose deficits predict later development of a psychotic disorder it may be feasible to attempt to remediate those cognitive deficits and decrease the likelihood that psychosis will occur. Unfortunately, the cognitive deficits which have been shown to occur in patients who gain a

GILLIAN HADDOCK AND PETER D. SLADE

diagnosis of schizophrenia cover a wide spectrum of areas, and although successful attempts have been made to remediate areas of cognitive deficits for some patients, the results do not appear to endow any particular benefits in relation to the psychosis or to social functioning (Spring and Ravdin, 1992).

Tertiary prevention

In psychosis, tertiary prevention has been the main focus of intervention and the chapters contained in this book have demonstrated that psychological approaches can be an effective way to reduce the impact of distressing psychotic experiences, improve social functioning and reduce stress in families. Despite this, the long-term impact of psychological approaches on the developing course of psychosis is, as yet, unknown. This is because researchers carrying out controlled studies in this area have begun only relatively recently. It is imperative that long-term follow-up of patients undergoing psychological treatment is carried out in order to help fine-tune the treatment approaches currently in use.

CONCLUSIONS

Considerable developments have taken place in our understanding of psychotic disorders over the last few decades. This has contributed to the development of treatments aimed at successfully ameliorating psychotic symptoms and their associated disabilities. The chapters in this book have described approaches which have been successfully applied to a large number of patients and indicate that psychological approaches (particularly cognitive–behavioural approaches) are viable ways of working with patients with psychotic symptoms. This conveys considerable optimism for the future of services for individuals experiencing psychosis, although, as outlined above, there is still considerable progress to be made. It is likely that the progress which can be made could be considerably enhanced by the increasing interest in the viability of these approaches and the amount to which this interest is carried from researchers and clinicians to fund holders and policy makers, who will ultimately be responsible for determining the future of services to individuals experiencing psychotic symptoms.

REFERENCES

Bentall, R.P. (1990) 'The syndromes and symptoms of psychosis: Or why you can't play twenty questions with the concept of schizophrenia and hope to win', in R. P. Bentall (ed.), *Reconstructing Schizophrenia*, London: Routledge.
Bentall, R. P., Claridge, G. and Slade, P. D. (1989) ' The multidimensional nature of schizotypal traits: A factor analytic study with normal subjects', *British Journal of Clinical Psychology* 28: 363–75.

Birchwood, M. and Tarrier, N. (eds) (1994) *Psychological Treatment of Schizophrenia*, Chichester: Wiley.

Brenner, H. D., Hodel, B., Volker, R. and Corrigan, P. (1992) 'Treatment of cognitive dysfunctions and behavioural deficits in schizophrenia', *Schizophrenia Bulletin* 18: 21–6.

Brooker, C., Tarrier, N., Barrowclough, C., Butterworth, C. A. and Goldberg, D. (1992) 'Training community psychiatric nurses for psychosocial intervention: Report of a pilot study', *British Journal of Psychiatry* 160: 836–44.

Brown, G. W., Birley, J. L. T. and Wing, J. K. (1972) 'Influence of family life on the course of schizophrenic disorders: A replication', *British Journal of Psychiatry* 121: 241–58.

Chadwick, P. and Birchwood, M. (1994) 'The omnipotence of voices. A cognitive approach to auditory hallucinations', *British Journal of Psychiatry* 164: 190–201.

Chapman, L. J. and Chapman, J. P. (1980) 'Scales for rating psychotic and psychotic-like experiences as continua', *Schizophrenia Bulletin* 6: 476–89.

Claridge, G. (1985) *The Origins of Schizophrenia*, Oxford: Blackwell.

Claridge, G. and Broks, P. (1984) 'Schizotypy and hemisphere function 1: Theoretical considerations and the measurement of schizotypy', *Personality and Individual Differences* 5: 633–48.

Drury, V. (1994) 'Recovery from acute psychosis', in M. Birchwood and N. Tarrier (eds) *Psychological Treatment of Schizophrenia*, Chichester: Wiley.

Falloon, I. R. H. and Talbot, R. E. (1981) 'Persistent auditory hallucinations: Coping mechanisms and implications for management', *Psychological Medicine* 11: 329–39.

Green, M. F. (1992) 'Information processing in schizophrenia', in D. Kavanagh (ed.) *Schizophrenia: An Overview and Practical Handbook*, London: Chapman and Hall.

Haddock, G., Bentall, R. P. and Slade, P. D. (1993) 'Psychological treatment for auditory hallucinations: two case studies', *Behavioural and Cognitive Psychotherapy* 21: 335–46.

Heaton, R. K., Baade, L. E. and Johnson, K. L. (1978) 'Neuropsychological test results associated with psychiatric disorders in adults', *Psychological Bulletin* 85: 141–62.

Kavanagh, D. (ed.) (1992) *Schizophrenia: An Overview and Practical Handbook*, London: Chapman and Hall.

Kingdon, D. G. and Turkington, D. (1994) *The Cognitive–behaviour Therapy of Schizophrenia*, Hove: Lawrence Erlbaum.

Lancashire, S., Haddock, G., Tarrier, N., Baguley, I., Butterworth, C. A. and Brooker, C. (submitted for publication) 'The impact of training community psychiatric nurses to use psychosocial interventions with people who have severe mental health problems'.

Launay, G. and Slade, P. D. (1981) 'The measurement of hallucinatory predisposition in male and female prisoners', *Personality and Individual Differences* 2: 221–34.

Morrison, A. (1994) 'Cognitive behaviour therapy for auditory hallucinations without concurrent medication', *Behavioural and Cognitive Psychotherapy* 22: 259–64.

Nuechterlein, K. H. and Dawson, M. E. (1984) 'A heuristic vulnerability/stress model of schizophrenic episodes', *Schizophrenia Bulletin* 10: 300–12.

Onyett, S. (1992) *Case Management in Mental Health*, London: Chapman and Hall.

Owen, F. and Cross, A. J. (1992) 'Biochemistry and schizophrenia', in D. Kavanagh (ed.) *Schizophrenia: An Overview and Practical Handbook*, London: Chapman and Hall.

Roberts, G. W. and Bruton, C. J. (1990) 'Notes from the graveyard: Neuropathology and schizophrenia', *Neuropathology and Applied Neurobiology* 16: 3–16.

Romme, M. A. R. and Escher, A. D. M. A. C. (1989) 'Hearing voices', *Schizophrenia Bulletin* 15: 209–16.

Siegel, R. K. (1984) 'Hostage hallucinations. Visual imagery induced by isolation and life-threatening stress', *Journal of Nervous and Mental Disease* 172: 264–72.

Slade, P. D. (1974) 'The external control of auditory hallucinations: Information theory analysis', *British Journal of Social and Clinical Psychology* 13: 73–9.

Spring, B. and Ravdin, L. (1992) 'Cognitive remediation in schizophrenia: Should we attempt it?', *Schizophrenia Bulletin* 18: 15–20.

Tarrier, N. (1987) 'An investigation of residual psychotic symptoms in discharged schizophrenic patients', *British Journal of Clinical Psychology* 26: 141–3.

Tarrier, N., Beckett, R., Harwood, S., Baker, A., Yusupoff, L. and Ugarteburu, I. (1993) 'A trial of two cognitive–behavioural methods of treating drug-resistant residual psychotic symptoms in schizophrenic patients. 1. Outcome', *British Journal of Psychiatry* 162: 524–32.

Wing, J. K. (1975) 'Impairments in schizophrenia: A rational basis for social treatment', in R. V. Ivert, G. Winokur and M. Roff (eds) *Life History Research in Psychopathology, vol. 4.*

Zubin, J. and Spring, B. (1977) 'Vulnerability: A new view of schizophrenia', *Journal of Abnormal Psychology* 86: 103–26.

INDEX